PLANTATION AIRS

Southern Literary Studies

FRED HOBSON, SERIES EDITOR

BRANNON COSTELLO

PLANTATION AIRS

RACIAL PATERNALISM *and* THE TRANSFORMATIONS OF CLASS IN SOUTHERN FICTION, 1945–1971

Louisiana State University Press
Baton Rouge

Published by Louisiana State University Press

Manufactured in the United States of America
First printing

Designer: Michelle A. Neustrom
Typeface: Adobe Jenson Pro
Printer and binder: Thomson-Shore, Inc.

Library of Congress Cataloging-in-Publication Data
Costello, Brannon, 1975–
Plantation airs : racial paternalism and the transformations of class in southern fiction, 1945–1971 / Brannon Costello.
p. cm. — (Southern literary studies)
Includes bibliographical references and index.
ISBN-13: 978-0-8071-3270-8 (cloth : alk. paper)
1. American fiction—Southern States—History and criticism. 2. Paternalism in literature. 3. Race relations in literature. 4. Social classes in literature. 5. Literature and society—Southern States. 6. American fiction—20th century—History and criticism. 7. Race in literature. 8. Paternalism—Southern States. 9. Southern States—Intellectual life—20th century. 10. Poor in literature. I. Title.
PS261.C59 2008
810.9'358—dc22

2007016576

The paper in this book meets the guidelines for permanence and durability of the Committee on Production Guidelines for Book Longevity of the Council on Library Resources. ♾

For Gina

CONTENTS

ACKNOWLEDGMENTS

I have been the grateful recipient of many kinds of assistance while writing this book, including a Louisiana State University Council on Research Summer Stipend and a Manship Summer Research Fellowship. I am particularly thankful for the many people who helped me shape and hone the arguments and analyses in this book. Noel Polk guided this project in its very earliest incarnation and has been a consistent source of support and encouragement. I owe a tremendous debt of gratitude to Mary Papke, Tom Haddox, and Chuck Maland, my dissertation committee at the University of Tennessee, whose challenging questions, thoughtful suggestions, and great patience were crucial to this project's transition from idea to book. Many friends have been kind enough to endure long discussions of this project and to offer distractions from it when they were most needed, including Matthew Evans, Ethan Krase, Darren Hughes, Jack Butler, David McCarty, Dan Novak, and Laura Mullen. Much appreciation is due my friends and colleagues at Louisiana State University who, in conversation and in close reading, helped me see this book with new eyes, including John Lowe, Katherine Henninger, Rick Moreland, and Susannah Monta; I owe particular thanks to Sue Weinstein, Pallavi Rastogi, and Robert Hamm, who by now might know these pages better than I do. It has been a pleasure to work with John Easterly and everyone else at the LSU Press, and I am grateful for the insightful comments and suggestions offered by Fred Hobson and the press's anonymous reader.

Finally, I am especially thankful for the unwavering support of my parents, Joe and Annette Costello. And most importantly, this book might never even have begun were it not for the inspiration and encouragement of my wife, Gina, who never doubted even when I did.

Some portions of this book were published previously, and I extend my thanks to the publishers for the permission to use them here. A version of chapter 2 appeared as "Playing Lady and Imitating Aristocrats: Race, Class, and Money in *Delta Wedding* and *The Ponder Heart*" in *Southern Quarterly: A Journal of Arts in the South* 42.3 (2004): 21–54. An earlier version of a portion of chapter 5 appeared as "Hybridity and Racial Identity in Walker Percy's *The Last Gentleman*" in *Mississippi Quarterly: The Journal of Southern Cultures* 55.1 (2001–2002): 3–41.

PLANTATION AIRS

INTRODUCTION

THE PROBLEM OF FLEM SNOPES'S HAT
Southern History, Racial Paternalism, and Class

Recent years have seen a steady flow of important scholarship in southern literary studies, work that has opened up new avenues of exploration in terms of race, gender, history, and the American South's relationship to the Caribbean. The concept of "class," however, is situated along an avenue which, as Fred Hobson has noted, southern literary scholars have seldom trod (*But Now I See* 143). To be sure, critics of southern literature have paid increasing attention to the works of socially marginalized white southerners—the so-called poor whites or "white trash"—such as Erskine Caldwell and Dorothy Allison, and well we should: understanding the works of these writers is essential to understanding class in the South. Yet I fear we have let the spectacular, often grotesque descriptions of poverty and deprivation in these works distract us from other important aspects of class in the South. It can be difficult to wrest our gaze from the sight of Jeeter and Ada Lester burning to death in their dilapidated home in Caldwell's *Tobacco Road*, or from the sight of young Harry Crews's skin being boiled from his body in his memoir, *A Childhood: The Biography of a Place*. Of course, the spectacular nature of these depictions makes them no less complicated, as much insightful scholarship on these writers attests. Too often, however, our only answer to the question "What about class?" is to offer a list of these writers and the critical works about them.[1] But we make a dangerous mistake when we conflate "class" and "trash," much as earlier generations of critics conflated "race" and "black" or "gender" and "woman." Such a conflation ignores both the slipperiness and instability of class hierarchies and the often confounding variety of other ways in which "class" operates in the South.

One such crucial aspect is the relationship between class and racial paternalism. I contend that well into the twentieth century, the performance of attitudes and behaviors—including, most significantly, racial paternalism—associated with an idealized version of agrarian antebellum aristocracy was essential for wealthy white southerners to validate their identities as "aristocrats" and for upwardly mobile white southerners to separate themselves from "trash." Take the example of Flem Snopes. *The Mansion* (1959), the final novel in Faulkner's Snopes trilogy, chronicles the last stage of Flem's climb from poverty and obscurity in the rural community of Frenchman's Bend to what seems the pinnacle of wealth, prestige, and respectability as a bank president in the town of Jefferson—just before his murder at the hands of kinsman Mink Snopes. Widely considered a money-hungry upstart by his neighbors, Flem takes care to exhibit his success in symbols and language associated with an agrarian-oriented southern aristocracy. Veteran Snopes-watcher V. K. Ratliff describes Flem's new abode, Manfred de Spain's "rejuvenated ancestral home" (458), as "jest a house," and notes that it would have been a perfectly acceptable house for de Spain or even Colonel Sartoris, since Sartoris "had been born into money and respectability too, and Manfred de Spain had been born into respectability at least even if he had made a heap of the money since" (469). However, Flem knows that since he had to earn the house and the bank presidency, had to "snatch and tear and scrabble both of them outen the hard enduring resisting rock," such an ordinary house would not do for him; instead, his house "would have to be the physical symbol of all them generations of respectability and aristocracy that not only would a been too proud to mishandle other folks' money, it couldn't possibly ever needed to" (469). Because the town does not see Flem as legitimately heir to the Old South tradition that is for them synonymous with aristocracy, Flem must "put on airs" that align him with that tradition. His new upper-crust status, then, is precarious and requires constant reinforcement, requires a performance that, paradoxically, represents both his skill with a dollar and his indifference to the base world of economics. Therefore, he sets about converting this "jest a house" into a replica of an antebellum mansion, white columns and all (469). But the house alone does not suffice: Ratliff goes on to point out that Flem only becomes "completely complete . . . with a Negro cook and a yard boy that could even drive" him to and from work each day (470). Similar servants, Ratliff mentions, did the same for previous bank presidents. That Flem requires such servants to "complete" him implies that a true southern aristocrat must maintain a paternalistic relationship of dominance over African Americans, a relationship rooted in an idealized version of antebellum society.

However, a slip in ostensibly the most minor and cosmetic aspect of Flem's performance of his new status becomes a major problem for the residents of Jefferson and prevents them from ever truly accepting him as a southern aristocrat, largely because this gaffe indicates his incomplete understanding of the racial performance necessary to authorize the class identity he seeks to attain. Ratliff reveals that when Flem ascended to the bank's presidency, he relinquished the old cloth cap that he had brought from Frenchman's Bend in favor of a black "planter's hat suitable to his new position and avocation" (453). Flem's move here seems a smart one, calculated to further his re-creation of himself as a classic agrarian aristocrat. However, Ratliff notes that the hat "even after five years still didn't look like it actively belonged to him" (465). Ratliff further implies that Flem's new hat fits him so badly because of how he disposed of his old hat, a hat which now rests on the head of a young African American boy. Normally, passing down a bit of old clothing to a needy black child would perfectly exemplify the paternalist ethic that organized relations between aristocratic southerners and African Americans. But, according to Ratliff, the "legend [was] he sold it to a Negro boy for ten cents" (452). This transaction proves to be a sticking point in Jefferson's vision of Flem. According to Ratliff, the citizens of Jefferson still see Flem as the same man because his old cap was "not throwed away or even give away, but sold, even if it wasn't but jest a dime because ten cents is money too around a bank, so that [they] could look at the hat and know that, no matter how little they might a paid for one similar to it, hisn had cost him ten cents less" (470). Though an adept social climber, Flem's violation of the aristocratic ideal of noblesse oblige, his privileging of profit over paternalism, prevents him from ever completely achieving the status he has so long sought.

The example of Flem's hat reveals a fascinating but underexamined intersection between race and class, an intersection that I argue is central to southern culture and is of central concern to southern writers in the years following World War II. The racial paternalism that Flem forsakes is crucial to understanding the way class operates in the South. "Paternalism" encompasses a whole range of racialized social practices stemming from a belief that African Americans are fundamentally inferior, even childlike, and, as such, require the almost parental care and protection of well-to-do whites who claim to have their best interests at heart, though they may in fact be ruthlessly exploiting them. Kind-hearted whites might give African Americans money, clothes, food, shelter, and advice, but, typically, only if their beneficiaries conform to the proper social roles. Well into the twentieth century, to behave paternalistically toward an African American was an effective and public way for the wealthy to display their power and for less affluent but upwardly mobile white southerners to demonstrate their worthiness for a place higher in the social echelon.[2] According to Eugene Genovese, paternalism lay at the heart of black-white relations on the antebellum plantation: he describes the relation of master to slave as "an extension of the relationship of father to perpetual child" (121). Although the South's economic and social structure was changing rapidly in the early twentieth century, becoming more business and urban oriented, white southerners nevertheless conceived of class in terms of a mythical but powerful vision of the Old South aristocracy—a vision in which racial paternalism played a central role.

In order to theorize the relationship between racial paternalism and class structure, I draw upon the consumption-oriented economic theories of Max Weber and Thorstein Veblen. Weber and Veblen are especially useful here because of their close attention to the ways in which class is never simply a product of wealth or income, but, rather, of the way in which that wealth or income is put on public display. Weber draws a clear distinction between what he labels a "class" and what he labels a "status group"; a "class" is comprised of individuals who are equally likely (or unlikely) to "procur[e] goods," "[gain] a position in life," and "[find] inner satisfaction" (302). Thus, a Weberian "class" is defined according to its "market possibilities"—a quality that correlates closely, if not exactly, with wealth (49). But if possessing wealth largely defines a Weberian "class," *consuming* that wealth in the proper manner defines a "status group." One may have great wealth and still not belong to the exclusive status group to which one aspires; as Weber argues, "status honor is normally expressed by the fact that above all else a specific *style of life* is expected from all those who wish to belong to the circle" (50). Consumption is at the heart of Veblen's theory of social stratification as well; he argues that wealth is not enough to ensure membership in the upper class but must be displayed conspicuously. However, Veblen offers an insight crucial to understanding racial paternalism: according to the Veblenian axiom, "In order to be reputable [consumption] must be wasteful" (96). As Flem Snopes's example indicates, wastefulness is a crucial component of racial paternalism; the charity bestowed upon African Americans must seem casual and natural, must occur without an apparent concern for compensation. Flem, of course, completely fails to understand this fundamental truth ("not throwed away or even give away, but sold. . ." says Ratliff of Flem's hat), and this failure prevents his ascendancy to the aristocratic role he covets. All his wealth avails him little if he cannot waste it properly.

For the sake of consistency and clarity, I will use the term *class* to refer to a social stratum whose membership is determined both by possession *and* consumption of wealth. An important question that recurs throughout the chapters to come concerns the rationality of this wasteful consumption, for while each of these authors agrees that wasteful paternalism is central to a particular class stratum in the South, their analyses of the nature of the benefits of paternalism often differ. The example of Flem Snopes seems to bear out Weber's argument that "economically irrational consumption patterns" characterize societies stratified by more than the mere possession of wealth (307). After all, despite the low esteem in which much of the town holds him after the rumors of his failed paternalism become widely known, it is not at all clear that Flem's failure truly costs him anything in economic terms: he retains his position as bank president and his columned mansion. Though he remains an outcast from Jefferson's most exclusive social circle, his economic situation changes little; thus, there seems to be little reason, in strictly economic terms, for him to give away the hat rather than sell it. However, Pierre Bourdieu has offered a persuasive account of the rationality underlying apparently irrational economic actions. For Bourdieu, traditional analyses of class, status, and capital err by treating economic capital, narrowly defined, as the only meaningful factor in an exchange. He argues that to characterize all economic transactions that do not appear calculated directly to increase or maintain one's wealth as "irrational" is fundamentally to misunderstand the relationship between economic capital and what he terms "symbolic capital," which he describes as a type of credit that may take the form of the "honour and prestige" associated with a family (*Logic of Practice* 118). According to Bourdieu, "economic and symbolic capital are so inextricably intertwined" that displays of symbolic power often attract economic profits (*Logic* 119). Thus, it is only "by drawing up a comprehensive balance-sheet of symbolic profits, without forgetting the undifferentiatedness of the symbolic and the material components of a family's wealth, that it becomes possible to grasp the economic rationality of conduct which economism dismisses as absurd"—or irrational (*Logic* 120).

Some of the writers considered here offer support for Bourdieu's theories by demonstrating how an economic action that may initially seem irrational may prove very rational indeed in the long term. For instance, in Zora Neale Hurston's *Seraph on the Suwanee* (1948), upwardly mobile Jim Meserve and his wife Arvay clash over extra wood left over from the construction of their new home. Jim pretends that he does not notice his African American employees carting it off, but Arvay protests that they are stealing, and, moreover, that she and Jim could use the wood themselves. Jim explains that if he forces them to stop, "Then I wouldn't be a gentleman no more, Arvay, and that would cost me something. That's like broken food from the table. The help don't look for the ladies and gentlemen to trace up a thing like that. If I act like I don't notice it, I got a lot of willing friends, and nobody will ever steal a thing off this place" (673). Jim's characterization of his laborers as "friends" bears out Bourdieu's argument that paternalism works as a form of "symbolic alchemy" which transforms "relations of domination and submission into affective relations" (*Practical Reason* 102). Thus, Jim's performance of aristocratic noblesse, a performance that at first seems highly irrational to his low-born wife, in fact serves a specific purpose: it not only reinforces his "gentleman" identity but also affords him an economic advantage in cheap labor from local African Americans who ostensibly see him as a friend and father figure.

One possible explanation for the different levels of "rationality" apparent in Faulkner's and Hurston's depictions of paternalism is, of course, that they take place in different historical moments and in different economic contexts: Jim and Arvay rely on their African American laborers to help them carve out a life and a livelihood in a cash-poor land not far advanced from wilderness, while Flem lives in a town in which he can purchase whatever he needs with cash. Though displays of symbolic capital are still important for advancing in the social hierarchy of Jefferson, their necessity as a means of organizing labor is diminished—although to be sure a sufficiently "comprehensive balance-sheet," to borrow Bourdieu's terminology, might still reveal that paternalism creates material benefits for someone like Flem more subtle than those Jim Meserve acquires so obviously.

The issue of economic rationality, of what these paternalists gain from their paternalism, from their aristocratic status, is prevalent in all of the texts under consideration here, and each text helps us to understand the relationship between racial paternalism and class in a different way. For instance, how does the variety of economic situations in which characters of these works find themselves affect their perceptions of class? That is, how does the meaning of "aristocratic" or "paternalistic" behavior differ for the extravagantly wealthy businessman as compared to a struggling farmer? How does paternalism change as traditional race relations become unstable? How do African American writers analyze and represent racial paternalism in comparison to white writers? Although Veblen, Weber, and Bourdieu provide a helpful foundation for considering these questions, I also draw upon the works of contemporary theorists such as Erik Olin Wright, Homi Bhabha, and Michel Foucault in order to articulate fully the complications and contradictions of southern class. As Zora Neale Hurston's *Seraph on the Suwanee* (1948), Eudora Welty's *Delta Wedding* (1946) and *The Ponder Heart* (1954), William Faulkner's *The Mansion* (1959) and *The Reivers* (1962), Ernest Gaines's *Of Love and Dust* (1967) and "Bloodline" (1968), and Walker Percy's *The Last Gentleman* (1966) and *Love in the Ruins* (1971) reveal, the racial paternalism that was so central to class formation and mobility in the South was becoming unworkable in the years after World War II, years in which the increasing business orientation of the South and the push for civil rights drastically altered southern life. These writers produced a rich and diverse body of literature that demonstrates a keen awareness of the ways in which the changes sweeping the South complicated the deeply embedded structures governing the relationship between race and class. The collapse of racial paternalism as a means of organizing class lies at the heart of each of these texts. By examining the way in which these novels depict and critique this collapse and its confusing aftermath, we may better understand the role that racial paternalism has played in constructing and defining class, and, further, we will see how these writers attempt to suggest alternate, less oppressive models of race and class identity and interaction to replace the paternalism of the romanticized plantation.

My argument regarding the continuation of Old South racial ideology (or some version of it) in the twentieth-century South has close ties to the larger debate in southern historiography over how long and to what degree the ideals of the agrarian "plantocracy" influenced an increasingly industrial and urban South and, indeed, what the exact nature of those ideals was. In his still influential and oft-contested *The Mind of the South* (1941), W. J. Cash argued that a distinct set of values characterized both Old South and New, including a propensity to violence, a resistance to change, and the tendency of lower-class whites to identify more strongly with wealthy whites than with the African Americans whose material conditions they often shared. He further asserts that plantation values continued to dominate this industrial society, claiming that "the *plantation* remained the single great basic social and economic pattern of the South" (205). C. Vann Woodward took exception to this view in his *Origins of the New South* (1951), arguing that the influence of middle-class industrialists has dominated the South since Reconstruction, resulting in the rejection of plantation values in favor of a profit-minded bourgeois individualism.

However, as James C. Cobb argues in *Redefining Southern Culture: Mind and Identity in the Modern South* (1999)—and as the example of Flem Snopes's hat suggests—the very terms of the debate are fundamentally flawed. Cobb asserts that reading southern history as a polarized conflict between planters and industrialists "overemphasize[s] the social and political distance between" the two groups (5). Discussing transformations in the South's economic infrastructure in the first four decades of the twentieth century, Cobb further posits that "so long as industrial-development initiatives posed no threat to white supremacy, labor control, fiscal conservatism, and political stability, the interests of the region's planters were in no danger of compromise" (16). Planters and industrialists, then, found themselves in a sometimes uneasy but ultimately complementary relationship, but one that did not immediately alter the landscape of southern culture in a dramatic manner. Even with the growth of industrialization, the plantation remained central to social and economic life in the South until the 1940s (Bartley 138). Indeed, generous government subsidies and the rapid mechanization of agriculture in the years leading up to World War II at least temporarily increased both planters' wealth and their control over the dwindling, largely African American agricultural labor force. With segregation and oppressive labor practices firmly in place, the southern agrarian elite—understandably if mistakenly—could feel comfortable that their power would not face a significant challenge (Bloom 86–87). Thus, despite transformations that seemed sure to unseat the planter elite, some version of the values of the nineteenth-century agrarian South adapted to technological and economic changes and managed not only to survive but to thrive well into the twentieth century—though, as we shall see, in many cases the longer term effects of these changes worked to the planters' detriment.[3]

Of course, in some important senses, what we often consider the familiar values of the Old South emerged from the mind of the New. Though observers as philosophically and chronologically diverse as Cash, Woodward, and Cobb differ over the precise relationship between "agrarian" and "industrial" values in the modern South, they all agree that the mythology of the antebellum plantation exercised a powerful hold on the New South. Perhaps Woodward put it best when he famously remarked that "one of the most significant inventions of the New South was the 'Old South'" (154). Woodward saw that, paradoxically, as the South began to look more like the rest of the United States, many white southerners became invested in a nostalgic, idealistic vision of the Old South, a vision in which the violence, oppression, and cruelty of the plantation system were pushed far to the side and heroism, honor, and chivalry were brought to the fore. As Woodward argued, this idealized image of antebellum life had repercussions for contemporary southern society: "Drippings from the plantation legend overflowed upon race and labor relations, public charities, and even the organization of factory villages" (157). It makes sense, then, that the plantation myth would play an important role in the stratification of social classes. As Cash argues, "if money was necessary to social position, pride in its possession almost invariably translated itself into terms fixed by the aristocratic complex as it had been brought forward from the Old South" (240)—a complex that, I would argue, includes racial paternalism.

Though emancipation ended chattel slavery, paternalism continued to influence social and labor relations between African Americans and whites after the Civil War. William Alexander Percy, Delta planter, lawyer, poet, foe of the Ku Klux Klan, and eulogist for the values of the southern elite, offers in his 1941 memoir *Lanterns on the Levee* an evocative description of persistent paternalist relations between white and black southerners: "To live habitually as a superior among inferiors, be the superiority intellectual or economic, is a temptation to dishonesty and hubris, inevitably deteriorating. To live among a people whom, because of their needs, one must in common decency protect and defend is a sore burden in a world where one's own troubles are about all any life can shoulder. . . . Yet such living is the fate of the white man in the South" (298). Percy even figures the racial relationship in familial terms that Genovese might recognize, noting that "the black man is our brother, a younger brother, not adult, not disciplined, but tragic, pitiful, and lovable; act as his brother and be patient" (309). Yet his text also reveals the coercive nature of such ostensible affection. For instance, during the legendary flood of 1927, Percy's cook, Minerva, refuses any longer to serve the family breakfast at six in the morning. Faced with this potential loss of the benefits to which he believes himself entitled, Percy confronts the woman and threatens to expel her from her shelter in his home and to force her to take up residence in a leaky tent on the levee with her abusive husband. As Percy smugly notes, "The insurrection collapsed" (261). It seems that Percy concerns himself with her welfare only insofar as she concerns herself with his comfort. Not only did the allegedly benevolent system of racial paternalism allow for individual violations such as Percy's badgering of Minerva, but its rootedness in fundamental assumptions about the essential immaturity and immorality of African Americans meant that paternalism authorized "civilized" whites to define the very terms in which African Americans constructed their communities and their selves (Bloom 120).

The firsthand investigations into southern life by such observers as John Dollard (*Caste and Class in a Southern Town*, 1937) and Gunnar Myrdal (*An American Dilemma*, 1944) indicate that W. A. Percy, though perhaps more poetically inclined than most wealthy southerners, was not otherwise an aberration, but that a brand of paternalism characterized upper-class whites elsewhere in the South well into the twentieth century. Indeed, in dire economic times, some upper-class whites clung to their paternalist behaviors even at great cost to themselves in order to keep themselves separate from the poor whites. Stark Young, staunch defender of the values of the southern elite and author of "Not in Memoriam, but in Defense," an essay in the Agrarian manifesto *I'll Take My Stand* (1930), argued that a true southern aristocrat maintained his paternalism even when he could ill afford to do so. He offers as evidence the example of a "poor cousin" who gave "a third of his day's salary to a negro for a small service, too proud to be thrifty or to resemble the white trash, whom the negro despised and my cousin's family had never invited farther than the front steps" (352). Notably, however, both Dollard and Myrdal recognized that wealthier whites acted more kindly toward African Americans because, unlike their working-class racial peers, they were not in direct economic competition with them. Dollard turned an especially skeptical eye on this supposedly paternal relationship. He remarks that a "tolerant, poised affection" for African Americans often characterized upper-class southerners, but that this affection only extended to the "'old-timy' ones who draw out this friendliness in the class to which they were once related as slaves" (82). And as historian Grace Hale has persuasively argued, this reenactment of an idealized version of antebellum race relations was crucial to white southerners who, though they may have made their money in the shops of Jackson instead of the cotton fields of the Delta, wanted to establish themselves as legitimate heirs to the political power and social prestige of the Old South aristocracy (87).

However, the denial of racial realities upon which such a paternalist ethos depends became increasingly difficult as the South felt the effects of the New Deal and World War II. Certainly, New Deal reforms in the South initially seemed to benefit only the agrarian elite and to tighten their stranglehold on southern politics and culture. Often, for instance, funds meant to help struggling farmers went not to the sharecroppers but to local administration boards controlled by the planters—the group with the most to gain from the continued oppression of African Americans—who dispensed aid as they saw fit (Sitkoff 118). Further, the shift away from sharecropping and toward wage labor, combined with increasing mechanization, meant that planters could now make more money and farm more efficiently without having to offer the paternalistic care that was such a fundamental component of the old system (Daniel, "The New Deal," 45, Sitkoff 122, Fite 153). With the government providing capital and with mechanization reducing their reliance on black labor, the agrarian elite seemed poised to maintain their grip on the politics, economy, and culture of the South. But the reforms that increased planter power in the short run had long-term ramifications that, combined with the effects of World War II, worked to create a South in which these same planters found themselves growing superfluous. The increasing assertiveness of African Americans and the transfer of population and therefore political power to the South's growing cities would soon undermine them. Agricultural laborers suddenly deemed unnecessary by modernizing planters found work in the growing cities of the South, where an increasing metropolitan elite was finally becoming aware that its interests might not always align so neatly with those of the planter class (Bartley 143, Bloom 2).

The move to the city proved crucial for the reconstruction of African Americans as individuals striving for full citizenship outside of the degrading paternalist system, and, again, New Deal reforms that at first seemed of only questionable help to blacks, combined with the effects of World War II, paved the way for this reconstruction. As Numan Bartley argues, "The breakdown of the paternal order generated an expansion of individualism . . . that underlay the civil rights movement" (146). The New Deal, though by no means an unqualified success when it came to racial equality, helped promote that new spirit of self-reliance, not least in the way that it promoted the hiring of African Americans to work middle-class, white-collar federal jobs (Sitkoff 129, 133). World War II only encouraged such a belief among African Americans in the possibility of change. As Jack Bloom observes, the war "opened up jobs for blacks, took them off the farms, and set them in the cities; it put guns in their hands and trained them to use them; the war exposed blacks to education and to the world and made them more cosmopolitan. As a result, by the war's end blacks were becoming more self-assertive" (128).

This combination of increasing African American self-determination and the rise of what Earl and Merle Black call the "entrepreneurial individualist" in business would prove the undoing of the planter elite (29). The South's business elite had little interest in actively promoting the long-standing traditions of segregation and planter power, but nor did they desire any changes in the political landscape that would negatively affect their ability to do business in the South (Black and Black 29). Yet, if they were no more interested in effecting social change than the planters, they were much more susceptible to the influence of those who were (Bloom 215). Thus, in order to effect change in the 1940s, 1950s, and 1960s, African Americans used boycotts, protests, and other forms of economic and social pressure to send a clear message: southern businesses that chose to adhere to the traditional model of race relations so necessary to planter power would find it increasingly difficult to turn a profit.

When African Americans refused to accept their allotted place in southern society, agrarian power began to fall apart, and the cultural myths that both supported it and emerged from it became harder to maintain. According to Cobb, "The eruption of grassroots civil rights activism made it obvious enough that the remarkable stability of the Delta's racial hierarchy had less to do with the happiness and satisfaction of Delta blacks than with the historic effectiveness of Delta whites in maintaining, through the appropriate combinations of reward, coercion, and repression, a status quo that fed not only their bank accounts but their delusions of omnipotence as well" (*Most Southern Place* 232). In the wake of civil rights landmarks such as the *Brown* decision in 1954, some whites traded their paternalism for a stricter insistence on the rules of the color line, while some, according to Cobb, "retired to their country clubs and private dining and drinking establishments, where they lamented the black 'takeover' of the Delta" (251)—a withdrawal from society that made it easier for them to preserve their memories of allegedly simpler racial times. The impact of the 1963 *Baker v. Carr* "one-man, one vote" decision, which "ruled illegal all districting that gave disproportionate power to the votes of any one district," further lessened agrarian power and increased agrarian anxieties (Bloom 215). To these reforms were added the Civil Rights Act of 1964 and the Voting Rights Act of 1965. All these reforms combined to thwart the efforts of some white southerners to maintain traditional patterns of southern race relations (Black and Black 125). Importantly, the withdrawal of paternalism spurred by these changes ultimately served to undermine accommodationist leaders in the African American community, leaders who had risen to prominence on their ability to wrangle favor from the white leadership, and it paved the way for the ascension of independent black leaders better capable of achieving the African American community's political and social goals (Bloom 219).

The civil rights era in the South was not marked, however, by endless onward and upward progress for the region generally or for African Americans in particular. True, the war-accelerated change in the economic structure did much to undermine the agrarian elite and created a space for African Americans to assert their political power. Nevertheless, this economic development directly aided whites to a much greater extent than it did blacks: as the Black brothers point out, even in the 1980s, black political participation in many rural communities in the South exhibited patterns not much different from those of earlier decades (Black and Black 120–21). Though southern boosters promoted the new ideal of the "Sunbelt South" in the 1970s, this new vision of the South as friendly to business and unconcerned with racial ideologies obscured the poverty and dislocation of an undereducated and unskilled workforce left behind in the transition from an agrarian to an industrial economy (Grantham 279).

As this historical overview suggests, the novels I focus on emerge from a critical time for the race and class structure in the South, a time in which radical changes in the racial, economic, and political landscape greatly complicated—but by no means demolished—a system of class formation rooted partially in agrarian racial performances. These texts are of course not the only southern novels written from 1945 to 1971 that deal with this issue; however, they offer the most intriguing and challenging engagements with the relationship between racial paternalism and class. Although they share a common subject, these works of fiction exhibit a richly varied range of responses, both in terms of which aspects of that relationship they critique and of the alternatives they imagine. Some authors are concerned primarily with exposing the mechanisms that allow the social positions authorized by paternalism to appear natural and essential, while others focus on the costs of paternalism for women or African Americans. The relationship between paternalism and labor is central to some of these texts, while in others paternalism appears as a hyperreal construct in which that relationship is merely incidental. Many of these texts are concerned with imagining alternative economic and social practices as a way of resisting racial paternalism. These alternatives are as varied and idiosyncratic as the texts themselves, and they encompass alliances between poor whites and poor African Americans, the usefulness of racial hybridity as a means of disrupting the rigidly defined boundaries of race upon which paternalism relies, and even the potentially subversive implications of consumerism. The broad range of approaches to the intersection of racial paternalism and class evident in these texts indicates the richness and complexity of literary responses to this relationship. Understanding how many of the South's writers imagined and engaged with the many facets of racial paternalism in their fiction is crucial to the task of constructing a more comprehensive picture of the complications and contradictions of class in the South.

1

PATERNALISM, PROGRESS, AND "PET NEGROES"

Zora Neale Hurston's *Seraph on the Suwanee*

Zora Neale Hurston's 1948 novel *Seraph on the Suwanee* follows the rise of Jim and Arvay Meserve, poor white southerners who overcome poverty and tragedy to become wealthy land- and business-owners, new aristocrats for a New South. Their journey is not without its pitfalls, however, chief among them the feelings of inferiority that keep Arvay—daughter of a poor white family of turpentine "Crackers"—from believing that she is truly worthy of Jim, the scion of a once rich, now ruined family of planters. Late in the novel Arvay returns to her hardscrabble hometown of Sawley to attend to her dying mother and to reconnect with the "piney-woods Cracker" roots that she feels her more aristocratic husband does not appreciate or even accept. Arvay quickly finds, however, that the rest of her family does not share her mother's joy at her homecoming. Her jealous, spiteful, and litigious sister Larraine and brother-in-law Carl resent Arvay's wealth and material comforts, emblems of success and status which stand in stark contrast to their own misery and squalor. In a particularly telling scene, Larraine and Carl express their bitterness in terms that speak directly to what I see as one of Hurston's central concerns in this text. When Arvay asks Carl to drive into town and inform the funeral home of her mother's death, Carl bristles and tells her that she should "let that rich and noblefied husband of yours run into town for you" (857).

We might merely chalk Carl's phrasing here—"rich and noblefied"—up to Hurston's colorful rendering of lower-class rural white dialect.[1] But Hurston, I would argue, has something more complicated in mind. The suffix *-fied* implies that Jim's nobleness is not an essential, fixed part of his identity, but is, rather, the result of a long process of, for lack of a better word, noblefication. Moreover, by framing "rich" and "noblefied" as discrete terms, Carl unconsciously indicates that he sees them as related but not necessarily automatically synonymous; as Max Weber might have it, "rich" might refer to Jim's "market possibilities" and "noble" to his status or his style of life. Presumably, then, when Jim first arrived in Sawley and married Arvay, he was not noble, or at least not *as* noble as he has become. I would argue that "noblefication"—the process of climbing the ladder of class—is inextricably linked to racial paternalism, an economic and social performance in which upwardly mobile white southerners demonstrate their allegedly essential superiority by treating African Americans as inferior and childlike. In *Seraph on the Suwanee,* Hurston offers a skillfully drawn portrait and a cutting critique of the ways in which white New Southerners such as Jim Meserve deploy racial paternalism both to increase their wealth and to constitute their elite class status along "noble," aristocratic lines adapted from a romanticized version of the Old South plantation ideal.[2] Yet this process has potentially disastrous results for all involved: relying on a performance of racial paternalism to validate an "aristocratic" class position commits white southerners to an attitude of sycophancy, a permanent performance that keeps them from meaningful engagement with the world and with each other. Hurston argues that this sycophancy is particularly a problem for women, who, despite even the most successful performances of paternalism, remain subordinate to the power of their husbands. Further, Hurston suggests that the paternalist system threatens to render African Americans unfit for any kind of success outside that system, unable to capitalize on the opportunities that may arise for achievement on their own terms.

The immediate post–World War II years during which Hurston worked on *Seraph* were crucial years of change for the racial, social, and economic structures in the South. The experience of the war only amplified the reform spirit and desire for self-determination that had been gaining force in the 1930s, partially because of the New Deal. After the war, many African Americans exhibited a refreshed, robust interest in politics and voting rights, and they demonstrated an independence that threatened the racial logic of the paternalist system (Goldfield 45, Burton 30–31). The rise of the business elite, who were less invested in traditional racial mores than the still-influential planter class was, increased opportunities for African Americans to achieve and articulate that independence. To be sure, change did not occur instantly. Though the business elite had fewer commitments to the racial ideologies of the planters, they had no commitment to challenging those ideologies, either. In fact historian David Goldfield cites "a rash of racial violence that had erupted in the South since the end of the war as some southern whites, unwilling to participate in the season of hope, sought swiftly to reassert their dominance before contrary ideas motivated returning black GIs" (53). Yet despite such outbreaks of violence, African Americans could take hope in President Harry Truman's encouraging stance on civil rights. For instance, his President's Committee on Civil Rights issued a controversial report in 1947, the year before *Seraph* hit the shelves, entitled *To Secure These Rights*. The report called for "transforming race relations not only in the South, but in the nation: an antilynching law; the abolition of the poll tax; laws to prevent voter-registration discrimination"; and numerous other reforms (54).

Thus, while racial paternalism had survived well into the twentieth century as a key component of the plantation system that continued to define social, political, and economic southern life, dramatic alterations in the long stable arena of race relations, particularly the growth of African American independence, meant that racial paternalism would no longer necessarily serve as the main paradigm for interactions between wealthy whites and African American laborers. During this period of change, some individuals of both races longed for the stability of traditional race relations. Thus, Hurston had good reason to consider the historical roots and workaday practices of racial paternalism. By setting her novel from roughly 1900 to the early 1930s, Hurston is able to offer us a picture of both the grave problems and the seemingly limitless possibilities offered to those southern whites who adopted the paternalist ethic in a relatively more stable historical moment. Further, she could explain to her contemporaries how central this now threatened system was to a certain way of southern life and expose the often brutal realities that lay just beneath the veneer of nostalgia.

In order to trace Hurston's interest in and understanding of the ways in which paternalism functioned in the twentieth-century South and to illuminate her critique of paternalism in *Seraph*, I will turn first to the 1943 *American Mercury* essay "The 'Pet Negro' System," Hurston's own unique entry into a discussion that already included Stark Young, W. J. Cash, John Dollard, William Alexander Percy, and others. These writers, like Hurston and many who would come after, identified racial paternalism as a crucial distinguishing feature of the upper-class white South in the early twentieth century, though each one viewed it through his or her own ideological lens. Hurston's particular biases are not necessarily clear from a cursory reading of the piece. The introductory editorial blurb bills the essay as addressing "An aspect of the race problem ignored by zealous reformers" (593), a phrase that seems to offer a sly wink to more reactionary readers. Yet it becomes clear that, for her part, Hurston wishes to illuminate complexities that she feels have been ignored by both camps in the polarized debate between the "zealous reformers" and their opponents.[3] She treats the "pet Negro" system as a piece of southern tradition as firmly entrenched as Christianity. Writing in a mock-biblical vein, Hurston explains that "every white man shall be allowed to pet himself a Negro. Yea, he shall take a black man unto himself to pet and to cherish, and this same Negro shall be perfect in his sight. Nor shall hatred among the races of men, nor conditions of strife in the walled cities, cause his pride and pleasure in his own Negro to wane" (593). More seriously, Hurston argues that this system serves as evidence of the complicated nature of race relations in the South, and she notes that the system "symbolizes a web of feelings and mutual dependencies spun by generations and generations of living together and natural adjustment. It isn't half as pretty as the ideal adjustment of theorizers, but it's a lot more real and durable, and a lot of black folk, I'm afraid, might find it cosy" (594).

The reasons for Hurston's fear are clear. The "pet" system assists certain individual African Americans at the whim and to the benefit of the white patron and "with little thought of the ability of the person promoted" (598). Her fears are much in line with the criticisms of paternalism voiced by observers such as historian Jack Kirby, who reminds us that "paternalism bound blacks to whites, apprenticed them not only as laborers but also as moral creatures" (16). Paternalism served as an insidious form of social control, a means by which the white upper class could control both the material circumstances of black life and even the desires and aspirations of the black community (Bloom 120). Yet, Hurston's description of the daily workings of the "pet Negro" system also helps us to understand why African Americans in a time of both de facto and de jure discrimination might find the system so "cosy": it offered them modest protection and a limited structure for economic gain and social mobility.

Hurston illuminates this system by telling us about Colonel Cary and his pet, John. Though the Colonel is a "strictly unconstructed Southerner, willing to battle for white supremacy," he makes exceptions for John. Hurston claims that "he found John truthful and honest, clean, reliable, and a faithful friend. He *likes* John and so considers him as white inside as anyone else" (595). Colonel Cary sees to it that his pet is well cared for: he sends him to college, has him appointed principal of the local African American high school, and even gets his wife a job. Hurston explains that, if John is accused of any crime short of raping a white woman or assaulting a white man, the Colonel will intervene to prevent John from spending any serious time in jail. Importantly, Hurston notes that this intervention serves not just to help John but also to establish the Colonel's prestigious status in the community: "It would be a hard-up Negro who would work for a man who couldn't get his black friends out of jail" (595). Of course, the fact that violation of certain taboos involving whites would cancel the good colonel's sense of obligation suggests the hollowness of his belief in John's internal "whiteness."

Although Hurston does not develop in much detail the notion that Colonel Cary receives certain benefits from this exercise of noblesse oblige, near the essay's end she alludes to one benefit to which she will devote much more attention in *Seraph on the Suwanee*. Hurston claims, "I am not defending the system, belov-ed, but trying to explain it. The low-down fact is that it weaves a kind of basic fabric that tends to stabilize relations and give something to work from in adjustments" (597). Indeed, racial paternalism serves exactly this "stabilizing" function in *Seraph*: despite the gradual social and economic "adjustments" occurring as the New South business ethic gains momentum over the first four decades of the twentieth century, paternalism serves as a stable platform from which Jim and Arvay Meserve can exploit black labor and re-create themselves as wealthy, aristocratic elites. However, as Hurston demonstrates, that re-creation comes at a cost.

Seraph opens at the turn of the twentieth century in Sawley, a poverty-stricken town whose life revolves around the sawmill and the turpentine still. Hurston describes it as a place where "there was ignorance and poverty, and the ever-present hookworm. The farms and the scanty flowers in front yards and in tin cans and buckets looked like the people. . . . Work was hard, pleasures few, and malaria and hookworm plentiful" (600). Arvay Henson, the young, white, and beautiful daughter of a family of turpentine "Crackers," finds herself, much to her surprise, being courted by an attention-getting newcomer, Jim Meserve. Jim stands out in this community of poor whites because of his lofty background. His "ancestors had held plantations upon the Alabama River before the War. In that respect, Jim Meserve differed from the rest of the inhabitants of Sawley, who had always been of the poor whites who had scratched out some kind of an existence in the scrub oaks and pines, far removed from the ease of the big estates" (604). However, even though Arvay thinks of him as "first-class" and as "no common Cracker boy" (620), Jim's aristocratic background offers him no immediate material advantages over his hardworking, hungry neighbors. In fact, he has never known firsthand the luxuries of a posh lifestyle: "The fortunes of the War had wiped Jim's grand-father clean. His own father had had no chance to even inherit" (604–5).

But according to Hurston, despite Jim's ill economic fortunes, he "had a flavor about him. He was like a hamstring. He was not meat any longer, but he smelled of what he had once been associated with" (605). Note that Hurston does not imply that Jim's aristocratic legacy is somehow essential to his identity, a fundamental and genetic part of his self waiting to emerge. Jim is "associated" with that history; he does not embody it. Indeed, he seems to disavow any connection with his plantation past: "When my old man was sitting around and reading and taking notes trying to trace up who did what in the Civil War, and my two brothers were posing around waiting for the good old times that they had heard went on before the War to come back again, I shucked out to get in touch with the New South" (782–83). However, we may recall that even a historian such as C. Vann Woodward, whose work focused on the ways in which industrialization changed cultural attitudes in the post–Civil War South, admits that a nostalgic fascination with Old South culture—including racial paternalism—influenced race, labor, and business practices in the New South. As Woodward puts it, "Drippings from the plantation legend overflowed upon race and labor relations, public charities, and even the organization of factory villages" (157). Woodward continues, "this idealizing of the past proceeded from the mouths of the most active propagandists for the New Order. And this with no apparent sense of inconsistency, certainly none of duplicity" (157). Thus, though Jim does not explicitly extol the virtues of plantation life, we should not too quickly assume that his rejection of his family's obsession with the Old South is complete; indeed, Hurston's text reveals that the main difference between Jim and his brothers has more to do with motivation than with attitude. While his brothers "pose," Jim sets out to parlay some of the skills, behaviors, and attitudes gleaned from his "associations" with an idealized version of the Old South into economic gain and aristocratic standing, and to bring back a modern version of the "good old times" for which his brothers pine.

To be sure, Jim's process of "noblefication" takes him on a long and sometimes strenuous journey, but he balances his own hard work with a paternalistic manipulation of black labor. He finagles a job as a woodsman in a turpentine camp from Arvay's father, Brock Henson, and before too long rises to the position of overseer, where he strikes up a relationship with African American employee Joe Kelsey, his soon-to-be "pet." Joe and Jim's relationship reinforces the stereotype of African Americans as shiftless and immature that enables the "pet Negro" system. Hurston depicts Joe as an underachieving worker who blames his poor performance on "family worries, the slick and tricky way that moonshine likker had a way of slipping up on him, and so on and so forth" (638). When Joe pesters Jim for money, Jim mock-angrily exclaims that it "Look like that's all you colored folks live for on this camp, Saturday night." Joe does not disagree: in fact, he responds with "But if you ever was to be a Negro just *one* Saturday night, you'd never want to be white no more" (639). Thus, Joe garners financial rewards and favor from Jim by enacting a safe, familiar, "typical" African American role as lazy and concerned largely with pleasure and caprice.

Indeed, for Jim this love of frolic and frivolity far outweighs Joe's limited skills as a turpentiner, since he rises to become Jim's "right-hand man around this camp" (653). In Jim's view Joe has "the best-looking smile that [he] had ever seen on a man. It always lit him right up. It always made Jim feel like playing and joking. Just seeing Joe put him into a playful mood" (637–38). Later in their relationship, when Joe occupies the role of "Uncle Joe," a guardian, companion, and guitar instructor for Jim and Arvay's son

Kenny, he continues to maintain his favorable position with the Meserves by making them smile. He mocks his own laziness and entertains them with an at least partially fictitious story of his failed grocery store business, an enterprise funded with his proceeds from a moonshining partnership with Jim. His story keeps Jim and Arvay in stitches, but "not a grin out of Joe though. He was acting out a drama of misfortune, and he had masked his face to fit the part. Until the curtain fell he was a modern Job, and suffering many things" (824). Hurston's use of theatrical metaphors here underscores the performative, constructed nature of the black "face" Joe presents to them. And, true to form, his paternalist audience offers him a form of payment for his trouble—in this case, hand-me-down clothes from Jim (827). Although Christopher Rieger argues that their illegal side business benefits both Jim and Joe (115), it seems that only Jim reaps any lasting rewards. For his part, Joe cannot conceive of success outside of the paternalist framework. Indeed, all he can do with his stake is turn its failure into a comic story to purchase his re-entry into the social and financial economy of paternalism. Though Joe left the Meserve place with big plans and a financial stake that resulted directly from his paternalist relationship with Jim, his long decades as a "pet" seem to have undermined his ability to succeed independently.

Hurston's description of the service that Joe provides for Jim recalls W. A. Percy's own nostalgic ruminations in *Lanterns on the Levee* about the ways in which his African American friends tempered his essentially intellectual nature with the knowledge of "gaiety and casualness and inventiveness" (54) and served as his "only tie with Pan and the Satyrs and all earth creatures who smile sunshine and ask no questions and understand" (296).[4] Significantly, when Jim tells Arvay about his affection for Joe, Arvay, a "Daughter of the South," understands: "Joe is your pet, I'll bound you" (653). Hurston then elaborates in a passage that echoes much of her earlier essay "The 'Pet Negro' System":

> Arvay sympathized and understood. Every Southern white man has his pet Negro. His Negro is always fine, honest, faithful to him unto death, and most remarkable. Indeed, no other Negro on earth is fitten to hold him a light, and few white people. He never lies, and in fact can do no wrong. If he happens to do what other people

> might consider wrong, it is never his Negro's fault. He was pushed and shoved into it by some unworthy varmint. If he kills somebody else, the dead varmint took and run into the pet's knife or bullet and practically committed suicide just to put the pet in wrong, the low-life-ted scoundrel-beast! If the white patron has his way, the pet will never serve a day in jail for it. The utmost of his influence will be invoked to balk the law. Turn go *his* Negro from that jail! (653)

Although both here and in her earlier essay Hurston describes this relationship as characteristic of "every Southern white man," as though it applied to all men no matter how affluent, she makes it clear in both texts that the white participant in the "pet Negro" system is, in fact, almost always an aristocrat. For instance, we never see Arvay's poor father, Brock Henson, nor any of the other poor white Sawley-ites with a "pet," only "associate" aristocrat Jim Meserve. And in "The 'Pet Negro' System," the white man is named "Colonel Cary"; "colonel" connotes a very traditional southern aristocrat. In both instances, Hurston describes the white man as someone of power and prestige, someone who can throw his weight around in the public sphere in order to procure advantages for his pet, even to the point of interfering with the (admittedly often rusty) wheels of justice. Evidently, the white patron must be a powerful man in the community, with moving-and-shaking abilities that far outstrip those of the average "piney-woods Cracker." Hurston further develops the class implications of the system in her essay when she notes that "if ever it came to the kind of violent showdown the orators hint at," the pets and their white patrons would protect each other so that only the "'pore white trash' and the 'stray niggers'" would be caught in the crossfire (596). Thus, less prestigious whites do not have pets; rather, white participants in the system must first attain a certain level of wealth and social status. Indeed, she argues, "Class-consciousness of Negroes is an angle to be reckoned with in the South. They love to be associated with 'the quality' and consequently are ashamed to admit that they are working for 'strainers'" (that is, whites who do not know the appropriate racial codes and aristocratic etiquette) (596). The Colonel's last name is no coincidence: he requires his "pet" to "carry" him apart from the rabble of common strainers. Clearly, Hurston argues that "petting" is a style of life (in the Weberian sense) associated with, and perhaps definitive of, the southern upper class. Without the "pet" as an aristocratic accessory, southern whites run the risk of being labeled low-class and no-count—and of lacking an important economic resource as well.

The course of the novel, then, follows Jim's largely successful attempts to deploy paternalism generally, and the "pet Negro" system specifically, to increase his wealth and to create a new kind of aristocratic identity for himself, even as it also emphasizes Arvay's initial discomfort with and eventual embrace of the paternalistic attitudes that enable their new class position. *Seraph* highlights the centrality of an Old South paternalist ideology in the creation of a New South society and economy, but it also subtly underscores the manner in which a reliance on paternalistic performance to create an aristocratic class identity can slavishly commit upper-class whites to an attitude of sycophancy.

Some critics have argued convincingly that Jim and Joe's relationship is ultimately symbiotic and genuinely affectionate, and indeed, I would agree that the men seem to feel genuine emotion for each other. However, Hurston also foregrounds the exploitative nature of their relationship in Jim and Joe's very first scene together.[5] Under the guise of a "practical joke," Jim "[crept] up close to Joe's back and made a sudden howl like an angry bob-cat on the kill. At the same time, he clawed his fingers and stuck them into Joe's broad back" (638). Though the men both find the faux attack funny and shift smoothly into a familiar riff on Joe's love of "likker and women," it is hard to ignore in this striking imagery a true picture of the structure of labor relations between the two men, one that recalls Colonel Cary and his "pet": Joe the broad-backed worker must *carry* the beclawed, parasitic Jim on his long road to noblefication. Indeed, the "pet Negro" system is a version of Bourdieu's "symbolic alchemy," that process by which "the relation of domination and exploitation . . . [is] enchanted in such a way as to transform it into a domestic relationship of familiarity through a continuous series of acts capable of symbolically transfiguring it through euphemization" (*Practical Reason* 101). The elaborate system of jokes, stereotypes, social roles, and perhaps even true affection that characterizes Jim and Joe's relationship does not prove that their relationship is nonexploitative; to the contrary, their familiar relationship is in fact a necessity for the exploitation to work most efficiently.

Both Hurston's description of Jim and Joe as well as Percy's characterization of the racial roles necessary to constitute a paternalist relationship recall Hurston biographer Robert Hemenway's depiction of the relationship between Hurston and one of her early patrons, New York matriarch Mrs. Rufus Osgood Mason. According to Hemenway, "Mrs. Mason thought of Zora as an unspoiled child of nature, an impression that the younger woman did little to dispel" (104). Indeed, continues Hemenway, "Louise Thompson, another woman supported by Mrs. Mason for a time, eventually came to feel that the patron was 'indulging her fantasies of Negroes,' that she was in fact racist. Her black guests were either primitive, or they were not being themselves" (107). Recent Hurston biographer Valerie Boyd notes that Mason held strongly to the "conviction that black people—if they'd only be their 'savage' selves—could save whites from the aridity of civilization. Mason believed in cosmic energies and intuitive powers, and she was sure that 'primitive' people . . . were innately more in tune with these supernatural forces than were whites" (157). Though Hemenway charitably grants Mason the sincerity of her intentions and accepts some of Hurston's claims that their relationship was sincere, he also notes that "it is hard to believe that Hurston did not recognize Mrs. Mason's wealth as a key to her future" (108). As Susan Meisenhelder argues, "the strategy Hurston adopted to survive in a publishing world controlled by whites and a few black men necessarily became a flexible one, a give and take affair in which she constantly had to weigh what she censored (or submerged) in order to get published and what she could openly express" (7).Together with the analysis of paternalism in "The 'Pet Negro' System," the implication here that Hurston was perhaps performing a racialized role in exchange for economic support suggests that she had a more complex understanding of the working of paternalism than a reading of Jim and Joe's relationship as characterized by friendship and symbiosis would suggest.[6]

When Jim and Arvay move to Citrabelle to become citrus farmers, Jim continues this relationship with Joe Kelsey, but he also extends the scope of his noblesse oblige to other African Americans in the area in order to learn the tricks of the citrus trade and to facilitate the building of his new home. His initial, uninformed forays into agriculture bear no fruit until he realizes that "since the colored men did all of the manual work, they were the ones who actually knew how things were done," and so he spends much time around the "jooks and gathering places in Colored Town," where, in addition to chatting and telling stories, he "stood treats" for the men there in order to get information (666). Jim's buying of rounds for the bar patrons conforms to the Veblenian ideal of conspicuous consumption; standing treats for a group of African American workers is no doubt a conspicuous way for Jim to announce his relative wealth, and it certainly *appears* wasteful, though it proves quite efficient in the long run, for it favorably disposes the men to Jim.[7] Moreover, Jim's noblesse allies him with the men in a way that separates him from poor whites in the area. For instance, he enlists the aid of many African American workers by providing flour, liquor, and shotgun shells—and, significantly, by not asking the purpose of the last item in that list, since "too many Crackers saved hog-feed by letting their hogs run wild in the woods until just before time to butcher for Jim to want to know too much. If a big barbecue was going to be held on his place to get it cleaned up, he knew nothing about where all that meat came from" (672). Already, then, Jim has begun to reenact classic plantation roles, earning the favor of black laborers and scorning working-class whites as "Crackers" and "trash."

Jim puts this combination of noblesse and conspicuous waste into practice on an even grander scale when he begins to build his house. When Arvay complains about his letting African Americans "steal" leftover wood that they themselves could put to good use,[8] Jim explains to her that doing so garners him an economic advantage in the form of eager black labor while at the same time confirming his status as an aristocrat, a "gentleman" who dispenses gifts to his "help." Jim's paternalism is expressed here through the conspicuous (though putatively covert) waste of lumber.[9] Indeed, Jim's increasing wealth keeps pace with new technologies, and he and son-in-law Hatton Howland soon have African American workers clearing out the swamp behind the Meserve home to make way for a country club and posh housing development: "As Jim had predicted, modern machinery and methods had cleared the swamp in an amazingly short time. Arvay, from her seat on the front porch, watched the gangs of husky black roustabouts rumbling past in truck loads, singing, chanting, laughing as they went to the swamp and moved about in their high boots, and swinging shining axes to rhythm, felling the giant trees" (775–76). In her description of a "horde of black men" (776) carving an expensive estate out of a barren wilderness, Hurston appropriates and updates the Old Southern strivings of another would-be aristocrat, Thomas Sutpen, whose story does not end as happily as Jim Meserve's. Hurston notes that, once completed, the development "exerted a tremendous effect on Citrabelle and the surrounding country. It came along and stratified the town. . . . Those who belonged moved west" (777). Perhaps Jim's intimate family associations with those who once stood inside of the threshold that Sutpen was barred from crossing grants him a fuller understanding of the racialized codes and practices needed to authorize an aristocratic identity. Again, Hurston suggests that the habits of the plantation persist in the most successful entrepreneurs of the New South.

However, as the incident of the wood suggests, although Jim's gentlemanly attitude toward waste and race dramatically increases his family's wealth and standing in the community, Arvay cannot initially understand the behaviors and attitudes that her new elite position requires of her. Though Jim tells her he is "scuffling" to place her "higher up"—on the pedestal of exalted southern womanhood, specifically—Arvay repeatedly disappoints him by her reversion to ways, including racial ways, he considers beneath her (838).[10] Her profound sense of class inferiority—reinforced, in part, by the birth of their first child, the deformed, mentally handicapped Earl, who reminds Arvay of her "queer" Uncle Chester and thus, Arvay believes, proves her essential trashiness—expresses itself as an overt, aggressive racism that prevents her from fully adopting Jim's ostensibly benevolent paternalistic ethic.[11] True, she initially enjoys the company of Joe Kelsey and his family and exhibits behaviors consistent with paternalist ideals, even going so far as to refer to their daughter Belinda as "my little girl" (703).[12] Yet the Kelseys also prove easy targets for Arvay's displaced frustrations with Jim. When she discovers that Jim and Joe have been running a moonshine business on the side, she takes her anger "out on Joe. He was leading her husband astray, and on top of that, she had a half-grown son, and he too was in danger of being ruined by Joe and his likkery ways" (705). For Arvay, then, in a moment of stress, Joe's more stereotypical African American traits—his "likkery ways"—become not an opportunity to exercise noblesse oblige but to attack him for sullying the moral purity of her white family. Even when Jim explains that he masterminded the moonshine operation, Arvay continues to act coolly to Joe (705). Ultimately, the chilly atmosphere drives Joe and his family to leave the Meserves and move to Colored Town.

Even with the Kelseys no longer living on the Meserves' place, Arvay still obsesses over the class inequalities between herself and Jim. She broadly allegorizes these inequalities as a conflict between the great plantations and the piney woods, a conflict in which African Americans such as Joe Kelsey rank higher in aristocratic estimation than poor whites like herself. She tells Jim, "You come from some big high muck-de-mucks, and we ain't nothing but piney-woods Crackers and poor white trash. Even niggers is better than we is, according to your kind. Joe Kelsey's word stands higher than mine any old day. . . . You give him more credit for sense than you do me" (713). Arvay further reflects, "He was that same James Kenneth Meserve of the great plantations, and looked down on her as the backwoods Cracker, the piney-woods rooter" (716–17). Moreover, "The great river plantations were too powerful for the piney woods" (718). Faced with what she perceives as an inability to stand on an equal class footing with Jim, Arvay, on two separate occasions, attempts to affirm and celebrate her Cracker roots. Importantly, she figures this affirmation as a renunciation of Jim's model of race relations: "Let Jim strain with his house and his impudent, biggety niggers his ownself" (845).

But Arvay's attempted affirmations fail. Frustrated with the incomplete understanding she shares with Jim, with his frequent absences and devotion to his new shrimping business, and not least with the increasingly ill-disguised disdain shown her by Jeff Kelsey, Joe's son and Jim's new right-hand man—whose seamless transition into his father's role suggests that southern paternalists see their "pets" as interchangeable cogs in a wheel, not as individuals—Arvay imagines herself returning to the simple town of Sawley and its honest, hardworking people: "The corroding poverty of her childhood became a glowing virtue, and a state to be desired" (845). She imagines a plain but honest life free of the "impudence" she must tolerate from African Americans who view her inability to behave in the appropriate paternalistic manner as sign of her unsuitability for aristocracy. But the reality she encounters destroys her romantic illusions. When she returns to Sawley to attend to her dying mother, she finds her humble but once well tended childhood home in filthy disarray: "Arvay could hear two things: the rattle of cook-pots in the kitchen, and the squeak and patter of rats in the walls. What was worse, she could smell the strong odor of rat-urine over everything" (849). The rats force her to ponder the kinds of questions that never seem to arise in Citrabelle: how to keep her mother's body from being eaten by animals, for instance (858). Nor does she find that her family conforms to her ideal of good-hearted country contentment. She discovers that her sister and brother-in-law resent her relatively luxurious lifestyle and have been leeching off her mother (852). When Carl and Larraine discover that Mrs. Henson has left her modest estate to Arvay, they sue her. When that fails, they destroy all of Arvay's heirlooms and mementos and abscond with everything of value from the home, including most of the sturdier boards from the back porch.

Realizing that she no longer belongs among the shabby denizens of Sawley, Arvay elects to return to Citrabelle and embrace her husband's lifestyle. Significantly, the way in which she chooses to express her acceptance of this "aristocratic" upper-class life is through racial paternalism. While preparing for her return trip, "she ordered a bag of paper shell pecans as a present for Jeff and Janie. Let them know that she appreciated them too. Maybe Jeff was not snappy for just nothing" (871). But when she encounters Jeff and Janie again, and Jeff refers to them collectively as "us Meserves," his casual evocation of the ostensibly familial relationship that characterizes paternalist relations makes her feel once again "all of the turmoil and uncertainty that [she] had felt before she went away" (883). She manages, however, to regain "command of herself." Hurston tells us that "Arvay took an attitude that she would have died before adopting before she went away," insisting that Jeff and Janie come up to her house so she can show them their present (883). Her paternalist gesture earns the desired response: Jeff tells her she "sure is folks," and continues, "Just like Mister Jim, ain't she Janie? And everybody knows that Mister Jim is quality first-class. Knows how to carry hisself, and then how to treat everybody. Miss Arvay's done come to be just like him. . . . You felt for us and remembered us. Made us feel like we amount to something with you. We feel proud and glad to work around you. You'se quality all the way" (884). Thus, by adopting Jim's paternalist ethic, Arvay not only receives Jeff and Janie's endorsement as "first-class" and "quality" but also their eager labor—"We feel proud and glad to work around you."

It would have been easy for readers of Hurston's day to see this as a sort of happy ending, a narrative of upward class mobility, with Arvay as the backwoods Cracker who has become a fine lady and worthy wife of a New South aristocratic husband through learning the ropes of nouveau-plantation racial paternalism. But Hurston, as we might expect, is subtly critical of the costs of Arvay's transformation. The idealized version of the "pet Negro" system and of racial paternalism in general holds that these structures of race relations promote understanding, harmony, and meaningful relationships between the races, yet Hurston makes it clear that, instead, it imprisons wealthy white elites like Arvay in an attitude of sycophancy. Their confidence in their class position relies on maintaining a paternalistic, aristocratic performance that in many ways precludes their sharing themselves with their black "friends." Indeed, Jim implicitly evokes this constant need to maintain an aristocratic performance when he tells Arvay that he wouldn't "*be* a gentleman no more"—not that the African Americans would not *consider* him a gentleman—if he did not allow them to take the excess lumber. Hurston more explicitly underscores the central, if certainly not final, role of the African American gaze in determining class during a scene in which, after Arvay refuses to help Jim wrestle with a poisonous snake, "Jeff gave her a look that halted her where she was. The look forbade her to approach the person of Jim Meserve. It called her unworthy of such an honor and pleasure and privilege by reason of cowardice and treason and *trashiness*" (831, my emphasis). As we recall, in "The 'Pet Negro' System" Hurston argued that "class-consciousness of Negroes is an angle to be reckoned with in the South. They love to be associated with 'the quality' and consequently are ashamed to admit that they are working for 'strainers.' It is amusing to see a Negro servant chasing the madam or the boss back on his or her pedestal when they behave in an unbecoming manner." Thus, Jeff, who idolizes Arvay's aristocratic husband, also polices the boundaries of Jim's class position to maintain its coherence by preventing anyone unworthy—or "trashy," a term obviously loaded with class significance—from sullying his master's good name.

In a remarkable scene shortly after the incident of the snake, Hurston makes clear just how constant and inescapable is Jeff's surveillance of Arvay, his continual evaluation of her suitability for Jim. One afternoon, when Arvay takes a nap on the sleeping porch that Jim has built for her—an area that he intends to serve as a kind of "throne room" that proves she has come "a long, long way from the turpentine woods" (811)—she awakens to find "Jeff standing with a 'lazy boy' in one of his big brawny hands, the other hand on his hip, and his face pressed against the screen wire, staring at her. His face was pressed so hard against the screening that his nose was flattened, and his lips were distorted into purple blobs. His eyes were fixed on her and unmoving. Neither did he jump away when he saw her see him. . . . That look was so powerful and intense" (843). Hurston quickly assures us that "Jeff was not longing after her body," but, rather, that his look "was anger and dislike" (843). This scene stands in marked contrast to Jeff's later evocation of "us Meserves"; while that phrase suggests solidarity and familial closeness, the manner of his surveillance here stresses the distance between them. Not only does Jeff stand outside of her porch of privilege, but the distortion of his facial features—the "flattened" nose, lips like "purple blobs"—emphasizes his racial otherness by conforming to stereotypical images of primitive Africans. Hurston even notes that when he turns away, he does so with a "*savage* abruptness" (843, my emphasis). Significantly, Jeff's features become distorted *because* he is pressing "so hard against the screening," as though, since he considers himself to be a "real" Meserve much more than Arvay is, he longs to be on the porch himself. The screen, then—a transparent, semipermeable boundary that allows Arvay to experience the natural world with all of her senses while also protecting her from its dangers—becomes a metaphor for the fundamental contradiction at the heart of paternalist ideology. Jim and his aristocratic ilk make much of the alleged closeness and familiarity of interracial relationships organized on paternalistic lines. Yet there always exists a barely visible boundary that, if violated, renders the African American utterly Other.

Although—or because—he cannot ever gain access to the porch and become a Meserve in the truest sense, Jeff polices the boundaries of his employer's family vigorously, lest anyone unfit should sully his master's good name. As these scenes indicate, Arvay lives under a condition of constant surveillance that recalls Foucault's concept of the Panopticon, which induces "a state of conscious and permanent visibility that assures the automatic functioning of power" (470). Though Jim is not present to encourage and exhort Arvay to adopt the paternalist behaviors that go along with his aristocratic lifestyle, he still manages to exert his power and express his disapproval through the gaze of Jeff and other African Americans. Indeed, Arvay very much identifies Jeff with Jim's power and emphasizes his observing function when she notes that although she wants to run "the impudent scoundrel-beast" off the place, Jeff would only "remind her that *Mister* Jim had put him on the place, paid his wages, and gave him his orders. . . . She couldn't fire Jeff—nothing of the kind—and Jeff knew it" (843, original emphasis).

The stress Arvay places on the word "Mister" as she frets about her tenuous position on the plantation is significant: she has begun to realize that, though performances of paternalism are necessary to maintain her status, she wields no true power over the workers. As a woman, the highest station she can hope to achieve is that of wife of the master; her goals and desires are validated only insofar as they conform to Jim's view of what the wife of a Meserve should desire. Thus, Arvay at rest on her sleeping porch is simply another version of the Southern Woman standing on her pedestal—privileged, yes, but also eternally on display as another piece of evidence of her husband's lofty status. Arvay is caught in a double bind: she must perform racial paternalism in order to maintain her status, but that performance does not offer her the same power to coerce and organize African American workers that it offers Jim. Hurston thus emphasizes the masculine nature of racial paternalism, a masculinity that is of course inherent in the term itself. Even when enacted by a woman, the effect is always the creation and maintenance of power for the fatherly aristocrat.

Hurston construes Arvay's acceptance of her role as a highly visible, perpetually performing indicator of Jim's upper-class status in a manner very much consistent with Foucault's claim that "he who is subjected to a field of visibility, and who knows it, assumes responsibility for the constraints of power. . . ; he becomes the principle of his own subjection" (471). Arvay at least unconsciously realizes that a restored relationship with Jim and the material comforts that that relationship guarantees her depend on Jeff and Janie's evaluation of her conformity to "first-class" mores, and so she carefully considers what sort of face to present to them, what facts she should reveal and conceal. For instance, when she tells them about her mother's funeral, she emphasizes "her mother's casket and the flowers" (884) and "the visits and the meals and other entertainments which the Carys," Sawley's richest family, had furnished, but she leaves out "how Larraine and Carl had behaved towards her" (883). When Arvay does mention the seamier side of the trip, she does so quickly and only to distance herself from her family and assert her solidarity with Jim: "She told them that she had burned the house, and turned her back on what it stood for for good and all. She had found that she did not belong there after all. Without realizing, she had come to prefer Jim's way of handling things" (885). Hurston pointedly notes that when she relates the story to Jim, "she did not leave out the part about Larraine and Carl" (892). After all, Jim already has firsthand experience with her "trashy" family, and so she cannot hope to downplay her connection to them as she does with Jeff and Janie.

Though Arvay frets that her conversion to Jim's paternalistic, aristocratic ways may have come too late, she does manage to win her way back into Jim's noble graces by demonstrating a paternalistic attitude toward Cup-Cake, the African American cook aboard one of Jim's shrimping boats. A shrimping boat on the high seas may seem an odd, even inappropriate place for Arvay to exercise her newly adopted paternalism, but in certain ways Jim has already brought the paternalistic spirit of the plantation to bear on his shrimping business. True, this enterprise at first appears to be run as a racially egalitarian meritocracy in which the only thing considered important "was who could go out there and come back with the shrimp" (893); indeed, "White and Negro captains were friendly together and compared notes," and "some boats had mixed crews" (893). According to Rieger, "the racial egalitarianism of the shrimping community even surpasses that of the muck [of *Their Eyes Were Watching God*], where white bosses supervise work, intraracial prejudice abounds, and the neighboring Seminoles are mocked" (121). Yet I would argue that this egalitarianism is less radical than it initially seems. Crucially, though Jim and Alfredo, a "husky Negro," might both serve as ship's captains, in this novel, only Jim and other white men serve as *owners* of those ships. Moreover, when Jim tells Arvay about the lives of the shrimpers as they "ma[k]e the round of the Jooks," he does so in a way that very much recalls his conversation with Joe Kelsey about the fundamentally pleasure-seeking nature of African Americans who live for Saturday night: "A man had to enjoy himself while he could. The very next trip might be his last. So if they bought likker and love recklessly, what of it? Arvay noted that he relaxed when she agreed that they had a point there. Even though most of them spent their money right away, and depended on going out there and getting more" (894). Perhaps it is not too much of a stretch, then, to note that the repeated exclamations of "Captain! My Captain. . . . Oh Captain!" from the mate of Jim's ship would sound equally appropriate spoken by a field hand to a plantation owner. In any case, Arvay's paternalistic gesture toward Cup-Cake works perfectly: She effusively praises his cooking, and "a half second later she knew that she had said just the right thing. Jim smiled and opened his eyes wide and looked at her with pleasure. Cup-Cake grinned all over himself" (901). Significantly, Jim's response, jokingly telling Cup-Cake that he hopes Arvay "don't take and spoil you too rotten," puts Cup-Cake in the position of a precocious child and Arvay in the position of an indulgent parent.

Jim's treatment of his seafaring underlings as just another group of carefree, impulsive laborers who need his paternal care—and Cup-Cake's apparent confirmation of that need—helps him and Arvay make an ostensibly seamless transition from citrus to shrimp. And to be sure, the fact that Jim does labor alongside his employees rather than simply amassing wealth from afar is a point in his favor. However, his breezy confidence that the men look up to him the way Joe and Jeff Kelsey do blinds him to a subtle undercurrent of resentment, and perhaps budding resistance, evident in the shrimpers' attitudes toward him. On his first voyage in the *Arvay Henson,* Jim asks his mate Stumpy if he fears sailing out with a new captain. Stumpy tells him, "I ain't scared of a thing but old Bozo" (800). When Jim expresses his puzzlement, Stumpy mock-incredulously informs Jim that he "ain't no real fisherman until you meet old Bozo and fight him" (800). The Third Man fills Jim in on the details: in order to find Bozo, an intrepid adventurer must return to shore and traverse a fantastical, decidedly un-Floridian landscape, to confront the mythical Bozo, who lives, significantly, on a plantation: "Bozo seemed to have a plenty. Rich and well-to-do. All you had to do then was to go right up and knock on the door, and when Bozo opened it, challenge him to a fight. The man who whipped Bozo would be the king of the world" (801).

The Third Man's own trek to vanquish Bozo ended abruptly when he caught sight of Bozo's cat, "as big as a yearling calf to start off with. . . . If his cat was that big and tough I didn't want to meet that Bozo riding nor walking" (801).

Jim laughs off the tale as part of his "initiation" into the world of fishermen, and it would be easy for the reader to laugh it off as well. Yet, we should not get so caught up in this paternalist's worldview that we miss the unrest, dissatisfaction, and anger brewing among the workers. The Bozo story reveals a measure of class-consciousness and indeed class resentment that should perhaps make Jim, ostensibly an astute observer of folk culture, at least a bit uncomfortable. After all, Jim is the scion of a great plantation family who has appropriated a form of plantation logic to make himself, like Bozo, "rich and well-to-do" and to build himself a "big house." Though the fishermen fear this Jim-like character's power, they also dream of conquering him by force in order to gain his wealth and become "king of the world." Jim's joking dismissal of the story may indicate that he misses the story's potentially troubling implications for his own way of life.

A similar myopia characterizes Jim and Arvay's response to another instance in which the men express their dissatisfaction with their working conditions and class position, an instance which should signal to Jim that things are not as simple as they had seemed in Citrabelle and Sawley. Arvay observes that the fishermen "all cursed out the owners. Everything that went wrong on a boat was named after the owner. Did the fuel pump on the engine go bad? It was a Toomer, Meserve, or whatever the owner's name so-and-so of a bastard! . . . Arvay found that Jim knew about it, as did the other owners and laughed it off" (893). Certainly, Jim's privilege and prestige allows him to "laugh it off" and insulates him from any real offense. But the gauzy shroud of wealth and power that he wears softens this harsh image like Vaseline on a camera lens, preventing him from perceiving the true nature of the men's demonstration: they impotently vent the anger and frustration that they feel toward their bosses on these inanimate avatars. Indeed, bestowing the owner's name upon every broken piece of machinery implicitly makes the statement that, like a faulty fuel pump, the owner stands in the way of their material gain. Jim characteristically misses this critique: when Arvay worries aloud about the practice,

Jim tells her, "Cussing the boss out behind his back is a lot of pleasure. I forget that I'm the owner and cuss my ownself out at times" (893–94). Of course, this "forgetting," this ability to move easily between roles, is a privilege only afforded to wealthy elites like Jim—he can slum with the shrimpers, but they cannot own a fleet of shrimp boats.

Ultimately, then, if Hurston holds out any hope for meaningful social action that can undermine the paternalist social order, she does so in her depiction of this nascent class resentment among the shrimpers, this dissatisfaction with Jim's New Old South management style. Their apparent impotence in the face of Jim's insulating power and wealth, however, qualifies this critique. But, as Hurston would have observed in the late 1940s, the seeds of independence evident in this multiracial coalition of laborers bode ill for those who rely on the established social order for a stage upon which to perform their power. True, Arvay learns how to pull herself—or to allow herself to be lifted by African Americans—onto the pedestal that Jim has constructed for her, learns the necessary racial performances that authorize her aristocratic upper-class position and make her a suitable mate for Jim.[13] At the same time, Hurston subtly criticizes the costs of Arvay's transformation. Admittedly, constantly performing paternalism with Jim, no matter how limiting or sycophantic, beats starving in Sawley with Carl and Larraine. But though racial paternalism does enable Arvay and Jim to increase their riches and to advance in status and proves useful even in nonplantation New South labor settings such as citrus growing and shrimping, it also places them firmly and forever on a very public stage and forces them to perform according to very strict rules for a watchful African American audience without whose approval they cannot maintain their wealth and standing—an audience whose approval would be less and less forthcoming in the years to come. Thus, in *Seraph* Hurston offers a sharp critique of the ways in which racial performances authorize an aristocratic class identity, and she makes clear for a contemporary white audience in a time of social unrest that the vanishing "stabilizing" force of paternalism for which they may long constrains not only the increasingly independent African Americans but themselves as well.

2

PLAYING LADY AND IMITATING ARISTOCRATS

Race, Class, and Money in Eudora Welty's *Delta Wedding* and *The Ponder Heart*

The central plot of *Delta Wedding* (1946), Eudora Welty's richly textured novel of plantation life in the Mississippi Delta of the 1920s, involves the marriage of Dabney Fairchild, daughter of an aristocratic family of planters, to Troy Flavin, the family's decidedly unaristocratic overseer from the hill country. Troy's position as a geographical and philosophical outsider and as a Fairchild employee complicates the Fairchilds' acceptance of him into their closely guarded ranks. As the wedding date draws near, he remarks to plantation mistress Ellen Fairchild (whose Virginia roots mark her as something of an outsider too) that he has finally discovered the trick to becoming a "Delta person" like the Fairchilds: "By now, I can't tell a bit of difference between me and any Delta people you name. There's nothing easy about the Delta either, but it's just a matter of knowing how to handle your Negroes" (125). Though Ellen protests that "if it was that at first, I believe there's more to it," she proves unable to articulate what exactly constitutes that something more. When Troy presses her for a more exact definition, she tells him vaguely, "The Delta's just like everywhere. . . . You keep taking things on, and you'll see. Things still take a little time" (125).

Ellen's inability to formulate a specific rejoinder to Troy's characteristically forward remark reveals a fracture in the Fairchilds' sense of their lofty place in Delta society. Though Ellen admits that "at first" their aristocratic status and the economic base that supported that status depended upon coerced African American labor, she and the other Fairchilds believe that they now lead a more refined and cultured life in which African Americans are not "handled" but rather form an integral part of the extended plantation "family," a belief that ignores the way in which familial behavior can serve as a coercive tool. Yet she cannot formulate a convincing explanation of what, exactly, makes a "Delta person"—a regional identity that Welty exposes as conflated with aristocratic whiteness—unique from a hill country bumpkin like Troy if *not* a particular relationship to their African American retainers. This concern with the nature of class identities is central both to *Delta Wedding* and to *The Ponder Heart* (1954). In *Delta Wedding* Welty explores the ways that paternalism serves both as a badge of status and as an economic tool and examines the reasons for Ellen's reluctance to admit this truth. Welty examines in particular how paternalism works to obscure the economic base of the Fairchilds' aristocratic status, a status that they perceive as natural and essential. The Fairchilds want to downplay the crass fact of money and its formative capacity in their privileged life, and paternalism as a form of labor relations helps them in this endeavor by enabling them to see their laborers as putative family members. Welty critiques this myth of an insular, self-perpetuating aristocracy by highlighting key moments at which the machinery of coercion and exploitation, the true relationship of employer and servant, becomes visible and disrupts the Fairchilds' carefully maintained façade. Though Welty seems to offer no compelling method of resistance to the Fairchilds' system of paternalism in *Delta Wedding*, she returns to this complicated intersection of race, class, and economics in *The Ponder Heart*, a text that offers a more hopeful model for relationships among classes and races.

Shifting historical, racial, and economic trends provided Welty good reason to turn her keen gaze on the complicated intersection of race and class in the Delta. As with Hurston's *Seraph on the Suwanee*, her *Delta Wedding* looks backward to a supposedly more stable historical moment for paternalistic race relations.[1] To be sure, the behaviors and attitudes necessary to "handle your Negroes," as Troy puts it, were clearer in the 1923 of the novel's setting than in the 1940s of its composition and publication. Written in the wake of New Deal reforms that set in motion forces that would irrevocably alter Delta life, and with the influence of World War II on the African American population already becoming apparent, *Delta Wedding* reflects anxieties about the naturalness, coherence, and perpetuation of aristocratic identity and traditional ways of life that many elite Deltans felt in the 1940s.[2] Welty has often noted that she chose not to set her novel in the contemporary 1940s because she wanted to tell a family story that would require the men to be home, and that she chose

1923 in particular because so little happened in the Delta that year. Yet, she has also observed that, despite the absence of wars, floods, or other catastrophes, the Fairchild way of life did not stand outside of history. In an interview with Charles T. Bunting, she described the way of life at Shellmound as "a fragile, temporary thing" (*More Conversations* 54).[3]

Indeed, the changes in Mississippi's racial climate contributed greatly to the fragility of Delta traditions. James Cobb describes the apparently stable Delta of the mid-1930s as a "region where extremes of white affluence and privilege were sustained by equally striking levels of black deprivation and powerlessness" (*Most Southern Place* 153). These conditions were the legacy of planters who, Cobb argues, "fanc[ied] themselves heirs to an aristocratic antebellum tradition" and sought to change "Old South fantasy to New South reality" (*Most Southern Place* 97). However, that "reality" required a large African American workforce to exploit, a situation that grew more difficult to maintain as the effects of the New Deal and World War II began to change the face of Delta life. Cobb states that responsibility for caring for impoverished African Americans shifted from aristocratic whites to federal programs, weakening the foundation of paternalism upon which the plantation economy rested. This decreased reliance on wealthy planters encouraged African Americans, especially those of the younger generation, to exercise their independence. Planters in turn found their need for black labor, and thus the need to adhere to the standards of paternalism, somewhat reduced by Acreage Adjustment Administration (AAA) subsidies and increasing mechanization (*Most Southern Place* 185–86).

Delta planters soon discovered, however, that the New Deal had not completely freed them from their reliance on black labor. Black workers left the Delta more quickly than mechanization could replace them, resulting in periodic labor shortages. The influence of World War II not only contributed to this exodus by drawing laborers to better paying jobs in the defense industry, but it also improved the lot of those laborers still in the Delta. Historian David R. Goldfield elaborates on the attractive opportunities that wartime industrialization offered to laborers accustomed to a system of debt peonage:

> A black sharecropper could leave his mule and plow and earn more money in one week of work in a defense plant than he ever saw at

> the end of a good crop year. He could enjoy the luxury of choosing a place to live, of paying other people to work for him—dry cleaners, taxi drivers, waitresses, and maintenance personnel. He could exercise choices in how and where to spend his money, assured that a drought or tumbling international markets or capricious landlords would not suddenly end his relative prosperity. Or, if he took up a gun, he could demonstrate his worthiness for first-class citizenship and visibility. And if both he and his nation were fighting to preserve democratic principles, how could his countrymen deny him his due? (32)

This new economic independence did nothing for the Delta's precarious racial détente: Cobb observes that "irritated planters in desperate need of cotton pickers could hardly endure the sight of blacks driving about the Delta enjoying their new leisure and flaunting their new sense of independence" (*Most Southern Place* 198). The 1944 Supreme Court decision in the *Smith v. Allwright* case, which ruled the all-white primary unconstitutional, contributed to the sense of unease for elite whites. The large population of eligible—if still unregistered and at times violently oppressed—black voters threatened the electoral supremacy of white Deltans and served as yet another signal of the gradual but permanent change in the planter way of life. Thus, in the Delta that Welty visited in the 1930s and 1940s, the once settled, familiar traditions governing interactions among races had become objects of contention. Welty's novel explores a time when those traditions could more easily be taken for granted, but she also exposes the often brutal reality that lay just beneath the apparently placid surface.

At first glance, the economic and racial strife that beset Deltans as Welty wrote *Delta Wedding* seems far removed from the privileged, carefree lives of the novel's main characters. The novel follows the Fairchilds as they traverse the expansive plantation grounds of Shellmound, visiting family members and carrying out the various domestic rituals necessary for Dabney's impending nuptials, all the while attended by a coterie of African American servants and ostensibly unconcerned with the grueling agricultural labor that makes such a gala affair possible.[4] A powerful sense of unity and entitlement characterizes their worldview: "no gap opened between them," writes Welty, and "all the Fairchilds in the Delta looked alike." As eldest daughter Shelley Fairchild puts it, "All together we have a wall, we are self-sufficient against people that come up knocking, we are solid to the outside" (110). This sense of privilege and familial coherence has drawn the attention of critics such as Douglas Messerli, who argues that the Fairchilds have almost created "a cosmos peopled by sons and daughters, uncles, aunts, and other relatives who in their similarity of appearance, ideology, and emotional temper repeat one another over and over again, insuring in that repetition—that complete oneness—a sort of immortality for each member of the clan" (108).

However, nine-year-old Laura McRaven, the Fairchild cousin—and a Delta outsider like Welty herself[5]—whose arrival at Shellmound opens the novel and through whose perspective we get our first look at the Fairchilds, perceives a taint of falseness in their supposed freedom. Although her recently deceased mother had said the Fairchilds "never seemed to change at all" (17), Laura sees that in fact "they changed every moment. The outside did not change but the inside did; an iridescent life was busy within and under each alikeness. Laughter at something went over the table; Laura found herself with a picture in her mind of a great bowerlike cage full of tropical birds her father had shown her in a zoo in a city—the sparkle of motion was like a rainbow, while it was the very thing that broke your heart, for the birds that flew were caged all the time and could not fly out. The Fairchilds' movements were quick and on the instant, and that made you wonder, are they free? Laura was certain they were *compelled*—their favorite word" (18). Laura further reflects that "maybe . . . their kissing of not only you but everybody in a room was a kind of spectacle, an outward thing" (18). Thus, even though each Fairchild may have a rich and "iridescent" internal life, the Fairchilds must subordinate that life to an outward "alikeness." The spectacle of privilege and unity belies the fact that their spectacular performance is "compelled," is necessary to maintain the illusion of freedom that Laura so quickly sees through. This performance of privilege that paradoxically constrains its elite white performers recalls Arvay Meserve's own paranoid performances of aristocratic behaviors in Hurston's *Seraph on the Suwanee*.[6]

But what compels this frantic performance? Welty offers us a clue at the end of this lively, noisy scene—a clue that ties their performance closely to racial and economic realities. As the family's activity winds down and they sit "sighing, eating cake, drinking coffee," Laura realizes, "The throb of the compress had never stopped. Laura could feel it now in the handle of her cup, the noiseless vibration that trembles in the best china, was within it" (20). This passage reveals that the Fairchilds' colorful clamor covers over—though always incompletely and impermanently—the material sources of their privilege, the evidence of the labor that allows them to enjoy their ostensibly carefree lifestyle. As Patricia Yaeger aptly interprets this scene, "What is vibrating in this china is not just the cotton compress, ceaselessly at work binding the just-picked cotton into bales, but the ceaseless vibrations of the pickers and the house servants, a vibration that trembles through the silverware and the best linens and every other expensive item in the house" (98). The Fairchilds make a great show of ignoring this vibration, of leading a hermetically sealed and self-perpetuating life, isolated from the brute realities of sharecropper sweat and cotton compress. Indeed, Laura recalls that on previous trips she saw the cotton lint that covered "ceilings and lampshades, fresh every morning," the airborne excess of the cotton economy, as a "present from the fairies," as though it appeared out of thin air and only for her pleasure. She perceives no relation between this fairy gift and the massive fields around her, and only notes in passing that it causes Vi'let, the black servant charged with cleaning it each day, to "moan" (8). Yaeger reads this lint as part of the "white detritus" that floats through many novels by southern women and "bespeaks a constant uneasiness about the meaning of whiteness" (20)—perhaps in this case because the moans it elicits from Vi'let reveal the constant black labor needed to maintain their comfort. Dabney Fairchild exhibits impatience when such economic matters impinge upon her romantic conceptions of plantation life: when she recalls the story of her grandfather's death in a duel over improprieties at a cotton gin, she wonders "what was the reason death could be part of a question about the crops, for instance?" and affirms her own belief that "all the cotton in the world was not worth one moment of life!" (158). But the insistent throb of the compress "within" even so delicate a household treasure as the best china cup reveals that mode of perception as fundamentally flawed and indicates that even the most refined existence rests on an economic base—in this case, one constituted by the labor of African Americans.

Although we might attempt to characterize Laura's and Dabney's attitude as juvenile naiveté or to argue that their viewpoint results from their exclusion from a male-dominated economic sphere, in fact the adult Fairchilds of both genders persist in the attempt to treat their rarified position as separate from the labor going on all around them. For instance, clan patriarch Battle Fairchild so ignores the crass details of cash and accounts that Troy's predecessor, former overseer Mr. Bascom, finds it simple to cheat him. Ellen (a Fairchild by marriage, and so perhaps not fully assimilated into their way of thinking) dreams sometimes about "the location of mistakes in the accounts and the payroll that her husband—not a born business man—had let pass, and discovered how Mr. Bascom had cheated them and stolen so much" (84). Further, when the Fairchilds absolutely must take heed of such petty details as the payroll, they do so in a way that indicates they consider such mundane concerns beneath them. Their aversion to the common physicality of cash money leads them to wash and iron the payroll, much to the more practical Troy's surprise. When he remarks, startled, "Is she ironing *money?*" Ellen tells him matter-of-factly, "Why, that's the payroll. . . . Didn't you know Aunt Mac always washes it? . . . I get the money from the bank when I drive in, and she hates for them to give anything but new bills to a lady, the way they do nowadays. So she washes it" (126). This revulsion toward old bills, bills handled and folded and sweated on by common whites and African Americans all over the Delta, suggests a fear of contamination by those whose fundamental otherness the Fairchilds depend upon, a fear that exposes the lie at the heart of the Fairchild ideal of plantation race relations as family relations. Further, this literal money laundering serves a function remarkably akin to money laundering in the legal sense: it mystifies and obscures the origins of the money, washing away the physical and figurative evidence of its history of exchange, thus allowing the Fairchilds to imagine themselves as unconnected to the common outside world. This ritual occurs regularly. At the novel's end, Welty informs us that "Aunt Mac, driven by Little Uncle, had set off to Fairchilds for the payroll, as she had decided to iron it this morning" (299). Thus, Battle's lack of business acumen makes sense, since he grew up in a family that treated money, in and of itself, as something filthy and contemptible, something that must be changed, purified, converted in order to have worth. Further, Welty suggests that the younger generation of Fairchilds will learn the same attitudes as their father and aunts. When they take a jaunt into the nearby town that bears their name, they visit the general store. There, "any member of the Fairchild family in its widest sense, who wanted to, could go into the store, walk behind the counter, reach in and take anything on earth, without having to pay or even specify exactly what he took. It was like the pantry at Shellmound. Anything was all right, since they were all kin" (178). No currency changes hands in these transactions; no money begrimes the soft palms of the sons and daughters of Shellmound. The Fairchilds trade on their status, not in cash. Moreover, the store only reassures them of their privilege, since "no matter what any of them could possibly want, it would be sure to be in the store somewhere" (178).

Thus, the Fairchild indifference to economic matters marks neither age nor gender but class. Max Weber and Thorstein Veblen would have recognized the Fairchild attitude toward money and found it consistent with many of their theories. For them, money itself did not offer an individual or group entrance to the highest social strata. According to Weber, "the status order would be threatened at its very root if mere economic acquisition and naked economic power still bearing the stigma of its extra-status origin could bestow upon anyone who has won them the same or even greater honor as the vested interests claim for themselves" (54). As Veblen puts it, "In order to gain and to hold the esteem of men it is not sufficient merely to possess wealth or power. The wealth or power must be put in evidence, for esteem is awarded only on evidence" (36). Such evidence must conform to a specific mold, a particular "style of life," in Weber's terms. His remarks recall W. J. Cash's claim that "if money was necessary to social position, pride in its possession almost invariably translated itself into terms fixed by the aristocratic complex as it had been brought forward from the Old South" (240)—a complex in which the Fairchilds are fully invested.

The Fairchilds' economic idiosyncrasies help us understand why racial paternalism is so important to their way of life. As James Cobb's work indicates, their wealth, privilege, and power is inconceivable without coerced black labor, but openly to acknowledge such a bluntly economic relationship would violate the fundamental tenets of the status order.

Indeed, Troy reveals his class origins when, in the discussion about ironing the payroll, "his hand started guiltily toward his money pocket," a clear reminder both of his financial dependence on the Fairchilds and of the payroll's physical, immediate reality for him (126). So, not only does paternalism form an integral part of Cash's "aristocratic complex," but, by conceiving of their servants, sharecroppers, and wage-hands as extended family members, as children whom they must benevolently guide, the Fairchilds can also imagine their plantation as an autochthonous, organic whole in which economics plays at most an incidental role and over which they rule as natural aristocrats. Pierre Bourdieu would recognize the Fairchild plantation as part of an economy "which, by its refusal to recognize and declare itself as such, is forced to devote almost as much ingenuity and energy to disguising the truth of economic acts as it expends in performing them" (*Logic* 114). The acts and attitudes associated with paternalism perform what Bourdieu calls "symbolic alchemy," in which "the relation of domination and exploitation" becomes "enchanted in such a way as to transform it into a domestic relationship of familiarity through a continuous series of acts capable of symbolically transfiguring it through euphemization" (*Practical Reason* 101).

In many ways the Fairchilds exhibit classic paternalist behaviors. Astute Welty scholars such as Jan Nordby Gretlund, John Edward Hardy, Michael Kreyling, and Dan Fabricant have noted the centrality of paternalism to the antebellum plantation ideals that the Fairchilds carry forward into the twentieth century.[7] We learn early in the novel that Battle Fairchild intercedes with the law on the behalf of African Americans just like William Alexander Percy or Colonel Cary of Hurston's "The 'Pet Negro' System" did: "When Negroes clear to Greenwood cut each other up, it was well known that it took Uncle Battle to protect them from the sheriff or prevail on a bad one to come out and surrender" (14). Elsewhere, a scene in which young "Roy [Fairchild] and a little stray Negro child were eating cold biscuits under Roxie's foot and feeding a small terrapin on the floor, and were sent out to the back yard" recalls W. A. Percy's claim that "any little boy who was not raised with little Negro children might just as well not have been raised at all" (46). Favorite brother George Fairchild offers the servants who greet him a stringer of just-caught fish, and Troy, stretching his noblesse legs, gives Pinchy a decidedly unscrumptious cake that Dabney has baked for him, encouraging Pinchy to "eat it or give it to the other Negroes. Now Scat!" (136, 197). Further, the childish qualities of carelessness and unreliability unite Fairchild youngsters and African American workers in Ellen's mind, since she often "dream[s] of things the children and Negroes lost" (84). Ellen affectionately cares for her black charges, as when she checks in on an older servant and Dabney's former nurse, Partheny, who is having a "spell," and Little Uncle's pregnant and ailing wife Sue Ellen. Of course, these missions to care for the servants conveniently serve to help Ellen organize their labor as well. For instance, her trip to Little Uncle's cabin also provides her an opportunity to "speak in person to Oneida too about helping to dress all the chickens" (85).

Significantly, Ellen's sometime inability to behave in an appropriately paternalistic manner subtly marks her difference from the natural-born Fairchilds. For instance, she bustles about the house in preparation for the wedding, even though "they said she had no need for hurry with a houseful of Negroes to do the first thing she told them. But she did not wait for them or anybody to wait on her" (24). Interestingly, Laura, watching Ellen's independent activity, recalls that previous summer when Aunt Tempe had remarked to her cousin India, "Your mother . . . . has never learned what is reprehensible and what is not, in the Delta" (25). Laura's recollection of this comment at a moment when other Fairchilds discuss Ellen's refusal to rely on her African American servants suggests that that very refusal might be "reprehensible" to the Fairchilds. Roxie, one of the chief house servants, proves sensitive to the ways in which Ellen's independence occasionally places her outside the Fairchild circle: when Ellen orders her out of the kitchen so that she can make a cake for George and his wife Robbie, Roxie replies, "You loves *them*. . . . You're fixin' to ask me to grate you a coconut, not get out," and Ellen acquiesces (29). Certainly, this incident could serve merely to confirm Roxie's faith in her superior culinary abilities, but her remark also implies that if Ellen loves the other Fairchilds, she will follow their rules and rituals, will accede to their reliance on black labor and their displays of paternalism. Though Ellen hails from Virginia, the state that even W. J. Cash, a staunch skeptic on the topic of southern aristocrats, credited as once possessing "a genuine, if small, aristocracy" (5), her life there did not prepare her to take on the role of plantation mistress. Ellen reflects that "she herself . . . was an anomaly," partly "for living on a plantation when she was in her original heart, she believed, a town-loving, book-loving young lady of Mitchem Corners" (286). She does not understand the intricate performances necessary to perpetuate the Fairchild myth. Note that Roxie does not say Ellen will *let* her grate the coconut, but that Ellen will *ask* her to grate the coconut, a small but significant distinction that emphasizes the codified, performative aspects of paternalism.

However, not all the Fairchild employees are as obliging as Roxie; indeed, some are disgruntled, hostile, and outright violent. For the Fairchilds to maintain the idealized conception of themselves as gentle paternalists attended by ranks of affectionate African American workers who accept their rightful place in the social hierarchy and who are bound to the Fairchilds not by economic forces but by love and respect, they must have some means of dealing with those unruly employees whose dissatisfaction with their working conditions threatens to reveal their nature as paid workers, not extended family members. Therefore, the overseer plays a crucial role in the family myth of organic, unconstructed aristocracy. Troy Flavin serves as a buffer between the Fairchilds and the economic world; he takes on disciplinary responsibilities that might threaten the Fairchild myths and thus allows them to maintain belief in their own benevolence, as Kreyling and Romines have also noted.[8] Indeed, the act of discipline, which acknowledges and legitimizes these disruptions of the paternalist narrative, seems not merely unpleasant but in fact downright traumatic for the refined Fairchilds. When Man-Son, a field hand whose name evokes the paternalist system's view of African Americans as perpetual children, raises his hat in salute to Dabney and wishes her connubial bliss, Dabney nods "sternly" to him and reflects that he should be at work in the fields (43). She chides Man-Son for this neglect of his duties: "Man-Son what do you mean? You go get to picking!" However, such forcefulness taxes her: "she trembled all over, having to speak to him in such a way" (46). This disciplinary gesture, restoring a worker to his assigned place on the plantation, causes Dabney great stress. Welty uses strikingly similar language to describe an exchange between Ellen Fairchild and groundskeeper Howard. When Ellen tells him her roses require attention, he grumbles, "I wish there wasn't no such thing as roses. . . .

If I had my way, wouldn't be a rose in de world. Catch your shirt and stick you and prick you and grab you. Got thorns" (298). When Ellen tells him to "hush" and returns to her own gardening, she realizes "to her astonishment she was trembling at Howard's absurd, meek statement, as at some impudence" (298). The literal "trembling" that both Ellen and Dabney exhibit in these passages is a result of figurative earthquakes: the smooth pedestal on which these aristocrats stand is revealed, if only for an instant, to be instead a mass of black laborers. The true nature of their relationship to their workers threatens to break through layers of repression and mystification.

The most striking example of this Fairchild revulsion toward such active engagement with their workers involves a long ago skirmish between Man-Son, his brother, and favorite son George Fairchild. Dabney recalls this incident as threatening to Fairchild myths of unity and coherence, since it was then that "she had discovered in Uncle George one first point where he differed from the other Fairchilds" (43). One morning, George happened upon a knife fight: "Two of their little Negroes had flown at each other with extraordinary intensity here on the bank of the bayou" (44). George intervenes in the scuffle. He catches the knife in the air, pins both combatants to the ground, and bandages the wounded one. As Dabney remembers it,

> The other little Negro sat up all quiet and leaned over and looked at all Uncle George was doing, and in the middle of it his face crumpled—with a loud squall he went with arms straight out to Uncle George, who stopped and let him cry a minute. And then the other little Negro sat up off the ground, the small black pole of his chest striped with the shirt bandage, and climbed up to him too and began to holler, and he knelt low there holding to him the two little black boys who cried together melodiously like singers, and saying, still worriedly, "Damn you! Damn you both!" Then what did he do to them? He asked them their names and let them go. (45)

If the Fairchild lifestyle is one of order and rigidly defined racial and social roles, this scene is its antithesis: violent, chaotic, and transgressive. George's intervention traumatizes young Dabney, for he has stepped down from his lofty, protected perch both to care for and to discipline these brawling youths; he thus enacts a performance that combines elements of two separate and even opposed identities—paternalist planter and disciplinarian overseer. As George stands there with "blood on his hands and both legs," he looks to her "not like a boy close kin to them, but out by himself, like a man who had stepped outside—done something. But it had not been anything Dabney wanted to see him do. She almost ran away" (45). The blood that covers George reveals to Dabney a glimpse of both the violence of plantation labor relations and the humanity of these young boys; moreover, it violates the distance the Fairchilds maintain between their own refined lives and the more messy, abject aspects of their workers' lives. Not surprisingly, she finds George's action revolting: "Disgracefully, he had taken two little black devils against his side" (46). Indeed, George seems to have committed the gravest sin a Fairchild could commit: "all the Fairchild in her had screamed at his interfering—at his taking part—*caring* about anything in the world but them" (46).

Further, the gray area that George temporarily enters threatens to engulf Dabney and to erase her aristocratic white privilege: her family prides itself on its insularity and solidarity, and so George's fatherly embrace of these two bloody, brawling African Americans is painfully disruptive for her, especially when George treats her almost exactly the same way when she screams in protest: "he saw her there in the field, and caught her when she ran at him. He hugged her tight against his chest, where sweat and bayou water pressed her mouth" (45). Dabney's horror at this scene indicates how ill-prepared she is to accept into her family someone who carries the ideals of paternalism to their logical end. George's actions equate these black children with Dabney, including them all in the Fairchild circle and thereby placing the coherence of that circle in jeopardy. Moreover, while their blood covers him, the "sweat and bayou water" that press against Dabney's mouth threaten to taint her pure, unsullied whiteness with the contaminants of labor, exertion, violence. (Indeed, Welty suggests that a taint of racial otherness lingers upon George still, perhaps the lingering residue of Man-Son's blood: when Ellen happens upon a napping George, she thinks, "In the darkened room his hair and all looked dark—turbulent and dark, almost Spanish. Spanish! She looked at him tenderly to have thought of such a far-fetched thing, and went out" [65].) George's intercession even threatens the economic ignorance so prized by the Fairchilds. Note, for instance, that Dabney only knows Man-Son's name because of his fight: "Dabney had never forgotten which two boys those were, and could tell them from the rest" (45). The fact that in the midst of remembering the fight Dabney thinks to herself that "Man-Son worked for them yet and was a good Negro" suggests that Dabney realizes a connection between George's keeping them healthy and the potential future value these two bickering boys might have as field laborers.

Significantly, both George and Dabney treat this event as alien, outside the bounds of Fairchild discourse. George declines to turn this small adventure into a tall tale: Dabney recalls, "he had not even laughed with them all about it afterwards, or told it like a story after supper" (46). Such reticence does not jibe with what we know of the Fairchilds, who tell another story of George's bravery—saving his mentally handicapped niece Maureen from the oncoming Yellow Dog—over and over again, each time with new details and grander embellishments. George's reluctance to speak may indicate that these aberrant moments with their African Americans should not form part of the public image of the Fairchilds, the smooth surface they show the world. For her part, Dabney responds by marking George as an aberration in the hegemonic Fairchild fold, excluding him for the sake of the family's coherence. She minimizes the damage to her sense of self and family by believing that the melee "was . . . something that the other Fairchilds would have passed by and scorned to notice," as indeed George's brother Denis did. Perhaps Dabney's exclusion of George from the Fairchild norm signals her awareness of the need to maintain the stories that keep their family "solid to the outside."[9]

These moments of attention to the labor and lives of their black employees threaten to disrupt the Fairchilds' façade and to reveal the throb of the compress that permeates the refined lifestyle at Shellmound. As Bourdieu might have it, these events threaten to violate the crucial "*taboo of making things explicit*" (*Practical Reason* 96). According to Bourdieu, in highly developed symbolic economies, "to say what it really is, to declare the truth of the exchange, or, as is often said, 'the truth of the price' . . . is to destroy the exchange" (*Practical Reason* 96). Paternalism mystifies the economic exploitation at the heart of interracial relations at Shellmound, and revealing the truth behind that mystification threatens the Fairchilds' aristocratic status. They have grown so accustomed to the ordered nature of their plantation household and to their servants' easy accession to their way of life that even these slight ruptures in the fixed pattern bring the individual nature of their employees to light and force them to confront the possibility that the ostensibly organic unity of Shellmound may be a sham. Dabney's shock at George's embrace of Man-Son and his brother makes sense when we consider that when not ill, pregnant, or needed for a specific task easily handled with a more "loving" gesture of paternalism, the Fairchilds often seem to take their retainers' labor for granted, to assume that they will do their chores without much need for guidance. As Suzanne Marrs puts it, the congeniality between the Fairchilds and their servants "mask[s] a very deep separation" (*One Writer's Imagination* 96). For example, on one lazy afternoon Laura reflects that "she could hear nothing, except the sounds of the Negroes, and the slow ceiling fan turning in the hall, and the submissive panting of the dogs just outside under the banana plants" (69). This construction—"nothing, except the sounds of the Negroes . . ."—implies that the noise of African American work is essentially background noise on a level with mechanical contrivances like the fan and submissive creatures like the dogs. Similarly, Laura happens into a room in which George sits "alone now—except, that is, for Vi'let, leaning from a stepladder with one knee on a bookcase, very slowly taking down the velvet curtains" (71). Thus, hard-working Vi'let barely qualifies as person enough to modify George's aloneness. As Yaeger puts it, blacks become merely "atmospheric" for the Fairchilds (104). This dim awareness of laboring blacks extends beyond young Laura. As Vi'let struggles with the dresses for the wedding party, Dabney grabs them up to show the newly arrived Tempe, heedless of Vi'let's cry: "Miss Dab, ain't you 'shamed, you bring my dresses on back here!" (131). In another striking passage, Tempe describes the despoiling of Roxie's domestic efforts as a tragedy—for Ellen. When George comes in with dirty shoes, Tempe exclaims, "Oh, Ellen—did you see how George tracked up your floor? It breaks my heart to see it. After Roxie spent the morning on her knees—now it all has to be done over" (141). These floors prove to be a recurring struggle for Roxie: later, after Laura and Roy come in from a trip to the Yazoo river, Roxie "with a cry of sorrow" falls "on her knees behind Laura to take up the water that ran from her heels" (236). And when Little Uncle drives the food to a picnic so the family can feast, Welty describes him as "invisible" to the Fairchilds (315).

Troy cannot afford this carefully maintained obliviousness to the work going on around him. His function at Shellmound is a continuation of the role of the antebellum overseer in the Delta, who, as James Cobb observes, "was expected to care for, supervise, and discipline the slaves, provide for the livestock, keep up the implements, and produce a bountiful crop of corn and grain as well as cotton" (*Most Southern Place* 24). True, Battle Fairchild intercedes with whites on the behalf of blacks across the Delta, and Ellen nurses ill and pregnant African Americans on the plantation. However, with the exception of George in the knife-fight scene, Troy is the only character in the novel who uses physical force in his dealings with the Fairchild workers or who intercedes in a skirmish between black laborers. The fact that Mr. Bascom, the previous overseer, got away with stealing from the family for so long because of Battle's lack of business acumen suggests that the overseer has a greater familiarity with the economic aspects of the plantation as well.

Not surprisingly, though the Fairchilds generally treat Troy with respect and courtesy, they also resent the intrusion of this low-born hill country native into their close ranks. As the incident with George on the bayou suggests, the Fairchilds consider Troy's type of work, though necessary, fundamentally un-Fairchild. Such class-conscious behavior is consistent with Cobb's description of "socially self-conscious planters" of the Old South who kept "the doors of the big house . . . [,] for the most part, closed to [the overseer] socially" (*Most Southern Place* 24). Indeed, the twentieth-century Fairchilds still have good reason to be self-conscious, since Troy's marriage to Dabney prompts much speculation from other Deltans: "Troy Flavin was the overseer. The Fairchilds would die, everybody said, if this happened" (38). The Fairchilds find some consolation in the fact that Dabney is not "going out of the Delta, of course" (56), yet they still find Troy threatening. When Aunt Jim Allen remarks that she has "never really *seen* Troy. . . . Not close *to*—you know," Welty notes that "she did sound actually frightened of Troy" (55). The more irascible Aunt Mac reflects that if she had charge of the family, "She would start by throwing Troy Flavin in the bayou in front of the house and letting the minnows chew him up" (87). Battle Fairchild shares Aunt Mac's predilection for imagining gory demises for his future son-in-law, and, indeed, for anyone of lower rank who dares marry into his family: when the discussion turns to Robbie Reid Fairchild, George's estranged wife, Battle declares, "If I weren't tied down! I'd go find little Upstart Reid myself, and kill her. No, I'd set her and Flavin together and feed 'em to each other" (82). The animalistic implications of Battle's fantasy come through more explicitly in other descriptions of Troy. For instance, he has "foxy skin" and "a luxuriant, petlike look" (123). Aunt Primrose comments, "I always think of him as part horse—you know, the way he's grown to that black Isabelle in the fields" (147). Here Primrose renders Troy not just as part horse but also as part black, a suggestion of racial otherness that recurs in other descriptions. Indeed, as overseer, Troy lives in a house closer to the African Americans' houses than to Shellmound (47). Riding by this house, India sees Troy as "a black wedge in the lighted window," a metaphor that suggests Troy's otherness is a "wedge" that divides the Fairchilds; or, perhaps, that Troy is a "wedge" that separates the Fairchilds from the reality of their African American employees' lives and preserves their ignorance (68). For the Fairchilds, then, to be other than an aristocratic planter is also to be other than human and, perhaps, other than white. Their speech marks humble-born Troy not just as vulgar and crude but also as of a fundamentally different species.[10]

However, Shelley witnesses a scene that causes her to question the value of such distinctions—though not, ultimately, to reject them. As she strides into Troy's office in "one of the houses none of the girls ever paid any attention to," she finds him in the midst of a tense confrontation between some feuding field hands. Two of them have "slashed cheeks," the work of Root M'Hook, who wields what Shelley at first thinks is a knife but soon realizes is an ice pick (257). When Root begins to fling his weapon at Troy, Troy shoots his finger and orders him removed. He then turns to another wounded hand, Big Baby, whose name, like Man-Son's, evokes the paternalist conception of African Americans as perpetual children. When Troy inquires about the nature of his injury, Big Baby tells him in "confessional tones," "Mr. Troy, *I* got my seat full of buck-shot." Troy sympathizes, even while he finds the situation amusing—"Troy groaned with him, but laughed between his drawn lips"—as one might find a scuffle between overserious young boys amusing. Troy sets about mending his charge, telling him, "Pull down your clothes, Big Baby, and get over my knee," a request that underscores Big Baby's supposed child-like nature by putting him in a position that suggests he is prepared to receive both discipline and care from a loving parent.

This scene strikingly parallels George's intervention in the bayou knife-fight. Once again, the brawling African Americans have wounded each other with a knife; once again, a white male figure breaks up the fight (if more violently) and tends to the injured, childlike worker with paternal affection. As in that earlier scene, here the white male protagonist embodies both "caring," paternalistic racial attitudes and disciplinary, patriarchal attitudes—two attitudes associated with distinctly different, even opposed, classes and jobs on the plantation—thus throwing into doubt the division of labor management along class lines that enables the Fairchilds to preserve their aristocratic image and status.[11] Troy is caught in this paradox, much as George was. African American blood, the evidence of the violence implicit in plantation labor relations, initially forms a barrier to Troy's full entrance to the Fairchild family, much as being covered with African American blood marked George's difference from his brothers and sisters: blood pools at the office threshold, and, suddenly, Shelley "could see the reason why Dabney's wedding should be prevented. Nobody could marry a man with blood on his door" (258). As Ann Romines puts it, this bloody scene startles Shelley "into a momentary awareness of the economic structure within which she has grown to (near) adulthood" (614). However, perhaps realizing that the wedding has its own momentum, she quickly decides not to reveal this incident for the sake of the family's coherence. She initially decides, like Dabney before her, to keep the incident a secret. She would "never tell anybody, for what was going to happen was going to happen" (258). As she flees back to the rehearsal—and past the site of Man-Son's knife-fight—she further ponders issues of class and authenticity:

> Running back along the bayou, Shelley could only think in her anger of the convincing performance Troy had given as an overseer born and bred. Suppose a real Deltan, a planter, were no more real than that. Suppose a real Deltan only imitated another Deltan. Suppose the behavior of all *men* were actually no more than this—

> imitation of other men. But it had previously occurred to her that Troy was trying to imitate her father. (Suppose her *father* imitated . . . oh, not he!) Then all men could not know any too well what they were doing. (259)

Troy's performance inspires Shelley to realize the constructed nature of an identity, that of an overseer, she had previously considered natural, "born and bred." This epiphany leads her to question the nature of other, more privileged types of identity such as "a real Deltan, a planter." Most importantly, the unfixed, flexible nature of Troy's performance causes her to doubt further the rigidity of social boundaries and social roles. He simultaneously exhibits the fatherly benevolence of the planter and the violent discipline of the overseer. Like George before him, he steps into a disruptive, liminal space between two conflicting class identities. If one individual can move between two such supposedly different and indeed opposed identities, then no identity is pure, natural, unconstructed. Though we might read her thoughts on her father—"oh, not he!"—as an attempt to preserve Fairchild identity as somehow unimitative, unperformed, I would argue that we may better read it as a brief internal exclamation of despair as the momentum of her logic leads her to question even this most cherished identity.[12]

In her reading of this scene, Ann Romines pays particular attention to Shelley's rumination that "women, she was glad to think, did know a *little* better—though everything they knew they would have to keep to themselves . . . oh, forever!" (259). As Romines notes, this thought represents a retreat into gender essentialism (615); the realization that such supposedly stable identities such as "planter" and "overseer" are inauthentic and constructed forces Shelley to fall back on the belief that women, at least, do not participate in this cycle of performance. However, though Shelley may endorse an essentialist conception of gender here, we should not too quickly assume that Welty does as well. As Romines points out, *Delta Wedding* "does not advocate an essentialist construction of 'woman's culture'" (616). I would note that the phrase "she was glad to think," which interrupts Shelley's assertion that women know better, implies that this belief may be merely a pleasant, necessary fiction that allows her to maintain some sense of herself, some anchor in this sea of imitation and performance. After all, we have already seen Aunt Tempe criticize Ellen Fairchild for behaving in a "reprehensible" manner unbefitting a Delta woman, and we have seen Roxie convince Ellen to conform to her family's ways; so it seems that women are not free from this cycle of imitation.

Shelley's new awareness of the performative nature of class and other identities leaves her in an ambivalent position. She realizes that class distinctions and social relations are slippery and malleable but realizes also that her family's status rests on a firm belief in rigid class differences. According to Romines, Shelley keeps her knowledge as "a potent secret beneath the fragile surface of the surviving plantation fiction" (615). However, she does not entirely keep the implications of this knowledge to herself. When she returns to the wedding hall, she objects to the way in which the wedding ceremony formally affirms Troy's class otherness: "Mama, I think it's so tacky the way Troy comes in from the side door. . . . It's like somebody just walks in the house from the fields and marries Dabney" (270). Now that Shelley has seen the falseness of the class distinctions so central to life at Shellmound, she sees no reason for her family to continue in their attempts to mark him as an outsider. However, I would hesitate to read Shelley's remark uncritically as evidence of a burgeoning progressive class ideology. After all, her main objection seems to be that this reminder of Troy's humble origins is "tacky," that it interferes with the wedding's otherwise refined, aristocratic atmosphere. Her concern lies more with keeping her family "solid to the outside" at this public event than with challenging the myths that sustain that solidity, and she certainly does not question the oppression of the African Americans whose labor and lives support those myths.

Shelley's minor protest, in any case, counts for little. The wedding goes off as planned: "Troy came in from the side door, indeed like somebody walking in from the fields to marry Dabney" (279). Even the flowers make him seem out of place: "His hair flamed. Had no one thought that American Beauty would clash with that carrot hair? Had no one thought of that?" (279). Thus, even if we read Shelley's objection as an act of resistance, however qualified and compromised, against her family's ideology, Welty does not offer us much hope that her act will have any real, lasting ramifications. In *Delta Wedding*, then, Welty explores the complicated logic of class, race, and paternalism, exposing the ways in which paternalism—

whether demonstrated directly by the Fairchilds or delegated to the subordinate overseer—obscures the sometimes violent, bloody nature of plantation labor relations and allows the aristocratic family to preserve a sense of itself as part of a natural, organic extended family with African Americans as perpetual, contented children. Though she makes clear that these supposedly natural identities actually result from an elaborate, intricate set of performances, she offers little in the way of strategies for resistance to this social order; in this novel, those whose prestige might be threatened by those critical moments when class differences blur or even vanish can afford to ignore them. Welty does, however, demonstrate for her contemporary audience that nostalgia for a supposedly more stable time in race relations, a time when everyone knew their places, is fundamentally wrongheaded. She reveals that even in the most tranquil and stable year of the Delta's recent history, the ostensibly stable racial and social hierarchies of the Delta existed in a state of flux and were only precariously, sometimes violently, maintained.

If in *Delta Wedding* Welty suggests that southern aristocrats require a deliberate blindness to the economic underpinnings of their elite status, a willful ignorance of the (usually African American) labor that enables their privileged lifestyle, she makes that suggestion even more explicit in *The Ponder Heart,* a short novel that again investigates the complicated intersection between racial paternalism, economics, and class. Originally published in *The New Yorker* in 1953 and issued in novel form the following year, *The Ponder Heart* chronicles the waning days of the Ponders, a prominent aristocratic family from the small town of Clay, Mississippi. Edna Earle Ponder, the story's narrator and sole proprietor of Clay's Beulah Hotel, recounts to a road-weary traveler the twisted and darkly comic tale of her crackpot Uncle Daniel's marriage to, and eventual murder of, the decidedly low-class Bonnie Dee Peacock. Edna Earle's narrative reveals a profound anxiety about her family's class position, their relationship to their African American servants, especially longtime cook Narciss, and how public discussion about the sources and uses of their wealth might affect their standing in the community—and everyone else's.

The Ponders occupy a lofty but complicated place at the pinnacle of Clay's social hierarchy. As Welty put it in an interview, they stand "right at the top" (*More Conversations* 131). Their prestige and influence make them famous throughout the surrounding area. According to Edna Earle, "people not knowing the Ponders but knowing *of* them are just about everywhere you'd look" (86). As one might expect of a prominent family in mid-twentieth-century Mississippi, they own an opulent home on a large cotton farm worked by African Americans and managed on a day-to-day basis by a poor white family. But the Ponders are also on the decline: Edna Earle and Daniel are the last of the line, and after his trial for Bonnie Dee's murder, Daniel abandons their country home, symbol of their prestige, to live in the Beulah Hotel with Edna Earle. The now dilapidated hotel symbolizes their loss of status. Although Grandpa Ponder used to let someone else run the hotel for him and thus reaped the profits of this business without having to deal with it directly and dirty his hands with the "wrong element" who zip through town on the new highway (13), now Edna Earle has taken the reins—after Daniel gives the hotel to her as a gift—and thus participates in the plebian world of commerce. Of course, Edna Earle runs the hotel with aristocratic aplomb, focusing mainly on "looking pretty" for the guests and keeping them entertained while her African American servants do the actual labor. Indeed, even the one time we see her directly engaged with any mercantile endeavor takes place in a framework of paternalism and charity: she runs a rummage sale for African Americans, with the proceeds going to missionaries in Africa (21).

But if Edna Earle occupies a gray area between the aristocracy and the petite bourgeoisie, Daniel occupies a more easily identified position. As Ted Ownby has observed, perennially white-suited Daniel "is almost a parody of Will Percy's ideal paternalist, who secures the affection of people he meets by giving his money away" (146). In a time of social change, Daniel is, in Rachel V. Weiner's memorable phrase, "a still-bright figurehead on an otherwise crumbling wall" (265). Like the Fairchilds, Daniel acknowledges no relation between his status and the money that enables it. According to Edna Earle, "Uncle Daniel was used to purely being rich, not having money" (50). Indeed, Daniel has never worked a day in his life. He understands his aristocratic status as a pure state of being, not something created or constructed. What little cash money he does have—a three-dollar weekly allowance from the bank—he generally distributes to children as soon as he gets it (50). Indeed, he gives away all kinds of things, and to all kinds of people. Edna Earle runs through a lengthy but not at all comprehensive list of his divestments: "a string of hams, a fine suit of clothes, a white-face heifer calf, two trips to Memphis, pair of fan-tail pigeons, fine Shetland pony (loves children), brooder and incubator, good nanny goat, bad billy, cypress cistern, field of white Dutch clover, two iron wheels and some laying pullets (they were together), cow pasture during drouth (he has everlasting springs), innumerable fresh eggs, a pick-up truck—even his own cemetery lot, but they wouldn't accept it. And I'm not counting this week" (8). One could even argue that Daniel's unbridled generosity leads to his wife's death, since Bonnie Dee suffocates as she presses her face into a pillow to escape the tickling that Daniel gives her despite her protests (140). Daniel's largesse thus goes well beyond the conventional bounds of racial paternalism; he does not just give worn-out shirts to needy African Americans but also gives banana ice cream cones to dancing girls at the fair, and so on. However, the text suggests that giving to downtrodden African Americans does perhaps uniquely satisfy him. Indeed, Edna Earle only singles out one adult to whom Daniel gives consistently, an African American man named Big John who, Edna Earle informs us, "worked for us out there since time was. . . . Always wore the same hat and shoes and overalls, and couldn't sign his name if life depended" (89). Big John's profound material deprivation provides a perfect complement to Daniel's openhanded ways: according to Edna Earle, "I expect he's been robbed a hundred times, among the Negroes, but he'll always ask you for money any time he sees you" (90). She continues: Uncle Daniel "always did like him—because of the money he could deposit on him" (91). Thus, Big John's persistent neediness provides Daniel with ample opportunity to demonstrate his paternalist ways.

Such paternalist behavior befits a man like Daniel Ponder, who sits "right at the top" of Clay's society; and, as in *Delta Wedding,* African American labor makes that lofty ranking possible. Daniel and, during most of their marriage, Bonnie Dee, live in the Ponders' enormous home on a large farm. Edna Earle itemizes their assets when she imagines how easily Daniel must have impressed Bonnie Dee with tales of his grandiose lifestyle: "Home on the hilltop! Great big car! Negroes galore! Homegrown bacon and eggs and ham and fried grits and potato cakes and honey and molasses for breakfast every morning to start off with—you know, you don't have to have all the brilliance in the world to sound grand, or *be* grand either. It's a gift" (30). The "Negroes galore" enable many of the other luxuries Edna Earle mentions. According to her, "If you know what you want done, you can just ask in the morning for how many Negroes you want that day, and Uncle Daniel hollers them in for you out of the fields, and they come just like for Grandpa" (54). Thus, the Ponders have an almost magical abundance of African American labor at their disposal. Moreover, as Eugene Genovese would have expected, the Ponders have maintained the Old Southern tradition of treating some of their black employees as inextricably entwined with the white family. According to Genovese, "Not accidentally, and by no means as a petty propaganda device, acts of the Confederate Congress referred to the obligations of citizens to their black and white families. Not infrequently, planters recorded births and deaths of slaves in their family Bibles" (196). The Ponders would find such attitudes familiar: for instance, we know that the Ponders' cook, Narciss, cared for Uncle Daniel as a child (98), and that she was essentially adopted into the family by Grandma Ponder. Edna Earle describes her as "a Negro we'd had her whole life long, older by far than I was, Grandma raised her from a child and brought her in out of the field to the kitchen and taught her everything she knew" (32).

But such close bonds do not relieve the Ponders of their stereotypical conceptions of African Americans. Edna Earle sees Narciss and other blacks as immature and shiftless. She tells her listener, "They don't know anything, but you can try telling them and see what happens" (54), and notes even of faithful Narciss, "You can't trust a one of them" (30). Moreover, Edna Earle exhibits some of the same condescension toward her African American workers at the hotel that characterized the Fairchilds' attitudes toward Vi'let, Roxie, and other Shellmound servants. When describing the rigors of innkeeping, Edna Earle rhetorically asks, "Could *you* hope to account for twelve bedrooms, two bathrooms, two staircases, five porches, lobby, dining room, pantry and kitchen, every day of your life, and still be out here looking pretty when they come in? And two Negroes? And that plant?" (10). With the placement of the "two Negroes" in that laundry list—between such decorative priorities as "looking pretty" and a plant—Welty not only signals the relatively low priority that Edna

Earle gives her two African American laborers but also suggests that they serve the same "atmospheric" role that Patricia Yaeger saw blacks fulfilling in *Delta Wedding*.

As a poor white, Bonnie Dee Peacock shares neither the Ponders' paternalistic attitudes about African Americans nor their indifference to money, and her inability—or refusal—to toe the Ponder line on those crucial issues threatens to expose the myths that enable the Ponders' aristocratic standing. Edna Earle sees low-class Bonnie Dee as a danger to her family, much as the Fairchilds saw Troy, and, also like the Fairchilds, she adheres to an essentialist ideology of class. For instance, when she visits the Peacock home in nearby Polk, she notes a cluster of stately, impressive tombstones in a nearby cemetery and reflects, "It may be that the Peacocks at one time used to amount to something (there *are* worthwhile Peacocks, Miss Lutie Powell has vouched for it to Eva Sistrunk), but you'll have a hard time making me believe they're around us. I believe these have always been just about what they are now" (79). Since she herself has never laid eyes on a "worthwhile" Peacock, Edna Earle can continue to believe that their degraded condition is essential and eternal, much as she sees the grandeur of the Ponders as a "gift," not something earned through skill, effort, or cunning (30). Animal metaphors pervade Edna Earle's descriptions of Bonnie Dee, evidence that she perceives her as of a fundamentally different species than the Ponders. She observes that Bonnie Dee "didn't know how to smile. *Yawned* all the time, like cats do" (42). Edna Earle connects this feline imagery directly to Bonnie Dee's class position when she notes that "Bonnie Dee, with her origins, could turn and spit like a cat" (49). A hint of racial otherness also creeps into Edna Earle's animalistic picture of Bonnie Dee: "I could tell by her little coon eyes, she was shallow as they come" (35).

Bonnie Dee's financial philosophies differ from the Ponders' as well. While Uncle Daniel thinks of himself as "purely rich" and Edna Earle handles money only long enough to pass it to the missionaries, Bonnie Dee works at the local Woolworth's. Such a position suits her, since, according to Edna Earle, "all she knew how to do was make change" (30). Edna Earle later reminds us of Bonnie Dee's pecuniary aptitude and her own lack thereof: "Bonnie Dee could make change, and Bonnie Dee could cut hair. If you ask me can I do either, the answer is no" (41–42). Of course, we should not trust Edna Earle without question: she has already admitted making change at the rummage sale, however altruistic her motives may be. Regardless of its truth, her claim emphasizes the significance of the relationship between economic practices and class position. As some critics have rightly noted, consumerism characterizes Bonnie Dee's attitude toward money. While the Ponders concern themselves with the symbolic value of their wealth, Bonnie Dee focuses on translating that wealth into things.[13] She clips the coupons out of her magazines to send off for various household items and appliances. As Edna Earle puts it, "Think of something to wear. Bonnie Dee had it" (67). She gets the house electrified—connecting it to the town of Clay in a way Grandpa Ponder would have abhorred—and even buys a washing machine, though, as Edna Earle notes, she kept it "on the front porch, just like any Peacock would do" (68).

Bonnie Dee's unaristocratic attitudes toward race and money make her transition into the Ponder home difficult; her refusal simply to assimilate into their aristocratic framework and accept their ways disrupts the Ponder lifestyle and challenges Edna Earle's essentialist ideas about class. Initially, ignorance about aristocratic racial mores lies at the heart of Bonnie Dee's discomfort in her marriage and contributes to her decision to leave Daniel after five years and six months. According to Edna Earle, Daniel "carried that child out there and set her down in a big house with a lot of rooms and corners, with Negroes to wait on her, and she wasn't used to a bit of it. She wasn't used to keeping house at all except by fits and starts, much less telling Negroes what to do" (48). Despite Edna Earle's grim appraisal of her aristocratic aptitude, Bonnie Dee turns out to be a quick study. When she returns, she kicks Daniel out of his ancestral home and lives there alone with Narciss; moreover, she proves newly adept at paternalist performance. For instance, she gives Narciss her old clothes when she tires of them. Says Edna Earle, "We saw Narciss in Bonnie Dee's pink voile dress she got married in, parading through Sistrunk's Grocery with a store-bought watermelon wrapped in her arms" (67). Such a paternalist gesture ostensibly represents her conformity to aristocratic racial customs and her understanding of the role of properly conspicuous waste. She also masters the ability to "tell Negroes what to do": during her testimony, Narciss reports that Bonnie Dee ordered her to drag an old parlor sofa away from the windows during a lightning storm—with Bonnie Dee still sitting on it (96). Narciss irons her expensive apricot dress, "all dem little pleats," and her first thought on seeing her deceased body is of "all dem little pleats to do over" (98).

Yet Edna Earle still resists accepting Bonnie Dee despite these exercises of paternalistic racial behavior. In a significant locution, she describes Bonnie Dee's newfound aristocratic manner as a game, a form of play. As Edna Earle puts it, "Bonnie Dee was out yonder dressing up and playing lady with Narciss" (69). Indeed, though she adopts paternalistic performances with aplomb, Bonnie Dee does not commit to them completely. As W. J. Cash might put it, she refuses to accede fully to the terms of the "aristocratic complex" brought forward from the Old South into the New. In some cases, she demonstrates an intimacy with Narciss that violates even the liberal allowances of the "pet" relationship. For instance, Narciss reports that in violent thunderstorms, "Us hides together under Miss Edna Earle's bed. . . . Another thing we does together, Mr. DeYancey, I occasionally plays jacks with her" (99–100). Indeed, this friendship has deep roots. When Bonnie Dee leaves Uncle Daniel, Narciss discovers her unaddressed farewell note, which reads, "Have left out. Good-by and good luck, your friend, Mrs. Bonnie Dee Peacock Ponder" (47). As Edna Earle observes, "We don't even know which one of them it was *to*" (47). Her note thus symbolically equates her wealthy husband and her impoverished cook, a collapse of social differences unacceptable to the Ponders. Further, the fact that she left it on the kitchen table implies that she intended it for Narciss and considers her a friend.

Bonnie Dee's violation of the boundaries of paternalist racial mores with Narciss highlights the gendered nature of racial paternalism. Like Arvay Meserve, another poor white woman who ostensibly marries up, Bonnie Dee comes to realize that, for women, the privileges of aristocracy come at the price of freedom and of genuine friendship with African Americans, without the compensation of power that men receive. Although she is expected to uphold and affirm the principles of paternalism for the sake of her family's honor and class position, her only rewards are material and in fact only incidentally hers at all, as they serve primarily to affirm the Ponders' social position. If Bonnie Dee's refusal to remain inside the bounds of her role—specifically her commitment to make friends with Narciss when she should remain content with the parody of friendship that is the "pet" relationship—marks her as a dangerous anomaly in the paternalist scheme, then Edna Earle in some ways represents the ideal female paternalist: someone who has so thoroughly internalized the priorities and prejudices of paternalism that she sees them as natural and whose every action and utterance is aimed at preserving family prestige. She recognizes no distinction between her own ideals and Daniel's, and she works tirelessly to uphold his status. Indeed, if Bonnie Dee Peacock recalls Arvay Meserve, Edna Earle in some ways recalls Jim Meserve's servant Jeff Kelsey, who so assiduously polices the boundaries of his employer's family to ensure that Jim does not associate with anyone who is not "quality." Of course, Edna Earle enjoys material wealth and social prestige far beyond that of the Kelseys, and so it would be too simple to claim that women and African Americans occupy exactly the same role in the paternalist ideology. However, their duties are nonetheless similar: to preserve and further the power and reputation of the clan patriarch and, by extension, the family entire.

However, Bonnie Dee chooses not to follow in Arvay Henson's footsteps and adopt her husband's paternalism, and her refusal to do so challenges the essentialist notion of class that enable the Ponders to maintain their status as aristocrats. Though Edna Earle means it as a slight, I propose we consider seriously the implications of her assertion that Bonnie Dee is only "playing" lady. The idea that she is "playing" at being an elite southern aristocrat, trying it on to see how it fits, using the role when useful and pleasant but discarding it when not, is consistent with the consumerist ideology that leads her to fill the already overstuffed house with new appliances ordered from the Memphis newspaper. Significantly, she agrees to marry Daniel only "on trial" (40). That is, Bonnie Dee accepts the marriage on a trial basis, much as she might buy a set of encyclopedias or a commemorative plate from the Franklin Mint "on trial," with the option of returning it if she is not satisfied. And, indeed, she *does* return it: as Edna Earle puts it, "So the marriage trial . . . went on for five years and six months, and Bonnie Dee, if you please, decided No" (48). We know that Bonnie Dee is accustomed to buying things on a trial basis because when Edna Earle stays with Daniel on Ponder Hill to comfort him, she sees that Bonnie Dee's magazines are full of "holes she'd left where she'd sent off for all kinds of things—you know, wherever they showed the postman smiling in the ad" (55). These purchases include perfume samples, a free piano lesson, and, most significantly, "a set of Balzac to examine ten days free of charge"; but, Edna Earle notes, she sent it back: "she must have decided against it—I looked everywhere" (56). Further, when Bonnie Dee does decide to commit to the marriage, she responds not to Daniel's heartfelt apologies or a romantic serenade but to a newspaper advertisement—and one that promises a better deal. Edna Earle and Daniel run "a three-day ad in the Memphis *Commercial Appeal*" (57). Edna Earle includes a poem in the ad promising that "all is forgiven," and, perhaps more importantly, "retroactive allowance will be given" (59). This claim has particular significance because Edna Earle has belatedly realized that Daniel inadvertently contributed to his marital strife by never giving Bonnie Dee any money. According to Edna Earle, "I don't think it ever occurred to him, to give anything to Bonnie Dee. Because he *had* her. (When she said 'trial,' that didn't mean anything to Uncle Daniel that would alarm him. The only kind of trials he knew about were the ones across the street from the Beulah, in the Courthouse—he was fond of those)" (49).[14]

In the same way that her tendency to clip coupons out of magazines leaves "holes in the stories all the way through" (56), Bonnie Dee's consumerist ideology pokes holes in the narratives that sustain the Ponders. By exposing aristocratic white ladyhood as a commodity that she can easily buy, return, and indeed haggle over, Bonnie Dee also exposes the myths of natural, essential class positions that Edna Earle clings to in this time of social change. For instance, the awareness of money as a useful tool that this change-making upstart brings to the Ponder family leads Daniel to attempt to purchase his acquittal when he can no longer count on his reputation to protect him. The terms of Bonnie Dee's return to the Ponder fold include twenty-five dollars in cash per week, which Daniel and Edna Earle deliver to her each Saturday (71). Perhaps this weekly transaction, this paying money to ensure his marriage remains more or less intact, gives Daniel the idea to bribe the entire town to avoid a guilty verdict. On the day of his trial, Daniel withdraws all his money from the bank—despite a long-standing order that bank tellers should "never, never, never let Uncle Daniel get his hands on cash" (147). When it seems that the prosecutor has Daniel on the verge of confessing his misdeeds, Daniel begins handing the money out to everyone in the courtroom—Sistrunks, Peacocks, Sampsons, and so on, regardless of class. Rachel Weiner offers one explanation for why Daniel's massive handout causes such problems and why Grandpa Ponder went to such lengths to keep him away from his cash. According to Weiner, for Grandpa Ponder "money has place neither among material possessions nor among the landed inheritances which determine family place. It represents the world of no-nonsense law that exists on paper among strangers" (267). I would extend her analysis a step further. As Weiner's statement implies, money is no respecter of persons; Grandpa Ponder worked hard to create a life in which Daniel could be "purely rich," trading on his reputation and prestigious name, but anyone can use money, not just, as Weiner rightly argues, strangers, but also individuals from any class.[15]

Thus, Daniel suffers the fate the Fairchilds worked so hard to avoid: this exposure of the crass, material money that enables the Ponders' lofty social rank further disrupts any claim to essentialist aristocracy they might have, since it inspires a vocal and public debate about the sources of their wealth. Trial spectator Florette Sistrunk fires the opening salvo, arguing that "the Ponders as I've always been told did not burn their cotton when Sherman came, and maybe this is their judgment" (147). Edna Earle clarifies, but does not help their case much: "The Ponders did not make their money that way. . . . Ours was pine trees and 'way after Sherman, and you know it." Another Sistrunk points out, however, that "'Twas the same Yankees you sold it to!" The chaos inspired by this sudden redistribution of wealth and the conversation about it spreads all across Clay, resulting in a muddled social hierarchy. As Edna Earle puts it, "The worst thing you can give away is money. . . . You and them are both done for then, somehow; you can't go on after it, and still be you and them" (149). Indeed, "that money has come between the Ponders and everyone else in town. There it still is, on their hands" (155). Edna Earle's desperate desire to maintain even the faintest vestiges of their status—and to help Daniel maintain his illusions of being "purely rich"—comes through clearly in the novel's closing passage. Edna Earle warns her guest that Daniel "may try to give you something—may think he's got something to give" (156). Her qualifier indicates that Daniel can no longer afford the generosity that assured him of his position. Nevertheless, she begs a favor of her guest: "Make out like you accept it. Tell him thank you" (156). Even if she must face the reality of their new position, she may still enlist the aid of others to preserve Daniel's belief in his own aristocracy.

Perhaps most damaging to the Ponders, this ambiguity about social "standing" extends into the realm of race relations. The consumerist-informed, flexible attitude toward race and class that Bonnie Dee brings to Ponder Hill—riding the sofa Narciss moves one minute, hiding under the bed with her the next—inspires Narciss to revolt, however subtly and ineffectually, and demonstrates the hollowness of paternalist claims to know their charges intimately. Indeed, Edna Earle's narration offers hints that she does not know Narciss as well as she thinks she does. Though Narciss does show considerable and apparently genuine affection to Uncle Daniel in her testimony, she also reminds the court of the distance between herself and the native Ponders. While defense attorney DeYancey Clanahan conforms to the paternalist model when he describes Edna Earle and Daniel to Narciss as "your best friends on earth," Narciss herself offers an alternate view (99). When prosecutor Dorris Gladney asks why she remained under the bed during the storm when she heard the Ponders at her front door, Narciss explains, "If white folks and ball of fire both tryin' git in you all's house, you best let *dem* mind who comin' in first" (102). Thus, while the white man sees Daniel and Edna Earle as her "best friends," Narciss lumps them in with "white folks" and puts them on par with the destructive and unpredictable fireball she so fears. Edna Earle's ignorance about her cook's personal preferences and talents further underlines how little she knows Narciss. For instance, when Narciss first arrives in the family Studebaker to announce Daniel and Bonnie Dee's surprise nuptials, Edna Earle comments, "I never in my life knew she knew how to drive" (31). Moreover, although Narciss clearly enjoys driving and spending time with Bonnie Dee, Edna Earle sees her only as a cook. According to her, "They had that grand Narciss—had her and never appreciated her" (42). Indeed, when she moves back to Ponder Hill, she observes that Narciss "had a black smear across all her aprons, that the steering wheel made on her stomach"; but Edna Earle remedies that: "I made her get back to the stove" (54). Grandma Ponder brought Narciss into the family as a child and taught her how to cook; for Edna Earle,

Narciss has not developed, changed, or grown more complicated since that moment in her youth. As her name suggests, Narciss serves merely as a vehicle for the Ponders' vanity; they see in her their idealized conception of themselves.

By contrast, Narciss misses Bonnie Dee in a way that suggests she considered her a true friend, or at least truer than the Ponders: "She claims she's lonesome in town," even though she lives in the Beulah Hotel with Daniel, Edna Earle, and whatever visitors happen by. Though I do not wish to overstate the degree or depth of the friendship between Bonnie Dee and Narciss—after all, Narciss does a great deal of labor at Ponder Hill—the fact remains that we see a greater degree of intimacy between her and Narciss than between Narciss and Edna Earle, for instance.[16] Moreover, at the trial, Narciss refuses to provide an alibi for Daniel. As Edna Earle says, "She just washed her hands of us. You can't count on them for a single minute" (103). Most importantly, her time with Bonnie Dee has made her singularly unfit for the one role for which Grandma Ponder trained her: cooking. According to Edna Earle, Narciss could cook well, "if she just would. But Narciss don't cook good any more. I hate to tell you—her rice won't stand apart. She don't cook any better than Ada or Ada's sister" (155). When their longtime retainer refuses to play her role in the paternalist performance, the Ponders cannot "stand apart" from the denizens of Clay. Although Narciss's revolt does not amount to much—some bland rice and a turn on the witness stand that does not affect the trial's outcome—we may catch in her relationship with Bonnie Dee glimmers of Welty's vision for a more equitable relationship between African Americans and whites, a relationship outside the rigidly circumscribed boundaries of paternalism, a relationship in which social identities are not fixed but flexible. When asked in an interview for her thoughts on politics, Welty praised the advances of the civil rights era and criticized those who opposed racial equality as desiring "an idiotic return to something that was not any good in the first place" (*Conversations* 114). Most significantly, she further commented, "I do feel that private relationships between blacks and whites have always been the steadying thing" (*Conversations* 114).[17] In *The Ponder Heart,* however, she has created a story in which personal relationships between black and white do not steady an oppressive paternalist social order but disrupt it, with hopeful results.

Should we assume, then, that Welty prefers Bonnie Dee's consumerism to the Ponders' paternalism? Perhaps not; I would argue that Welty does not celebrate Bonnie Dee's urge to buy and spend in and of itself. After all, none of her many purchases seems to do her much good. In fact, when she succumbs to the lure of Edna Earle's ad and "buys" back her marriage even when she knows it is a bad deal, she seals her doom. However, perhaps Welty intends for us to take from Bonnie Dee an attitude of irreverence to long-standing southern class hierarchies, an attitude informed by an awareness of the economic underpinnings of southern society that offers the possibility of freedom from hidebound social and racial customs by making claims for essential, natural class positions impossible and by opening the avenues of genuine communication among races and classes. In both *Delta Wedding* and *The Ponder Heart,* Welty describes racial paternalism as a tool whereby wealthy white southerners simultaneously organize the black labor that supports their posh lifestyles and obscure the true nature of that labor so that their aristocratic positions appear essential and inevitable. But by exposing the mythical nature of their pretensions to aristocracy—their dependence on violently coerced black labor, for instance, or a poor white woman's ability to try on and take off elite ladyhood like a dress—Welty demystifies and delegitimizes the racist, elitist systems that support them and explores the possibility of creating new, more equitable, and more humane ways of interacting.

3

STOPPING ON A DIME

Race, Class, and the "White Economy of Material Waste" in William Faulkner's *The Mansion* and *The Reivers*

In 1940, William Faulkner offered a eulogy for Caroline Barr, his family's longtime African American retainer.[1] In it, Faulkner credited Barr, to whom he referred as "a fount of authority over my conduct," with teaching him many valuable lessons, including "to refrain from waste" (117). Such simple advice may seem only commonsensical, yet readers familiar with Faulkner's late-career literary production—not only *The Town* and *The Mansion* (the second and third volumes in the Snopes trilogy) and *The Reivers: A Reminiscence,* but also a wealth of speeches, essays, and public and private letters—may perceive that Faulkner's emphasis on this bit of practical wisdom presages his late 1950s preoccupation with the role waste plays in the intersections of race, class, and economics. Indeed, in much of his late work, most significantly *The Mansion,* Faulkner probes this complicated relationship in order to understand more thoroughly the ills of a southern class system based on acquisitive, competitive individualism and to offer an alternative model of race and class relations based on communal need.[2]

An essay entitled "On Fear: Deep South in Labor: Mississippi, 1956" suggests Faulkner's shifting emphasis in his treatment of race toward the end of his career. Claims Faulkner, "it is our southern white man's shame that in our present economy the Negro must not have economic equality; our double shame that we fear that giving him more social equality will jeopardise his present economic status; our triple shame that even then, to justify our stand, we must becloud the issue with the bugaboo of miscegenation" (105). The casual dismissal of miscegenation as a "bugaboo" may initially seem surprising to readers accustomed to viewing Faulkner's entire body of work through the lens of his ostensible "Major Phase"; after all, miscegenation lies at the heart of three of the works typically considered among his greatest—*Light in August, Absalom, Absalom!* and *Go*

Down, Moses. Even if we question Edouard Glissant's claim that "Creolization is the very thing that offends Faulkner: *mestissage* and miscegenation, plus their unforeseeable consequences" (83)—if it surely repulsed many of his characters, it less clearly repulsed the author—we must still acknowledge that in the 1930s and 1940s Faulkner accorded the concept more attention than any mere "bugaboo" would warrant. And, though Faulkner's concern with the relationship between race, labor, and economics was certainly evident in those earlier works, as Richard Godden has ably pointed out, rarely did he articulate that concern so baldly as in this essay.[3]

For Faulkner, waste—or the lack of it—lay at the heart of his analysis of the reasons why white southerners feared economic competition from African Americans. In "On Fear" he argues that though the African American farmer has been free a scant ninety years, now

> he can own his land and farm it with inferior stock and worn-out tools and gear—equipment which any white man would starve with—and raise children and feed and clothe them and send them to what schools are available and even now and then send them North where they can have equal scholastic opportunity, and end his life holding his head up because he owes no man, with even enough over to pay for his coffin and funeral. That's what the white man in the South is afraid of: that the Negro, who has done so much with no chance, might do so much more with an equal one that he might take the white man's economy away from him, the Negro now the banker or the merchant or the planter and the white man the share-cropper or the tenant. (96)

Thus, Faulkner locates the white fear of African American economic competition in the impressive and wholly necessary efficiency of African Americans, workers who, because of their subjugation, cannot afford to waste a breath, much less a dollar. As he succinctly puts it in his notorious interview with Russell Howe, "the Negro won't come out on top because of anything to do with the race but because he has always gotten by without scope—when they are given scope they use it fully. The Negro is trained to do more than a white man can with the same limitations" (264). Similar sentiments appear in *The Mansion*. Faulkner's omniscient narrator explains that, before his political career, populist demagogue Clarence Snopes and his gang beat up African Americans out of fear: "they were afraid of that alien race. . . . not because it was black but because they—the white man—had taught the black one how to threaten *the white economy of material waste,* when the white man compelled the black man to learn how to do more with less and worse if the black man wanted to survive in the white economy—less and worse of tools to farm and work with, less of luxury to be content with, less of waste to keep alive with" (599, my emphasis). Of course, a similar attitude often validated oppressive economic practices. As Gilbert Fite points out, when local administrators controlled the distribution of New Deal relief payments, "black farm families received considerably less than their white neighbors. The prevailing attitude throughout the South held that blacks could live on less than whites"; withholding cash from African Americans maintained the paternalistic bond by ensuring that they would have to rely on planters for work and for other kinds of care (136). However, I would argue that Faulkner perceives African American efficiency not as an excuse for further subjugation but as a possible model for a reform in an economic and social system he finds corrupt.

In this context, Caroline Barr's simple admonition "to refrain from waste" takes on added resonance. Not just homespun wisdom, her advice evokes a type of African American economic practice fundamentally different from, and indeed subversive of, a white economic system based on "material waste," a system in which the participants' frantic economic activity means they end up with a houseful of unnecessary consumer goods (almost) paid for on the installment plan (644). Elsewhere in *The Mansion,* Charles "Chick" Mallison elaborates on the nature of this white economy. Discussing Jefferson's resistance to the efforts of a pair of immigrant Communist organizers, Chick argues that

> among us white male Jeffersons there was one concert of unanimity, no less strong and even louder at the bottom, extending from the operators of Saturday curb-side peanut- and popcorn-vending machines, through the side street and back alley grocers, up to the department store owners and automobile and gasoline agencies, against everybody they called communists now . . . [,] any and everybody who seemed even to question our native-born Jefferson

> right to buy or raise or dig or find anything as cheaply as cajolery or trickery or threat or force could do it, and then sell it as dear as the necessity or ignorance or timidity of the buyer would stand. (523)

In this sense Faulkner's treatment of exchange in *The Mansion* recalls John T. Matthews's analysis of trade in *The Hamlet* as "a game that yields pleasure, makes statements, and fabricates meaning" (179). However, in *The Mansion* Faulkner is clearer about the racial and class aspects of that meaning. Chick renders the competitive nature of free-market capitalism not simply as American but as fundamentally white, male, and southern; he implicitly portrays economic competition not just as a means of material gain but of certifying one's proper identity and one's place in the social hierarchy. Indeed, Chick describes the Finnish communists, who refuse to participate in this system, as nonwhite and fundamentally other: one is a "troglodyte," and both are "already well advanced outside the Jefferson *pale*" (523, my emphasis). The nonwhite Reds share their association of racial otherness with Meadowfill, a poor sawmill retiree who scrimps and saves and whose thriftiness leads him to shop in stores that cater to African American trade, buying "wilted and damaged left-over of food which even Negroes would have scorned" (626). The narrator later describes him as "too stingy or too perverse" to tend his "scraggy" orchard; the association of "stinginess" with "perversity" again makes clear that refusal to participate in economic competition marks one as other, perhaps even subhuman. But while white Jeffersonians treat the economic sphere as a proving ground for their race, class, and gender identity, African Americans cannot afford to waste effort or item: they must become masters of efficiency, wresting every last erg of use from impoverished land and worn-out tools.

To understand better how waste might serve so vital a function in a competitive market economy, I turn again to Thorstein Veblen. White Jeffersonians participate in conspicuous consumption, and, indeed, in what we might call conspicuous commerce. Their competitive exchanges create a social field in which each individual white male may define his position relative to other white males. Veblen clarifies the relation between "material waste" and this competitive activity when he argues that "in order to gain and to hold the esteem of men it is not sufficient merely to possess wealth or power. The wealth or power must be put in evidence, for esteem is awarded only on evidence" (36). Yet not just any evidence will serve. According to Veblen, "In order to be reputable it must be wasteful" (96). Further, this waste must conform to "established usage" (115). In the early-twentieth-century South, such "established usage" conformed to a romanticized antebellum ideal—what W. J. Cash termed the "aristocratic complex" (240). Thus, if "material waste," according to Chick Mallison, organizes the white social structure, then these wasteful gestures of paternalism represent the pinnacle of achievement in the economic arena: they simultaneously signify financial superiority and disinterest in the process of "cajolery," "trickery," "threat," and "force" that characterizes the economic struggles of lesser men. Moreover, wasteful paternalism reinforces the racial difference between African Americans and whites; African American southerners are disqualified from competition in the economic arena by dint of the favors they receive—though, as Faulkner's Charles Mallison notes, the skills they learn by having to make do with less mean they threaten the very system itself. The white men of Jefferson thus inhabit a world in which money and commerce are imbued with a fetishized social significance far beyond their economic value.

Flem Snopes's rise from poverty in the community of Frenchman's Bend to what seems the pinnacle of wealth, prestige, and respectability as a Jefferson bank president illuminates the importance of paternalistic waste to the construction of class in *The Mansion*. As I discussed in the introduction, though the citizens of Jefferson clearly consider Flem to represent a new profit- and business-centered ethic that they find alien and other, Flem takes care to exhibit his success in symbols and language associated with an agrarian-oriented southern aristocracy.[4] Veteran Snopes-watcher V. K. Ratliff describes Flem's new abode, Manfred de Spain's "rejuvenated ancestral home" (458), as "jest a house," and notes that it would have been perfectly acceptable for de Spain or even Colonel Sartoris to live in, since the social position of these men was well established (469). However, Flem knows that since he had to earn the house and the bank presidency, such an ordinary home would not do for him; instead, he must use his house to connect himself to the fabled planter class and its aristocratic values. His home "would have to be the physical symbol of all them generations of respectability and aristocracy that not only would a been too proud to mishandle other folks' money, it couldn't possibly ever needed to" (469). According to Ratliff, Flem's depositors must be able to lie down "undisturbed at night with their money that immaculate, that impeccable, that immune" (470). Ratliff's narrative suggests that the denizens of Jefferson expect their aristocrats to have transcended economic concerns so that they would never need to "mishandle" the bank's deposits. Presumably, outright cheating would fall outside of the realm of "cajolery, trickery, threat or force," would not be an acceptable way of advancing in the Jefferson hierarchy.

Ratliff's description of Harvard- and Heidelberg-educated lawyer Gavin Stevens's relationship to economics offers a comic picture of the aristocrat's proper relationship to economics. Discussing Gavin's involvement in the matter of Linda Snopes's inheritance, Ratliff describes his prestigious friend as "not only in the middle of that entire monetary and sepulchrial crisis but all around ever part of it too, like one of them frantic water bugs skating and rushing immune and unwettable on top of a stagnant pond" (463). Thus, though economic matters immerse Gavin, he nevertheless remains "unwettable"; like others in the upper ranks of southern society, he may be *involved* with money, but he is never *determined* by it—at least ostensibly. The fact that his "unwettable" status requires "frantic . . . skating and rushing" suggests the complicated performance required to maintain that arid state. In fact, the "skating and rushing" prove to be too much effort for Gavin, finally; in his mania to get the better of Flem, he mortgages his Cadillac convertible, strips it down, and refuses to make the payments in order to force Flem to repossess a defunct shell of a car. Noel Polk aptly describes Gavin's scheme as "fourth-rate lowgrade childish penny-ante chiseling and gouging" ("Idealism in *The Mansion*" 116).[5] Indeed, the fact that the aristocratic Gavin is guilty of such pettiness but does not suffer any demotion in the eyes of other Jeffersonians indicates that there may be forces at play, beyond simple achievement in Chick's "competition," that affect his class position, or at least Ratliff's description of it, as we shall see.

As Gavin's example indicates, Flem's new upper-crust status is precarious and requires constant reinforcement, requires a performance that, paradoxically, represents both his skill with a dollar and his indifference to the base world of economics. Therefore, he sets about converting this "jest a house" into a replica of an antebellum mansion, tearing off the mundane front gallery and adding Tara-worthy white columns (469–70), and he staffs his new showplace with the expected African American servants.

As first discussed in the introduction, however, a slip in Flem's performance of his new status indicates to the people of Jefferson his incomplete understanding of the role of racial paternalism in constructing an aristocratic identity. Even though the black planter's hat that Flem dons is the same type as worn by the unassailably aristocratic Colonel Sartoris, it never looks like it actually belongs to him, according to Ratliff, because of how he disposed of his old hat. The citizens of Jefferson still see Flem as the same man because his old cap was "not throwed away or even give away [in a conspicuous, paternalistic gesture], but sold" (470). Thus, Flem's privileging of naked profit over the sophisticated waste of paternalism prevents him from ever completely achieving the status he has so long sought.

Or does it? In Ratliff's version of the story, the dime, minute though it is, seems to form an impregnable physical barrier to Flem's social ascent. Ratliff treats the transaction as strictly mercantile and decidedly nonpaternalist—the boy gets a hat, Flem gets a dime. However, Montgomery Ward Snopes offers a slightly but crucially different version of the story that challenges the foundation upon which Jefferson bases its disdain for Flem. According to M. W., Flem "sold it to a nigger boy for a dime *that he took out in work*" (390, my emphasis). If we take his testimony seriously, then Ratliff has omitted a crucial fact: he lets the reader believe that Flem engaged in a goods-for-cash transaction when the exchange may, in fact, have conformed much more closely to the paternalist ideal which Flem seeks to emulate. If a dime does not literally change hands, then Flem's trade is decidedly less gauche, and Flem's customers would have reason to continue believing that their banker still keeps their money "immaculate" and has little interest in plundering their accounts. Thus, Jefferson's refusal to allow Flem to be "altered and transmogrified" (470) into an aristocrat has less to do with Flem's failure to adhere to the proper social conventions and more to do with Ratliff's manipulation of the story. We have reason to believe that Ratliff exerts considerable influence over the way in which the town perceives its upstart banker: according to Ratliff, Flem's addition of a small, bare, wooden footrest to his otherwise upscale mansion mantelpiece was initially known only to Flem's African American yardman but became "a Jefferson legend after he mentioned it to me and him (likely) and me both happened to mention it in turn to some of our close intimates: a part of the Snopes legend and another Flem Snopes monument" (479). Ratliff's parenthetical qualification—"(likely)"—suggests that he may in fact be the sole disseminator of this tale. Thus, the fact that the longtime Snopes-watcher chooses the particular detail of the hat as the point of attack in his campaign against Flem's impending respectability indicates the significance of paternalistic performance to elite status; if Ratliff can deprive Flem of his claims to paternalistic waste, then all the fancy columns and African American servants will avail him little.

Ratliff is Faulkner's most seductive and dangerous narrator; we want to trust him. His folksy, aw-shucks "wisdom" is a refreshing change from Gavin Stevens's pompous gasbaggery. And certainly, in his routing of the duplicitous politician Clarence Snopes, he performs a valuable service for Yoknapatawpha County and for the state of Mississippi. However, as Richard Godden has observed of Ratliff in *The Hamlet*, "Ratliff's perception of Flem needs to be recognized as partial, interested and class based. . . . Ratliff shares much with Flem, not least that both quit rented fields for versions of the store" ("Earthing *The Hamlet*" 87). Godden's insight holds true for the Ratliff of *The Mansion* as well. I would argue that Ratliff projects his own perceived inferiorities onto the story of Flem's ten-cent hat. He chastises Flem for not suitably adhering to the ideal of material waste, yet he has trouble adhering to that ideal himself. Rather than a heroic crusader enacting a Faulkner-approved model of resistance to crass, commercial Snopesism, Ratliff is in fact a zealous, if at times conflicted, adherent to the bankrupt model of social-economic relations that Chick Mallison describes as characterizing all white male Jeffersonians. Flem Snopes's only crime is that he excels at it.

Ratliff's ultimate inability to relinquish his position in the economic competition of Jefferson becomes clear when he and Gavin journey to New York to visit Linda Snopes and Barton Kohl in Greenwich Village. Gavin takes him to an exclusive designer necktie store run by Russian designer Myra Allanovna, where Ratliff orders two ties before he inquires as to the price. His discovery that they cost seventy-five dollars apiece puts him in a fiscal quandary. Though we might at first think that wearing an expensive tie would constitute the conspicuous waste so prized in Jefferson, we should remember that, as Veblen points out, conspicuous waste must conform to accepted social norms, and there is nothing especially paternalistic or antebellum about Ratliff's purchase. Indeed, one could reasonably argue that going to Greenwich Village and buying pricey designer neckties from a Russian haberdasher is the very antithesis of the romanticized antebellum ideal that reigns in Yoknapatawpha. Nor would such a purchase further his reputation as a smart trader and shrewd businessman, his position in the game of competitive commerce. Ratliff haltingly articulates these concerns: "I sells sewing machines in Missippi. I cant have it knowed back there that I paid seventy-five dollars a piece for neckties" (489). Yet as a merchant, Ratliff feels obliged to fulfill his contract: he attempts to pay for the ties but refuses to take them home; nor can he accept them as a gift. Myra Allanovna's next proffered solution horrifies Ratliff and startles him into revealing that the obsession with money that he ascribes to Flem truly belongs to him. She snaps open her cigarette lighter and prepares to burn the money that he has laid on the counter, but Ratliff quickly intervenes, placing his hands on the cash, and saying, with diction that indicates a kind of primal panic, "Wait! Wait! . . . Not burn money" (490). When Myra presses him for a reason, his first response is merely tautological: "Because it's money" (490). Ratliff's halting explanation does little to ameliorate this naked expression of affection: "Somebody somewhere at some time went to—went through—I mean, money stands for too much hurt and grief somewhere to somebody that jest the money wasn't never worth—I mean, that aint what I mean. . . ." Of course, it is Ratliff whose money is threatened; it does not seem unreasonable, then, to imagine that this "somebody" is him, that, because of the effort it has taken him to succeed in business, money has for him become overdetermined as a symbol of his own escape from poverty.

Faulkner's vision of Ratliff here is more pessimistic than in the novel with which he began his exploration of the Snopes clan. While many critics read *The Hamlet* as an indictment of the fetishization of cash money over an embrace of more personal, traditional values, the Ratliff of *The Mansion* perpetuates that fetishization and more.[6] While the Fairchilds of *Delta Wedding* strive to erase the traces of history from their money, Ratliff values money precisely because he sees it as the symbol of his history. Allanovna confirms as much: she responds to Ratliff's semicoherent rationale by saying, "I know exactly what you mean. Only the gauche, the illiterate, the frightened and the pastless destroy money" (490). Of course, she was perfectly willing to destroy money moments before, so she may only intend her remark to comfort Ratliff and offer him a vision of himself as noble instead of cash-crazy. Regardless, though her comment may gesture toward a critique of those who waste, Ratliff is not capable of articulating or enacting that critique. He offers no viable alternative, because, though he does not conform to the economy of material waste, he upholds its ideals by projecting his own money-fetish onto Flem. Here Faulkner makes visible the interestedness of those who claim to protect an allegedly natural social order: their appeals to tradition or essence often conceal a desire to maintain their privilege, or at least to remain within a system whose rules and restrictions they understand and can manipulate.

If Ratliff can provide no useful alternative, then we might logically turn next to Yoknapatawpha's African American community; after all, Faulkner describes their economic practices as opposed to the "white economy of material waste."[7] But for Faulkner, the post–World War II economic boom has resulted in an expansion of wealth and consumerism such that even the impoverished African American underclass can participate in the mainstream economy, an economy that he continues to identify as fundamentally flawed. Charles Mallison reflects that with the new prosperity comes an alteration in the social fabric of Yoknapatawpha: he believes that the "American knights-errant liberal reformers would be out of work now, with even the little here-to-fore lost places like Yoknapatawpha County, Mississippi, fertilised to overflowing not only with ex-soldiers' blood money but with the two or three or four dollars per hour which had been forced on the other ex-riveters and -bricklayers and -machinists . . . so fast that they hadn't had time to spend it" (644). Charles notes that even the two symbolically nonwhite Finn Communists, whom one might expect to oppose the expansion of individualistic capitalism, have become "capitalists and bull-market investors simply because they had not yet acquired any private place large enough to put that much money down while they turned their backs on it" (644). Most importantly, the African Americans now have "an installment-plan automobile and radio and refrigerator full of canned beer down-paid with the blood money which at least drew no color line in every unwired unscreened plumbingless cabin" (644). The language here echoes a prominent African American leader's earlier explanation to Gavin: "We both buy the same installment-plan automobiles to burn up the same gasoline in, and the same radios to listen to the same music and the same ice boxes to keep the same beer in, but that's all" (532). Thus, though this increased wealth seems a positive advance, it is still an advance within a system that Faulkner sees as problematic, if not downright corrupt. African Americans' halting entrance into mainstream economic practices—though it remains rigidly circumscribed by southern whites—is also an entrance into an economy of consumption and waste; instead of rewriting the economic master narrative, they have let it rewrite them. Thus, Yoknapatawpha's African Americans no longer enact the alternative, subversive economic practices that they did before the war.

I would argue that, although neither Ratliff nor Mississippi's African Americans can provide an alternate model of economic, race, and class relations, we may find one by following the unlikely figure of Mink Snopes. Faulkner uses Mink's journey from Parchman to Jefferson to explore one potential manifestation for a subversive, alternative paradigm of community economic practices made possible in the wake of drastic transformations wrought by World War II. First, though, let me make clear that I do not intend to offer a reading that sees Mink's journey from hardscrabble tenant farm to Flem's mansion, the scene of his crime, as a redemptive quest for him or for Jefferson. Critics such as Joseph Urgo, Noel Polk, and Theresa Towner have done much to challenge readings of the Snopes trilogy that posit Flem as a fundamental evil who must be heroically exterminated.[8] So, while I agree with Polk and others that we must not too simply read Mink as a hero who rids the world of Flem's pervasive evil, I would contend that Faulkner uses his travels in order to present an alternative method of organizing class and economic relations—an alternative that Mink, obsessed with petty revenge, misses.

Murderous Mink Snopes may seem a far-fetched suggestion for a source for a critique of the dominant economic and social systems in Yoknapatawpha County; throughout *The Mansion*, Faulkner characterizes him as so overwhelmed by economic pressures that he converts nearly all knowledge into economic terms, even knowledge about himself. When he hitches a ride to Memphis upon his release from prison, he surreptitiously enlists the driver's aid to determine his age: "He thought *Money*. He said: 'If you had twenty-five dollars and found thirty-eight more, how much would you have?'" When the driver does the math for him, he thinks, "*Sixty-three . . . So that's how old I am*" (428). Perhaps this tendency toward an economic epistemology of age results naturally from a life spent, with the exception of his years in prison, on the losing end of the competitive system of "cajolery or trickery or threat or force" by which Yoknapatawpha's white male citizens determine their relative worth. Indeed, his persistent obsession with money starkly contrasts with Ratliff's image of Gavin Stevens as "unwettable" by the swamp of financial affairs.

Further, Mink's impoverished economic condition threatens even his whiteness. He resents the African Americans who work for Jack Houston because Houston's paternalism provides them with more material comfort than Mink can provide for himself. Mink obsesses over the fact that Houston's servant has "a better house to live in than the one he . . . , a white man with a wife and two daughters, lived in" (339) and wears "warmer clothing than any he and his family possessed" (341); indeed, he curses "the Negro for his black skin inside warmer garment's than his, a white man's" (341). Mink particularly perceives his whiteness as precarious and unstable when in the presence of the wealthier and undoubtedly white Houston, who treats all those beneath him as fundamentally other: when he goes to Varner's store, "Houston ordered whoever was on the front gallery to step inside and fetch him out whatever it was he had come for like they were Negroes" (337). Mink finds this interpellation into racial otherness difficult to resist: when he goes to visit Houston to retrieve his cow, he can only confirm his whiteness in the presence of Houston's African American servant: Mink reflects that he does not need "to fawn and cringe yet because only the Negro with his hayfork would be in the lot now, the rich man himself in the house" (342); instead of having to "fawn and cringe," a phrase Faulkner repeats a few lines later, Mink can speak to Houston's servant "level and white-man" (342). Houston's presence, however, forces Mink into a performance of subservience that aligns him with stereotypical representations of "fawning and cringing" African Americans. Indeed, Mink's and Houston's interactions with the servant mark their class differences clearly: Mink tells his rich foe, "I dont listen to niggers: I tell them" (344); because his state of deprivation puts him on a lower level than even this African American servant, Mink cannot afford any gesture that would acknowledge social equality with him. On the other hand, Houston, whose class position makes his whiteness unassailable, can listen to his servant's advice without fear.

Mink has had little success, then, in the economic competition by which Yoknapatawphans confirm their whiteness. So perhaps it should come as no surprise that when he is sentenced to Parchman for killing Houston, he perceives his incarceration as a reprieve from that cutthroat system:

> He could drag dust up and down cotton middles from year in to year out and if nothing whatever sprang up behind him, it would make no difference to him. No more now to go to a commissary store every Saturday morning to battle with the landlord for every gram of the cheap bad meat and meal and molasses and the tumbler of snuff which was his and his wife's one spendthrift orgy. No more to battle with the landlord for every niggard sack of fertilizer, then gather the poor crop which suffered from that niggard lack and still have to battle the landlord for his niggard insufficient share of it. All he had to do now was just to keep moving. . . . At first he was ashamed, in shame and terror lest the others find that he felt this way; until one day he knew (he could not have said how) that all the others felt like this; that, given time enough, Parchman brought them all to this. . . . (414–15)

But this freedom from economic concerns is brief: "Parchman just changed the way a man looked at what he saw after he got in Parchman. It didn't change what he brought with him" (415). When his sentence is up, he receives "a pair of shoes, a shirt, overalls and jumper and a hat, all brand new, and a ten-dollar bill and the three dollars and eighty-five cents which were still left from the forty dollars Flem had sent him eighteen years ago" (424); thus, Mink is simultaneously released from a literal prison and returned to an economic one.

His first thought indicates that his long-standing obsessions with killing Flem and with needing money have not weakened during his long imprisonment: he immediately reflects that "it would probably take all of the thirteen dollars and eighty-five cents to buy a pistol even in a Memphis pawn shop" (425). Moreover, Mink quickly learns that he still lacks skill at competing in the economic arena. Even his shock at how inflation has driven up the price of bread and sardines cannot keep him from nearly blowing all his money in a pathetic small-scale spending spree: when he sees a case of soft drinks, "something terrible happened inside his mouth and throat—a leap, a spring of a thin liquid like fire or the myriad stinging of ants all the way down to his stomach; with a kind of incredulous terror, even while he was saying *No! No! That will cost at least a quarter, too,* his voice was saying aloud: 'I reckon I'll have one of them'" (564). His economic incontinence threatens both his mission and his manhood. Mink thinks, "If the bottles had been a dollar a piece, there was a definite limit beyond which temptation, or at least his lack of will power, could no longer harm him. But at only a quarter a piece, until he could reach Memphis and actually have the pistol in his hand, there was no foreseeable point within the twelve remaining dollars where he would have peace; already, before he was even outside the store, he was saying *Be a man, Be a man. You got to be a man, you got too much to do, too much to resk*" (566). Though he manages to resist this temptation, the storekeeper also short-changes him (by a dime, in fact), a result which perhaps indicates the ways in which Mink's desire to consume has gotten in the way of his success in the economic sphere, has blinded him to "cajolery and trickery."

Curiously, given Mink's apparent weakness in the economic arena, Gavin's plan to dissuade him from killing Flem fails, even though it is intended to exploit just this weakness. When Linda Snopes arranges to have Mink pardoned and released two years before he completes his sentence, she and Gavin decide to pay him two hundred and fifty dollars upon his release, with the same amount to follow every three months, as long as he leaves Mississippi and never returns. According to Ratliff, everyone (except Linda, of course) believes this plan will work because no prison should "contain nobody eccentric and antisocial enough to behave like he considered anything like free-will choice to even belong in the same breath with two hundred and fifty active dollars give him free for nothing so he never even had to say Much obliged for them" (675). But although Mink's refusal of the money constitutes a surprising display of willpower, it also conforms to the rules of the game that the wealthier

Gavin and Linda have established: accepting the money means that he would have to leave Mississippi and never seek his revenge on Flem; he refuses the money so that he can stay. Thus, though Mink's decision resists the blunt economic determinism that nearly everyone assumes motivates him, it does so in a way that indicates he has not realized that the rules of the system he is caught in are not neutral but in fact serve the interests of the wealthiest and most powerful. Ultimately, however, by refusing the money and pursuing the quest, Mink tacitly accepts the economic system imposed on him from above.

However, although Mink cannot conceive of an ideal of class and economics outside of the prevailing Yoknapatawphan norm, he does encounter, on his journey to Jefferson, a community that has organized itself around a fundamentally different model—a model that does not validate and reward waste, a community in which paternalism is unknown. Faulkner signals Mink's entrance into this alternate system when, after realizing he will need more money to buy a pistol, he finds a job performing the profoundly unwasteful task of sorting scrap wood from a collapsed house, "a jumble of beams, joists, window- and door-frames and even still-intact sections of siding" (569); his new employer, the Reverend Goodyhay, means to build a church with the salvaged materials. Mink begins to realize how this church differs from others when he sees their interim sanctuary—a former African American schoolhouse (579). Goodyhay has reclaimed this abandoned edifice for his unique congregation, a racially integrated group of working-class World War II veterans and their families. Mink pays particular attention to "two oldish couples, man and wife of course, farmers obviously, without doubt tenant farmers come up from the mortgaged bank- or syndicate-owned cotton plantation from which the son had been drafted three or four or five years ago to make that far from home that sacrifice" (583). Significantly, the group remains deliberately unstratified even by military rank: Mink "sense[s] that identity, similarity among them even beyond the garments they wore—more battle jackets, green army slickers, one barracks cap still showing where the officer's badge had been removed" (579). When Mink spots a black woman in the congregation and professes surprise that they accept African Americans as well as whites, one of Goodyhay's parishioners explains to him, "Her son had it too just like she was a white woman, even if they didn't put his name on the same side of the monument with the others" (579). Mink later watches as "the white people on the bench ma[ke] way for the Negress to sit down beside the young white woman and put her arm around her" (584).

This striking, moving vision of an integrated worship community founded on the common experience of loss and a renewed commitment to the democratic values for which the United States entered World War II is central to Faulkner's critique of the prevailing systems of race, class, and economics in postwar Mississippi. If, as Noel Polk argues, *The Mansion* is Faulkner's "kaleidoscopic record" of the impact of World War II on Mississippi life (138), then Reverend Goodyhay's congregation is clearly one central aspect of that record. In "Fighting for What We Didn't Have: How Mississippi's Black Veterans Remember World War II," historian Neil R. McMillen discusses the results of his interviews conducted with some of the 85,000 African American Mississippians who served in World War II. According to McMillen, the histories he collected, although diverse and idiosyncratic, in general suggested that the war "helped shape an emerging racial consciousness"—in white and black Americans—that more fully apprehended the "moral contradictions of a nation that professed human rights and practiced white supremacy" (110). McMillen notes that one hopeful—albeit problematically so—aspect of the military experience was the way in which it offered a space for white and black Americans to form friendships, though in many cases those friendships did not survive the trip home (99–100). In Goodyhay's congregation, then, Faulkner presents for us an idealized version of an alternative model of interracial community that could develop after World War II, a community characterized not by hate and fear but by a recognition of equality and common humanity.[9]

One of Mink's fellow scrap-wood sorters, a man named Dad, tells Mink that he does not believe that such a community can long survive: he argues that those who have not come around to this new way of thinking "aint going to put up with no such as this. The rest of the folks that already had to put up with that damn war for four–five years now and want to forget about it. That've already gone to all that five years of trouble and expense to get shut of it, only just when they are about to get settled back down again, be damned if here aint a passel of free-loading government-subsidised exdrafted sons of bitches acting like whatever had caused the war not only actually happened but was still going on, and was going to keep on going on until somebody did something about it. . . . trying to bring Jesus Christ back alive in the middle of 1946" (575). Thus, Dad's cynical remarks make it clear that Goodyhay's congregation threatens to disrupt the status quo by forcing the citizens of Jefferson to acknowledge the gap between their religious and political ideals and their social practices.

Most significantly for this study, however, Faulkner also depicts this community as enacting an alternative model of economic practice as well. Historian Jack Bloom has noted that the struggle for civil rights hinged largely on African Americans' becoming increasingly savvy in the economic arena, gaining purchasing power and learning to deploy it in a strategic manner to split the business and planter classes (219). But as we have seen, for Faulkner such success is always highly qualified, for it means adhering to a fundamentally corrupt economic system, one based on "cajolery," "trickery," "threat," and "force," one in which use value and the common good are at best secondary to the constant jostling for individual position on the social ladder. In contrast, he offers Goodyhay's church, whose congregants share economic resources in a manner reminiscent of the early Christian church. When Goodyhay tells his flock that Mink needs nine dollars to get home, one man, who has recently won thirty-four dollars in a crap game (in a manner somewhat *less* reminiscent of the early Christian church), volunteers to donate his winnings, and another volunteers to drive him to Memphis. With no concern for racial boundaries or class distinctions, no worry for how their economic expenditures will affect their whiteness, their maleness, or their southernness, this group enacts an economic practice based on mutual need and mutual sacrifice. Their economic system does not reward waste and acquisitive individualism; instead, it rewards the careful use of resources and affirms the bonds that tie individuals together. I would argue that here we may see Faulkner's vision for a radically countercultural interracial community that could stand in opposition to the grasping, vicious, isolating nature of contemporary consumer culture.

Initially, it may seem unlikely that Faulkner would locate his critique in such a community. After all, as Polk and Towner have observed, Faulkner's public statements from this era seem to indicate that he was convinced that only individual action was meaningful, and that any attempts to organize collective political action were doomed to failure since human beings are essentially corrupt and weak (Polk, "Faulkner and World War II" 137; Towner 126). Some of that individualist rhetoric is a natural product of his Jeffersonian individualism, though Faulkner also likely understood how much suspicion he could garner by speaking out in favor of collective action in the hysterical McCarthy era. Significantly, we should remember that, according to John Matthews, "Faulkner's texts almost invariably possess more complex, nuanced, and critical thinking about social and historical problems than Faulkner ever displayed in public remarks" ("Faulkner and Proletarian Literature" 175). Most importantly, as Polk notes, "if *The Mansion* is a narrative of social and political change in Mississippi during and after the War, it is even more significantly a record of the evolution of Faulkner's political sensibilities" ("Faulkner and World War II" 140). Further, in "On Fear" Faulkner expressed his frustration at the southern church's failure of leadership in the conflict over integration. According to Faulkner, "The Church . . . is the strongest unified force in our Southern life" (99), and he fears that by its silence it may be "tell[ing] us that it has no validity and wants none outside the sanctuary behind its symbolical spire," when it should be reminding southerners that "Christianity says: I am the only distinction among men since whosoever believeth in Me, shall never die" (101). Goodyhay's church, unorthodox though it may be in many ways, proclaims that truth loudly. Thus I would argue that in this church we may see Faulkner's attempt—and a graceful attempt at that—to describe a meaningful, effective model of communal action, one in which individuals may act together politically, economically, and personally without losing their individuality. Goodyhay's sermon clearly affirms the crucial value of individual effort, but it also suggests that such effort must take place in the context of a community. Further, Goodyhay asserts that he wants his congregation to crusade actively for their "salvation," and, though he refers explicitly to a religious salvation, I would suggest that we can also see in his sermon a vision of a community that actively crusades for social justice, that does not wait for it to be granted by benevolent superiors. According to Goodyhay, "Anybody that thinks all he's got to do is sit on his stern and have salvation come down on him like a cloudburst or something, dont belong in here. You got to get up on your feet and hunt it down until you can get a hold of it and then hold it, even fighting off if you have to. And if you cant find, then by God make it. Make a salvation He will pass and then earn the right to grab it and hold on and fight off too if you have to but anyway hold it, hell and high water be damned" (581). He then goes on to tell the tale of waking up on a battlefield, believing that he was dead. There, Goodyhay believes, God appeared to him in military dress and, calling him the "Top Soldier," ordered him to "Fall in"—but not before he also picks up, over his protests, the unconscious body of "the damned little bastard that had gone chicken at the exact wrong time, like they always do, turned the wheel aloose and tried to duck and caused the whole damn mess" (583). This ideal of the strongest "top soldier" helping the weakest and most cowardly animates the political and economic practices of his congregation and starkly contrasts with the individualism of the "white economy of material waste."

True, reading Goodyhay's congregation as a model of alternative social and economic practice raises some troubling questions. On one hand, it does seem that the forces of conspicuous commerce and individualism in the town worry about the influence of the church's ideology: when one of the congregants, Albert, explains that the plantation owner who had promised them a spot of land on which to build the church has reneged on his offer, he asserts, "Somebody changed his mind for him. Maybe the bank that holds his mortgage" (577). Here, Faulkner reminds us that the pretensions to economic "unwettability" that many white southerners associate with the plantation is but a sham, that the planter is just another participant in the "white economy of material waste" who cannot escape the economic underpinnings of his supposedly natural class position. Indeed, though there are two banks in Jefferson, and Albert notes that the American Legion might have had a hand in changing the planter's mind, it is tempting to imagine that Flem perhaps is the mortgage-holding banker who encouraged the planter to kick the church off his lands. Almost always a step or seven ahead of everyone else in Jefferson, Flem may simply be ensuring that no new system of social organization will rise up to threaten the one that he has spent his life mastering.

On the other hand, it is not entirely clear that such a preemptive strike is truly warranted, that the church can truly have exerted so powerful an influence on the community at large. Though cords of war and loss bind black and white Mississippians together, one could argue that this community does not know how to share its message with those who have not experienced such loss directly: when Albert tells Mink a story about the death of a black prostitute's son in combat, he repeatedly punctuates his narrative of foxholes and grenades with the phrase, "you know how it is" (580). Of course, Mink decidedly does *not* know how it is, and it seems that Albert and his fellow congregants have not yet managed to construct a way of talking about the principles that bind them together that does not rely on this shared experience; it may constitute a "distinction among men" other than Christianity. Further, the church's generosity does ultimately allow Mink to purchase the weapon with which he murders Flem, raising doubts about the church's effectiveness as a consciousness-raising agent.

However, Faulkner sets Mink up as a special case: he describes him as "not only unreconciled but irreconcilable" (583). Perhaps if he had either eyes to see or ears to hear he would have been dissuaded from his quest by Goodyhay's flock. Mink, however, cannot see past his obsession with his cousin to the hope embodied in the congregation, however poorly articulated it may sometimes be or how exclusive it might initially seem. He does kill Flem and, ultimately, ends up dying alone, absorbed back into the earth he so long struggled against and into the very anonymity and conformity that Faulkner abhorred: Mink passes into a world where he is "all mixed and jumbled up comfortable and easy so wouldn't nobody even know or even care who was which any more, himself among them, equal to any, good as any, brave as any, being inextricable from, *anonymous with all of them*" (721, my emphasis). Although one could argue that Mink's rubbing skeletal elbows with "Helen and the bishops, the kings and the unhomed angels, the scornful and graceless seraphim" (721) is a decided step up, perhaps even a reward, it seems to me that Faulkner's real point here is to stress how ultimately meaningless social hierarchies seem when even these glorified figures become "inextricable" from Mink Snopes.[10] When we consider the image of Flem sitting alone in his new mansion, chewing air, with the image of Mink being reclaimed by the earth and losing his self among the other corpses scattered there, we see that Faulkner uses these men to represent not divergent ideologies but a single critique: they represent the failure of the southern white mind to imagine an ideal of community, a model for society, organized upon a foundation other than materialistic individualism and concern for social status.

In a 1957 letter to the *New York Times,* written while the tensions over high school integration in Little Rock were at their peak, Faulkner pleaded with his fellow citizens: "What is important and necessary and urgent (urgent: we are reaching the point now where we haven't time anymore) is that we federate together, show a common unified front not for dull peace and amity, but for survival as a people and a nation" (230). In Goodyhay's church, Faulkner proposed one possible pattern for such a federation. *The Mansion,* then, stands as a rebuke to a southern social structure that rewards those most skillful in the game of "cajolery" or "trickery" or "threat" or "force," a game in which racial paternalism is celebrated not only because of its inherent wastefulness but also because of the way in which it keeps African Americans out of the game and thus protects the boundaries of white identity. Ultimately, Faulkner calls for a new model of social cooperation in which the commitment of individuals to one another is not merely metaphorical or rhetorical but fundamentally political and economic. He suggests that if southerners refuse to abandon their wasteful social and economic system and create a new one that ignores race and class divisions in favor of community need, then emptiness and injustice are the only alternatives.

The Mansion might have served well as Faulkner's culminating statement on the imperative for and potential structure of a new southern social model. Yet if *The Mansion* offers a vision of hope and possibility embodied in an alternative model of economics and community, Faulkner's final novel, *The Reivers,* offers a stark contrast: a vision of the emptiness and anxiety of the old model of wasteful paternalism. The narrator of *The Reivers*—an elderly Lucius Priest—spins a comic coming-of-age yarn in which his escapades with Boon Hogganbeck, his family's poor-white employee, and Ned McCaslin, an African American servant related to them by blood, serve mainly to teach him the importance of being a gentleman. Lucius is quite a tale-spinner, and his deft comic touch has led many critics to read his story as Kevin Railey does, as a "deeply romantic, nostalgic vision of people's places and possibilities in society" (169), a vision that "purposely has little to do with history" (173). But as Joseph Urgo wisely reminds us, we should no more take Lucius at his word than we do the narrators of Faulkner's other works (29–30). If Lucius's depiction of the era of his youth is obscured by nostalgia and selective memory, that obscurity is as much a function of the tale's fundamental connection to the historical moment of its telling—the late 1950s or early 1960s—as of its questionable relationship to the moment of its setting. Lucius's tale reveals anxieties about black labor and the changing nature of the race and class hierarchies that have traditionally organized life in the South. Ultimately, *The Reivers* not only reflects a desire on the part of wealthy, aristocratic white southerners to treat their class positions as natural and essential, as merely incidentally related to the economic exchanges and accumulation that make their privilege possible, but it also depicts their anxiety about the impossibility of fulfilling that desire in a changing South. *The Reivers,* then, is a narrative of failure: not a nostalgic victory lap through Faulkner's fictional world but instead a tour of the cracks in the façade of Yoknapatawpha's myths, cracks that expose the pernicious underlying ideology of race and class.

The Reivers opens with a scene in which the key components of Faulkner's analysis of waste, race, and class—efficient black labor and white paranoia about that labor—come together. When Boon comes crashing into the Priests' livery stable in search of a weapon with which he can avenge an insult, everyone realizes that, when his initial attempt to acquire his employer's, Maury Priest's, pistol fails, he will seek a pistol belonging to John Powell, an African American man who works there. Lucius recounts how John told them the pistol was the "living badge of his manhood, the ineffaceable proof that he was now twenty-one and a man" (728). The phallic symbolism is obvious, of course, but even more interesting is the emphasis Faulkner places on the strenuous labor that John must undertake in order to earn this symbol of his manhood. The pistol once belonged to John's father, but rather than simply inheriting it or receiving it as a gift, John works long hours to purchase the gun from his father: "He had earned the price of the pistol by doing outside work on his own time, on time apart from helping his father on the farm, time which was his own to spend eating or sleeping, until on his twenty-first birthday he had paid the final coin into his father's hand and received the pistol" (728).

The generally known but unacknowledged presence of the pistol sets up an interesting dilemma for Lucius's father. Because Powell sees it as the emblem of his maturity and manhood, he refuses to leave it at home; because Powell is a valuable worker, Maury, Lucius's father, cannot fire him. Thus they make what Lucius describes as a "gentlemen's" agreement that neither man will acknowledge the pistol's presence (729). Lucius's description of this arrangement includes both his father and Powell as "gentlemen"—an unusual use of the term to refer to a black man in the South, whether in 1905 or 1962. It is tempting, then, to read this usage as somehow progressive, as shaking the idea of the "gentlemen" loose from its particular race and class associations and redeploying it in a more general sense to refer to any man of honor. This reading would, however, neglect some crucial complications, such as the moment when Powell refuses to refer to Boon with the proper respect due him as a white man: as Lucius narrates it, "he didn't say Mister and he knew Father heard him: something he would never have failed to do in the hearing of any white man he considered his equal, because John was a gentleman" (730). Thus Powell seems *not* to consider Maury Priest his equal. In fact, he considers his employer to be *beneath* him—though he of course defers to *him* as "Mr." As Theresa Towner argues, "by making Maury choose which of the offenses of the code of *noblesse* deserves the strongest response, John [Powell] forces Maury to recognize his 'manhood'—the 'unforgivable' pistol—even as he acknowledges that he plays by stricter social rules than Maury does" (40). This revelation, parenthetical and not dwelt on by the narrator, makes the idea of "gentlemanliness" seem less a matter of fraternity among like-minded men, and more of an aspect of "manners" in the sense that Scott Romine has described: "a way of deferring conflict on an everyday basis" meant to "produce a commonly held view of reality" (*Narrative Forms* 1).

In Towner's analysis, the denied reality is the truth of the color line. She rightly argues that "Faulkner takes pains to show how" the code of gentlemanliness ostensibly "subsumes racial identity (and race relations) and promotes instead a moral code that avows itself colorblind," while at the same time he demonstrates how incidents such as Boon's thievery of John's pistol highlight the "tenuousness" of the code's alleged colorblindness (39). However, Faulkner also is careful to stress that the reality denied is not only racial and gendered but also economic: that John Powell has earned the emblem of his maturity through long and tireless labor—the very sort of labor that Faulkner identifies as at the heart of white anxieties about African Americans, the driven and efficient work that would, supposedly, make black southerners the masters of the southern economy were they to be given the chance. Such labor stands in contrast to Maury Priest's world of relative idleness: Lucius tells us that he tends to go home earlier than everyone else, and that his place of business is for him and many other white Jeffersonians really a place of conspicuous leisure: according to Lucius, a large part "of our Jefferson leisure class, friends or acquaintances of Father's or maybe just friends of horses . . . could have used the stable as a permanent business address—if they had had any business or expected any mail" (754). Lucius even spends his Saturdays "carry[ing] the burden of the requisite economic motions" so that his father will have only to count his money, a task that does not even occupy his entire morning (725). Of course, such conspicuous leisure, such conspicuous waste of time, is important to Mr. Priest and his friends because it indicates their class position in clear Veblenian fashion.

Boss Priest, Lucius's grandfather, is famed for wasting money in ways both extravagant and subtle—extravagant in buying a car only to have "eliminated it from circulation" (748) and subtle in employing a servant, Ned, whom he can clothe in his worn-out garments. According to Veblen, the employment of a servant who conspicuously fails to serve is an especially effective means of conspicuous consumption (59–60). Boss Priest sits near the top of the Jefferson hierarchy, a leader in the "white economy of material waste" because of his ability to waste with apparent impunity, to perpetuate the illusion that money is beneath him. Indeed, the adult Lucius's narration betrays a discomfort even with the fact that Boss Priest is a banker, someone who deals with money on a day-to-day basis. He frequently euphemizes the job description, referring to his grandfather not as a banker but as a "negotiable paper wizard" (753), one of the "dedicated priests"—pun surely intended—"in the impenetrable and ineluctable mysteries of Finance" (747). By recasting his idolized grandfather's job in terms of the magical and holy, he attempts to mystify its economic nature, to lift him above the violent game that Chick Mallison describes in *The Mansion*.

These restrictions, then, are at the root of the problem faced by the Priests and their fellow Jefferson aristocrats: waste is of fundamental importance to their hierarchy of class, to their ability to perpetuate the illusion that the trappings of their aristocracy have nothing to do with its economic base. Yet this wasteful attitude toward dollars and cents means that they have become less skilled workers, less capable of defending their positions at the top of the economic heap. And though John Powell, in 1905, might still be willing to keep the evidence of his earning potential hidden behind a "gentleman's agreement," in the late 1950s or early 1960s, when Lucius tells this tale, the evidence of what African Americans with money can and will do is everywhere: historians such as David Goldfield and James Cobb have illuminated the ways in which the industrial growth in the years following World War II, growth that gave many black southerners economic opportunities far beyond what they had known a few decades before, rendered problematic deeply embedded structures governing the relationship between race, class, and labor in the South. In this sense, *The Reivers* works as both a development and a complication of Faulkner's treatment of what Richard Godden has called the "primal scene of bound southern labor—[when] the master both recognizes and represses the fact that since his mastery is slave-made, he and his blacks are in whiteface" (*Fictions of Labor* 4).

Thus, Lucius's story moves in two directions at once: on the one hand, it is an attempt to recast his story and the history of his family as one in which money is merely incidental, in which their lofty class position has much to do with their moral character and little to do with their skills in the marketplace or their exploitation of black labor. Yet at the same time, his narrative constantly speaks the truth that he wants to silence. Not surprisingly, the economic truths that Lucius strives to conceal most frequently rupture the beguilingly placid surface of his story in scenes describing Boon Hogganbeck. The first time we meet Boon in this novel, lunging for the pistol that Maury Priest keeps in his desk, their altercation scatters the "neat stack of coins" that Maury has spent the morning carefully arranging, much to Maury's anger, for now he will have to spend the rest of the day gathering and reordering his money (726). This disruption is emblematic of Boon's role in the novel: wherever money is "neatly stacked," he knocks it over; wherever economic relations have become neatly ordered and nearly invisible he renders them visible again.

The most striking example of Boon's economically disruptive nature comes in his encounter, along with Lucius and Ned, with the proprietor of a "private mudhole" (809) in Hell Creek Bottom. Perhaps the shrewdest capitalist in the novel, the mud farmer plows the bog in front of his house to keep it soft and treacherous, so that anyone driving through in an automobile will inevitably get stuck and require his assistance, and for the not at all insignificant fee of two dollars per passenger. So it comes as no surprise that Boon would first endeavor to extricate the car by the sweat of his own brow—his, and then his and Ned's, and then his and Ned's and Lucius's. Boon's refusal to spend the money has a curious effect on the three adventurers. Their muddy labor transforms the aristocratic youngster, the poor white employee, and the family's black retainer into, as Lucius puts it, "three forked identical and now unrecognisable mud-colored creatures" (795). The mud, a byproduct of their labor, has concealed their identities, substituting three identical workers in place of a complicated hierarchy of race and class. Of course, this transformative labor is directly related to Boon's tight-fistedness: after all, if he had paid the money at the outset, then those identities would have been preserved intact and immaculate, would never have had to confront this moment of anonymous interchangeability. I do not mean to suggest that Boon's expenditure would be "wasteful," strictly speaking; six dollars is a significant amount to him. But then, the appearance of waste is sometimes what counts, as Stark Young reminds us when he relates the tale of his cousin, who gave a "third of his day's salary . . . for a small service" to an African American servant so that he would not "resemble the white trash, whom the negro despised and my cousin's family had never invited farther than the front steps" (352). Thus this scene at the mudhole makes clear how precarious those allegedly essential, natural class and race identities are: if ever the money—or simply the will to spend it or waste it—vanishes, then differences of class or even race are also imperiled.

Perhaps even more significantly, Faulkner indicates that the precarious distinctions between these men, distinctions in which they invest so much of their identities, matter increasingly less to the changing world beyond Jefferson. When Boon attempts to haggle with the mud farmer, arguing that he should not charge the full rate since Ned is black and

Lucius just a boy, the mud farmer famously replies, "Son . . . both these mules is color blind" (798). Traditional southern "manners" mean little to him. As Theresa Towner aptly notes, "the capitalist at the mudhole, in his infinite practicality, certainly would have acknowledged John Powell's pistol" (41). Indeed, the mud farmer may be a forerunner of what Earle and Merle Black call the "entrepreneurial individualist," a term that refers to those southern business leaders who emerged in the wake of the South's urbanization and industrialization after World War II and who had little investment in maintaining traditional race and class structures (29). According to Jack Bloom, such individuals eventually "developed as an economic, and ultimately as a political, competitor to the agrarian upper class" when it became apparent that they had little to gain by supporting race and class structures that benefited the agrarian elite (2). The mud farmer is no urban captain of industry, to be sure, but, as a farmer who works with classic farming implements such as middlebusters and mules and yet who raises no crop, who markets his commodity to all consumers in the same way with little regard for ideologies of paternalism or aristocracy, he symbolizes a transition between an agrarian past and a business-oriented future. His transitional nature may account for the fact that he charges the full fare for Ned but still insists that he adhere to a stereotypical racial role: he forgives a possible insult from Ned, who not-so-subtly mocks the mud farmer's low social status, only because Ned follows his insult with "hee hee hee," a laugh that is part of his performance as a servile "Uncle Remus" and that indicates he is not to be taken seriously (797, 872). So, while the farmer's business may be color-blind, he himself is not. Still, his relative indifference to the race and class distinctions of the three travelers anticipates the shift of economic and political power away from men like Lucius's grandfather, a shift that will help authorize the civil rights movement and the increasing social power of African Americans—the very thing feared by the participants in the "white economy of material waste." Thus, even if Boon had paid the farmer his due at the beginning, the traditional race and class structures that the payment would have maintained would have separated the men only temporarily.

Understanding the role of traditional ideologies of waste and paternalism in maintaining the wholly contingent distinctions among these men helps us to read Lucius's final meeting with Ned at the novel's end. After the series of horse races that dominates the novel's final sections, Lucius struggles to understand the meaning of all that has gone before. Although he is unsure of what lesson he should learn from the experience, he claims to be sure of one thing: "only that I wasn't doing it for money: that money would have been the last thing of all" (950). In fact, Lucius wishes that the spoils of their victory simply didn't exist at all: when their horse loses a final, additional race, Lucius says that if only they had bet their money on him, then it would be gone and they would not have to fret over how to dispose of it (969). Ned in fact encourages Lucius to treat the money as suspect and approves of his decision to dispense of it in properly paternalistic fashion by giving it away to Uncle Parsham Hood, an African American man who assisted them in their horse-racing efforts (952).

Parsham Hood, whom Lucius describes as "aristocrat of us all and judge of us all" (867), is an intriguing figure in terms of Faulkner's treatment of class and paternalism. He is shown great respect and deference by many of the white characters in the novel as well as by Ned and other African Americans. Given Faulkner's analysis of white paranoia about black labor, however, it is crucial to observe that Lucius describes Parsham Hood as "workless" (905). In addition to his positive moral attributes, then, it is possible that Hood is afforded such respect and courtesy because he no longer labors. His working days are finished, and, significantly, one of the primary things he has chosen to do with his money is mimic Boss Priest in dress and accessories, right down to the gold toothpick (925). I would suggest that his decision to invest his capital in this manner is evidence for Boss and others of north Mississippi's ruling class that he has adopted their values and poses no threat—that he is, perhaps, an even more strict observer of "manners" in Scott Romine's sense than is John Powell. Though Lucius describes him as "aristocrat of us all and judge of us all," the terms by which he judges them are Boss Priest's, and he is only an "aristocrat" in the sense that he functions as a stand-in for Boss, but with none of the attendant privileges or protections of aristocracy. Thus, I would agree with Railey's assertion that Hood "sees things the same way as white men," but I would disagree with his further claim that "Faulkner implies that all would have been well with Southern society if only these kinds of men existed to set matters straight" (172). By adopting the role of paternalist and giving Parsham Hood his winnings,

Lucius both solidifies his own position as an aristocrat and reinforces the clear racial and economic distinctions that separate men like Boss Priest and men like Hood regardless of their similarities of dress and manner.

Ned, of course, does not share Lucius's cash-averse perspective. In fact, we learn that he bet *against* Lucius in the final race and so collected a nice sum for himself—a sum that should rightfully belong to Boss Priest, who has had to pay $496 to rid himself of the stolen race horse. Yet Ned cannot offer to give him the money back. Ned asks, "Do you want Boss to insult me, or do you want me to insult Boss, or do you want both? . . . When I offers to pay his gambling debt, aint I telling him to his face he aint got enough sense to bet on horses? And when I tells him where the money come from I'm gonter pay it with, aint I proving it?" (970–71). Thus Ned directly profits from Boss's need to imagine himself above petty monetary concerns, from the social restrictions that prevent an African American man from ever making explicit how utterly his employer's wealth depends upon his employee.

Ultimately, then, and whether deliberately or not, the image of aristocracy that Lucius leaves his grandchildren with is one that is made possible only through a deliberate silencing that is also, as Faulkner well knew by the 1960s, ultimately unsustainable. If Goodyhay's church in *The Mansion* speaks a truth that terrifies and threatens elite white southerners, Lucius's story in *The Reivers* represents an attempt at a rhetorical counterattack: it promotes a romanticized version of southern history in which everyone knew their appropriate places in the social hierarchy as a contrast to the turbulent times of the 1950s and 1960s. Yet Lucius's tale reveals the very truths that he wishes to conceal: that the supposedly natural aristocracy of Jefferson is entirely contingent and constructed, dependent upon wasteful economic performances of racial paternalism that will no longer serve in a changing South.

4

MECHANICS AND MULATTOES

Class, Work, and Race in Ernest Gaines's *Of Love and Dust* and "Bloodline"

In Ernest J. Gaines's *Of Love and Dust* (1967), narrator Jim Kelly relates a tale of race and class tensions on a post–World War II Louisiana plantation. The central conflict involves the struggle among Marshall Hebert, a wealthy planter, Sidney Bonbon, his Cajun overseer, and Marcus Payne, a poor young African American man. Hebert has bonded Marcus out of jail to kill Bonbon, who has violated the boundaries of his appointed role by blackmailing the planter, stealing from him, and falling in love with an African American laborer. In one of the novel's crucial scenes, Marcus demonstrates his disdain for the traditional boundaries on the plantation. When Hebert reenters his home after conferring with Marcus in the yard, Marcus simply follows. Bishop, a longtime servant to the Hebert family, tells narrator Jim Kelly with horror, "He just pushed his foot in there. . . . The house his great grand-parents built. The house slavery built. He pushed his foot in that door" (215). Jim does not fail to grasp the significance of Bishop's dismay: "Bishop wanted me to understand that any black person who would stick his foot in a door that slavery built would do almost anything" (216).

Marcus's transgression quickly calls to mind other famous doorway confrontations in southern literature, most notably Ab Snopes's rug-ruining march in "Barn Burning," Thomas Sutpen's threshold rejection in *Absalom, Absalom!*, and, less renowned but perhaps just as significant, overseer Troy Flavin's entrance to his wedding to Dabney Fairchild via the side door that leads to the fields in Welty's *Delta Wedding*.[1] Like those earlier works, *Of Love and Dust* takes up the issue of the boundaries and borders that divide groups and individuals in the rural South. Gaines explores the ways in which racial paternalism divides white and black laborers into rigidly stratified and opposing communities, as well as the ways in which breaking out of the paternalist system requires violating the boundaries of those communities. However, Gaines also suggests that stepping across boundaries is not enough, and he examines the possible new models of interracial community and political action made possible in the wake of paternalism's collapse.

Gaines's novel is set in 1948, and although Hebert's plantation has begun to feel the combined effects of the New Deal and World War II, in many ways the life of the plantation remains unchanged. Planters, Cajuns, and poor African American sharecroppers coexist uneasily and, for the most part, separately. According to Jim, "The plantation (or what was left of the plantation now) had all its crop far back in the field. The front land was for the sharecroppers. The Cajuns had the front-est and best land, and the colored people (those who were still hanging on) had the middle and worst land. The plantation land was farther back still, almost to the swamps" (26). Segregation prevails in most social settings: when Jim gets a Coke after a long day on the tractor, he observes, "A colored person couldn't go through the back of the store to the yard. He had to enter the yard from the big gate" (84). Though he contemplates one day making a stand for equality, his exhausting labor deprives him of the energy and motivation for such a bold gesture: "Either I was too thirsty to do it, or after I had been working in the field all day I was just too tired and just didn't care" (43).

Like segregation, paternalism survives on the plantation and encourages its African American workers to see the social system as natural and inevitable. Most of Hebert's employees remain committed to the ideals of paternalism, and they believe that he does as well. Indeed, he does his best to look the part; his clothes offer an appearance of consistency that his actions subvert: "Winter and summer he wore a seersucker suit and a panama hat" (83). Hebert's refusal to acknowledge the changing of the seasons in his wardrobe choices indicates that his clothing has less to do with comfort and more to do with promoting and maintaining a particular idea of himself as a planter in the classic paternalist mold. His attempts are largely successful: nearly all of his workers see Hebert's bonding Marcus out of jail to work for him as a favor done for Miss Julie Rand, an elderly woman who was Hebert's longtime cook and who raised Marcus when his mother died and his father abandoned him. Rand herself tells Jim, "That white man been good to me. I went to him 'cause I didn't have nowhere else to turn" (14). When Jim fears for Marcus's survival on the plantation, he thinks, "I was hoping that when his trial came up they would lock him in prison, but after thinking about it I knew that wasn't going to happen. Not after Miss Julie Rand had given Marshall Hebert's people forty years of her life" (171). Even when Jim and others begin to suspect that Hebert has other motivations for freeing Marcus, Bishop, the most stalwart defender of Hebert's good name, insists that his master acts strictly out of paternalistic *oblige:* "He got him out for her. . . . He got him out 'cause she came there crying. He didn't know that boy from Adam" (218). Bishop and the other older folk on the plantation, in particular, cling to the ideals of paternalism as a way of making their lives make sense, as Karen J. Carmean has observed (52).[2] Thus, Bishop reacts with understandable panic when, as he tries to keep the door of the big house shut to Marcus, Hebert orders him, the faithful retainer, to "get out" and, finally, even strikes him. Bishop pleads, "Your people say I can stay here. Your people liked me. They say long as I was a good boy I could stay here. They say if I looked after y'all and I was a good boy, this house was my home till I died" (236). Bishop's greatest sorrow results from his belief that he has failed the paternalist order—the same order that has caused him to continue thinking of himself as a "boy" well into his old age. Jim tells us, "He was praying for Marshall and he was praying for the house. He was asking the old people who had died to forgive him for letting them down" (237). Paternalism has so firmly taken root in the psyche of many of the plantation's African Americans that all Marshall Hebert must really do is dress the part; he lives the dream that Flem Snopes could never quite achieve. His hat and suit become a screen upon which his workers can project the fantasies they have been conditioned to believe in.

Paternalism also helps to divide black and white workers exploited by the plantation system. Hebert makes this explicit when he tells Marcus, who is furious at the absolute terms of his bondage to the planter, that he should direct his rage at Bonbon instead: "The man killing you in the field out there" (188). Their close identification with Hebert and the ideal associated with his status as plantation owner leads most of the African American workers to despise the Cajuns and to see them as the root of all the trouble in the area. For instance, Jim notes that Bishop seems uncomfortable when he and other African Americans gather to discuss mounting tensions, not least because of the familiar way in which Jim calls Hebert "Marshall" instead of "Mr. Marshall." Says Jim, "Bonbon was a poor Cajun, and he [Bishop] would have talked about Bonbon all day. But things were a little different when they were about Mr. Marshall" (218). Even after Hebert's duplicity becomes apparent, Aunt Margaret blames the turmoil on the Cajuns (280). As Shane Bernard observes in *The Cajuns: Americanization of a People,* Cajuns historically held a marginalized status as whites-but-not-whites; according to Bernard, the perception of Cajuns as "white trash" extends as far back as the nineteenth century. He cites a post–Civil War journalist who "referred to them as 'good representatives of the white trash,' reviled even by local blacks as 'Acadian niggers'" (xvii). Carl Brasseaux also notes that the term *Cajun* signified "white trash" for most Americans in the late nineteenth century (104). Gaines clearly indicates that these attitudes have lingered: Marcus thinks of Bonbon as "not even a solid white man, but a bayou, catfish-eating Cajun" (57).[3] In their distaste for Bonbon, Bishop, Aunt Margaret, and others confirm Zora Neale Hurston's assertion in "The 'Pet Negro' System" that, as a way of surviving in a racist society, southern African Americans strive "to be associated with 'the quality' and consequently are ashamed to admit that they are working for 'strainers'" (596). Hurston also notes that "class-consciousness of Negroes is an angle to be reckoned with in the South," and she argues, "If ever it came to the kind of violent showdown the orators hint at," the pets and their white patrons would protect each other so that only the "'pore white trash' and the 'stray niggers'" would be caught in the crossfire (596). Hurston's prediction supplies an apt description of this novel's conclusion.

However, the ostensibly placid surface of the rigidly segregated plantation belies the abundance of complicated interactions and exchanges occurring across race and class boundaries. Though Bishop treats it as an earth-shattering aberration, Marcus's step across Hebert's threshold is only the most overt of these exchanges. Gaines finds the hope for change in these violations of the established order, and he explores them through his narrator Jim Kelly, whose complicated relationships with both Bonbon and Marcus lead him to a new understanding of the relationship between race, class, and power. Jim has a particular aptitude for sensing these tensions because of his unique status on the plantation. Unlike Bishop or the older African American workers, Jim did not grow up on the plantation; he has lived there for only three years, since responding to Hebert's request for workers who could "handle tractors" (147). Jim's expertise puts him in a unique position: he has more responsibility and authority than the other field hands, a closer relationship with Bonbon, and, thus, a certain degree of privilege and protection. Gaines suggests the relationship between mechanical savvy and privilege when Jim notes, "I drive the tractor and I have an umbrella. . . . The ones walking behind that trailer got the mean part of it" (18). Significantly, Jim nearly always describes the sun that his umbrella protects him from as white, thus suggesting that his skill affords him a certain safety from the realities of the racist power structure. In two notable examples, he describes the sun as "white, small, and still strong" (38), as "white as snow, hot as fire" (82). Further, Gaines has noted that, as the plantation system in Louisiana began to embrace mechanization, Cajuns and other whites, not African Americans, tended to use the machines, and that these machines gave Cajuns an advantage over African American farmers that further divided the two groups, a subject that Gaines explores both in this novel and in *A Gathering of Old Men*. According to Gaines, "My people had been slaves on the place and they had become sharecroppers when the owner of the plantation turned it over to sharecroppers. But then the Cajuns became sharecroppers as well. They got the better land. They got better machinery, and they produced more, and a lot of the blacks moved out because they could not compete" ("An Interview with Ernest Gaines" 186–87).

Thus, as an African American tractor driver supervised by a Cajun overseer and employed by a white plantation owner, Jim occupies a complicated position. Erik Olin Wright's concept of "contradictory class locations" helps to explain his unusual status on the plantation. Though Wright primarily directs his analysis toward fractures in the nebulously defined "middle class," we may usefully employ the concept in Jim's case as well. According to Wright, "if we want class structure to help explain class consciousness, class formation and class conflict, then we need some way of understanding the class-relevant divisions within the employee population" (19). Wright argues that the "possession of skills or expertise" (19) contributes to these divisions. Because of the scarcity of these skills, "employees who possess high levels of skills/expertise are potentially in a privileged appropriation location within exploitation relations" (22). Jim's abilities would indeed have been necessary for a postwar plantation. During and after World War II, historian Bruce J. Schulman notes, "the proportion of southern farms operating tractors skyrocket[ed], [and].... the new machinery diffused rapidly through the Cotton Belt, so that by the end of the war decade, the traditional southern mule farmer had all but disappeared from the regional landscape" (102). Though Jim works primarily with corn, not cotton, it seems that the same trend holds generally true on Hebert's plantation; while Jim elsewhere notes that Hebert has plenty of hands around, he has few capable of handling the new technology and must advertise for qualified workers. Although Jim does not use his unique position to appropriate any more capital than his peers, as Wright suggests experts do, it does afford him other advantages. In addition to the better working conditions that he experiences, Jim finds that his skill results in a close but cautious relationship with Bonbon. According to Jim, their relationship began "when I showed Bonbon I was good with any machine he had there. Maybe if I hadn't showed him how good I was he wouldn't have put so much trust in me. He wouldn't have treated me different from the way he treated all the others" (147). Bonbon does more than simply trust Jim with additional responsibility; he trusts him with revelations about his family and personality. Jim reports, "[He] told me things about himself, things about his family—things he never told anybody else. No, I had to show him how good I could handle tractors. And every time I did, he told me a little bit more" (147). Jim elaborates on the close connection between his skills and their relationship: "Bonbon needed somebody to talk to just like anybody else needs somebody to talk to. And since I knew all about trucks and tractors, I was the person he chose" (148). Thus Jim's status as an expert distinguishes him from the other African American workers; it sets him literally and symbolically above them and makes him worthy of Bonbon's confidence.[4]

However, Jim's expertise does not always work to his benefit. Marcus initially distrusts the older man, referring to him repeatedly as a "white-mouth," a loaded term indicating that though Jim's skin may be black, he gives voice to the ideology of those in power (6, 24, 46). Admittedly, Marcus's reservations have some validity. Jim often feels compelled to preserve the status quo of the plantation: he tells Marcus, "We don't want any trouble on this plantation, hear?" (122). Moreover, though Jim generally has a positive, respectful relationship with the other African American laborers, at times his unique job keeps him from communicating clearly with them. When he tries to speak with Aunt Margaret, who cares for Bonbon's daughter, Tite, "the tractor was making so much noise she could hardly hear me" (180). Perhaps Marcus realizes that Jim's privileged status means that when their interests come into conflict, Jim can use his limited power against him. For instance, Jim expresses his frustration with Marcus's frequent disruptions of plantation life by forcing the inexperienced hand to work as hard as a longtime veteran: says Jim, "I didn't have any pity on him. I drove the tractor just like I was supposed to drive it when three people were working back there" (173). Most significantly, his expertise keeps him from having to choose sides in the ultimate confrontation between Marcus and Bonbon. On the day that Marcus plans to leave with Bonbon's wife, Jim notes, "Just as we knocked off, the tractor went dead on me. My heart jumped in my throat because I didn't know how long it was going to take me to get the tractor fixed. . . . I started to leave with them [the field workers] and come back to fix the tractor later, but I told myself that fixing the tractor was my work just like driving it" (269). Further, Jim says that he wants to get back to the quarter so that he can tell Marcus he admires him: "I admired his great courage. And that's why I wanted to hurry up and get to the front. That's why my heart had jumped in my throat when the tractor went dead on me—I was afraid I wouldn't be able to tell him how much I admired what he was doing" (270). His profession of admiration notwithstanding, Jim still chooses to align himself with the interests of the plantation status quo, represented by the tractor, instead of with the other laborers who want to return from work before the fight between Bonbon and Marcus. Jim's expertise, and the obligations to Hebert's interests that come along with it, keep him from getting back to the quarter and perhaps preventing Bonbon from killing the rebellious Marcus. Indeed, the fact that Jim says that he told *himself* that "fixing the tractor was [his] work" suggests that the apparent freedom that his expertise gives him has also caused him to internalize the values of the plantation. He needs no overseer because he keeps himself under surveillance; in this respect, Jim's position high on the tractor seat seems less a position of exaltation than of perpetual examination. As with Arvay Henson in *Seraph on the Suwanee*, Jim is under constant surveillance in a manner that recalls Foucault's claim that "he who is subjected to a field of visibility, and who knows it, assumes responsibility for the constraints of power. . . ; he becomes the principle of his own subjection" (470). Thus Jim's privileges come with a price; his expertise and close relationship with Bonbon separate him from other black workers and put him in a position of panoptical surveillance.

However, if Jim avoids committing to Marcus's rebellion, he does not ultimately remain content on the plantation, either. In fact, at the novel's end, he rejects Hebert's gesture of paternalism and abandons the plantation, and I would suggest that by examining his relationships with Bonbon and Marcus, we may best understand how Jim comes to realize the necessity of breaking away from traditional plantation race relations. Marcus is a self-reliant city dweller who has little connection to the myths and memories of the plantation; further, since he was likely born in the late 1920s, he has spent most of his life in a South in which the New Deal, and, more recently, World War II have offered increased opportunities for individualism to African Americans. As Harvard Sitkoff argues, although the New Deal may not have delivered on all of its promises, its "reform spirit . . . helped create a psychological climate in which black southerners and their allies could struggle with expectations of success" (133). No surprise, then, that Marcus has few illusions about the supposedly selfless paternalism of elite planters like Marshall Hebert. Even before he completely understands his benefactor's plans, he is suspicious. Near the end of the novel, he shares with Jim a story from his past that helps explain his reluctance to believe in paternalism. In his early teens, Marcus got a job in a parking lot, where his supervisor, an older African American man named Big Red, extorted a dollar from him every day. He seeks help from the parking lot manager, but Big Red doubles his fee when he finds out that Marcus has gone over his head. When Marcus goes back to the boss, the boss repeats his earlier advice but refuses to tell Big Red himself. Says Marcus, "I didn't tell Big Red anything because now I saw what was going on. Big Red was his number one nigger, and he didn't care what Big Red did" (250). Marcus snaps and attacks Big Red, and he finds the same system at work in jail: a black man named Cadillac pummels Marcus for having no cigarettes. Marcus notes, "The next morning the jailer looked at me all bruised, but he didn't say a thing. He even gived Cadillac more food than he gived the rest of us. Cadillac was his nigger just like Big Red was the other white man's nigger" (251–52). These experiences inspire Marcus to look for salvation, or at least survival, in a fiercely held individualism. Though Jim protests that "they got the world fixed where you have to work with other people," Marcus insists, "When they let me out of jail, I promised myself I was go'n look out only for myself; and I wasn't go'n expect no more from life than what I could do for myself" (253). Marcus's experiences with Big Red and Cadillac are significant because they demonstrate the hollowness of the lofty rhetoric that figures racial paternalism and the "pet Negro" system as emerging from benevolent noblesse oblige on the part of selfless, wealthy aristocrats. His perception that the jail and the plantation are but two versions of the same institution anticipates Houston Baker's argument that the southern plantation was for African Americans essentially a forerunner of the modern prison-industrial complex, both institutions serving the ultimate goal of "black or African *immobilization*" (84). Indeed, when Hebert bonds Marcus out of jail to labor for him, he participates in the system Baker identifies as a "middle-passage" between the plantation and the prison—convict lease labor. As Baker argues, after the Civil War,

> southern jails and prisons were strained to their limits. Black "convictions" for such petty larceny as "theft" of a three-dollar suit could bring fines and court costs ranging up to a hundred dollars. Sentences in such cases could run in excess of ten years. Convicted blacks were seldom (if ever) equipped to pay exorbitant fines levied against them. Hence, they were released into the custody of the white person who covered their court costs and fines. Then the true incarceration began.
>
> Terms of "working off" the debt incurred to one's white debtor might include hard labor in mining, turpentine manufacturing, or railroad-construction camps and, of course, on southern *plantations*. In the South, whole southern state systems of "criminal justice" became sinister arrangements for the white criminalization of black bodies in order to supply labor demands of a New South. (91)

Thus, through Marcus's story, Gaines reveals paternalism as just another form of coercion used by whites in positions of power—even decidedly urban and unaristocratic figures such as a parking lot manager and a jailer—to exploit African Americans. By divorcing paternalism from the mystifying context of the mythologized plantation, Gaines lays bare the exploitative nature of this system that purports to bind white and black southerners together in a spirit of familial love.

Marcus's experiences prepare him to see Hebert's overtures as motivated by his own interests, not paternalistic goodwill, and, rather than accept Hebert's favors with the shame-faced humility expected of him, he behaves in a manner singularly inappropriate for plantation labor. He continues to wear his flashy dress clothes in the field, even though they offer him little protection from the blazing sun (31). Although crossing the threshold of the big house would suffice to get him killed on other plantations, Marcus goes even a step further: he decides that if he must do Hebert's bidding and kill Bonbon, then he will run away with Bonbon's wife, Louise. Indeed, his plan rests on the consistent and violent enforcement of southern racial rules. He intends to take Louise away and then kill Bonbon when he attempts to stop them. When Jim asks him why he can be so certain that Bonbon will follow, Marcus replies, "Because Bonbon own people'll kill him if he don't. Because this is the South, and the South ain't go'n let no nigger run away with no white woman and let that white husband walk around here scot-free. Not the South" (224). Thus, if Bonbon is to retain his standing in the community, and, indeed, perhaps his life, he must protect the honor of southern womanhood, an obligation which Hebert, who belongs to the class so ostensibly devoted to that lofty ideal, ignores in order to rid himself of his insubordinate subordinate. As Marcus tells it, "He got to get rid of Bonbon, not me. I'm a nigger, me. I ain't nothing but a nigger. Bonbon is the man" (224). Gaines indicates that the rhetoric of Southern Womanhood, like that of paternalism, is hollow. When either one stands in the way of economic advantage, it proves immediately dispensable.

Although the tacit validation of an interracial love affair by a wealthy planter potentially has subversive implications, Gaines does not hold up Marcus and Louise's relationship as a positive model. Jim describes Louise as still a child, sexually stunted: "Louise was about twenty-five, but she was the size of the average twelve- or thirteen-year-old girl. Most of the time she wore the clothes of a thirteen-year-old girl—she wore skirts and blouses instead of dresses" (119). Further, Marcus initially finds himself attracted to her only as a way to inflict pain on Bonbon (117, 118). And according to Jim, Louise actually wants Bonbon to kill Marcus so that Hebert will send him away and she can be rid of her husband, whom she does not love (165). Although the relationship between Marcus and Louise does seem to grow beyond these initial selfish motives, Gaines continues to characterize it as immature and unrealistic. Aunt Margaret tells the young lovers, "Y'all act like two black children or two white children playing in the yard. There ain't nothing to stop y'all from going North 'cause North right around the house. Well, North ain't right around the house, and y'all ain't no children. Y'all grown people, and y'all white and y'all black. And there ain't no North for y'all" (207). Of course, Aunt Margaret, like Bishop, feels a powerful loyalty to the Hebert family and their plantation, and this loyalty may bias her interpretation of their relationship. Certainly, Marcus does demonstrate a degree of empathy for Louise; he tells Jim, "She much slave here as I was" (261). But he ultimately reveals himself as mainly concerned with his own welfare. Gaines suggests the superficiality of Marcus and Louise's love for each other when Jim asks Marcus if he truly cares for her. Though Marcus first responds "Yeah," Jim notes, "He didn't say it too strongly, though." After repeated entreaties, Marcus answers as though he is attempting to convince himself as well: "Yeah, I think I do. Yeah, I do. Maybe I didn't till just now—till you asked me. Now, I know I love her. It wouldn't be the same 'thout her. Yeah, I love her—love that little woman. Ain't claiming she much to look at—nobody in his right mind can honestly say that; but I love her anyhow" (260). Further, though Marcus does feel drawn to her because of their shared status of captivity, he also reveals himself as largely concerned with the way in which she strokes his ego and tends to his needs. He tells Jim, "She said, 'Marky-poo, 'thout you I'll go crazy.' That's what she told me. 'Thout you I'll go crazy, Marky-poo. I need your arms round me. I need your arms round me all the time, Marky-poo'" (261). He continues, "Pretty good arm, huh? . . . Say she like the color of my arms," all the while "twisting his arm one way, then the other way" to admire his own perfection. This display prompts Jim to realize, "He was the same Marcus" (261). Ultimately, Marcus's vanity and superficiality undercut whatever revolutionary potential his individualism may possess.[5]

Although Marcus and Louise's escape attempt comes to naught—Bonbon kills Marcus and leaves the plantation—Marcus's repeated violations of the physical and metaphorical boundaries of his role on the plantation open up, if briefly, the possibility for social change and raise the question of what model of interracial and/or cross-class political action Gaines implicitly endorses. Gaines has noted of his rebellious young character, "You see, Marcus was pre-revolutionary, pre-Civil Rights. Marcus looked after Number One" (108). By examining the relationship between Jim Kelly and Sidney Bonbon, we can better understand the nature of the alliances that Gaines believes individuals must form in order to undermine the system of paternalism and rigid race/class divisions that characterize the plantation system.

Jim's position outside of and above the other African American workers makes it possible for him to understand Bonbon's similar plight. As overseer, Bonbon occupies a position of power that aligns him with Hebert and planter power: "The big house had given him a horse and a whip (he did have a whip at first) and they had told him to ride behind the blacks in the field and get as much work out of them as he could" (67). Most of the farmhands respect his authority: they do his bidding and fawn over his prowess with a gun (40). As with Troy Flavin in *Delta Wedding*, though, Bonbon's close relationship to African American labor complicates his racial identity and his relationship to the aristocratic planter, as does his Cajun background. Suggestions of racial otherness pervade Jim's descriptions of Bonbon. Jim tells us, "His mustache was lighter than his tan face and much lighter than his red neck" (79); thus, his long labor in the sun darkens his skin and associates him with the other dark-skinned workers in the fields. Jim notes of Bonbon's white-haired daughter Tite, "Her hair looked whiter still with his big red hands going through it" (167–68). Most notably, Jim observes, when they go to a bar in Baton Rouge congenial to mixed-race individuals, that Bonbon "was darker than many of them" (143–44). Bonbon's racial and class otherness means that Hebert does not have to treat him as an equal; in fact, Bishop has standing orders that Bonbon should come no further than the kitchen of his home.

Bonbon finds himself, then, caught in an ambivalent position. His Cajun identity means that he is considered "white trash," and this status complicates his difference from the African Americans whose work he supervises. As Constance Penley puts it, "If you *are* white trash, then you must engage in the never-ending labor of distinguishing yourself, of codifying your behavior so as to clearly signify a difference from blackness that will, in spite of everything, express some minuscule, if pathetic, measure of your culture's superiority" (90). Jim often describes Bonbon as wearing a "white cowboy hat" (79); when Bonbon first appears in Jim's narrative, Jim reports that he "still had on that sweat-stained white straw hat and he was still wearing the dirty, sweat-smelling khakis he had worn in the field that day" (4). On another occasion, Jim informs us that "his khaki shirt was wringing wet with sweat. His white straw hat was turned up at the sides like a cowboy hat; he even wore cowboy boots" (36). While the sweat serves as physical evidence of the labor he performs as Hebert's subordinate, the white cowboy hat, I would suggest, serves to separate Bonbon from the laborers beneath him. Clearly, its color aligns him with Hebert rather than with Jim, Marcus, and the rest of the crew. Further, Gaines has commented in an interview that, during his childhood on the plantation in Point Coupee Parish, one of his few escapes from the plantation and one of the few contacts with broader American culture occurred when he "went to the big city of New Roads every so often on Friday night to see cowboy movies" (224–25). Thus, perhaps Bonbon's hat and boots help him confirm his whiteness by associating him with an identity not implicated in plantation labor. Indeed, the late 1940s would have been an ideal time for Bonbon to attempt to reinvent himself through his clothes: according to Bernard, after World War II, "Cajuns cast aside the antimaterialism of their ancestors and embraced the age's rampant consumerism" (25). By having Bonbon and Hebert locate their class and race identities in their clothing, Gaines highlights the mutable, performative nature of social identities supposed to be essential.

However, Bonbon finds this perpetual process of affirming his whiteness too much to maintain, largely because of his love for Pauline Guerin, Marshall Hebert's African American cook. Their relationship causes him to violate the boundaries so crucial to life on the plantation. According to the plantation workers, no one was surprised when Bonbon began making "her lay down and pull up her dress" in the fields. But they fall in love. According to Jim, "He couldn't just take her like he was supposed to take her, like they had given him permission to take her—no, he had to fall in love" (67). Thus Bonbon simply cannot behave in a manner befitting a poor-white Cajun overseer, and his inability creates problems for those committed to maintaining rigid distinctions of race and class. Jim notes that sometimes he visits Pauline "at the big house while they made Bishop, Marshall Hebert's butler, look out for Marshall. Bishop hated what he had to do—but what else could he do? If he had mentioned to Marshall that Bonbon had gone farther than that kitchen, Bonbon, or Marshall himself, probably would have killed him" (66).

Gaines further invests their relationship with disruptive potential in his descriptions of their children, the twins Willy and Billy, whom Gaines describes as chaotic figures who destroy any boundaries they encounter. Jim points out that Pauline's neighbors, Aunt Ca'line and Pa Bully, "had this barb-wire fence that came up on the gallery all the way to the wall. The fence was brought up there, according to Aunt Ca'line, to keep Pauline and Bonbon's two little mischievous mulattoes on their side. But putting the barb-wire fence up there was like putting nothing there. The two little boys had ridden the fence so much, a grown person could step over it without touching a strain of wire" (60). We quickly learn, however, that the fence Willy and Billy so tenaciously wear down has significance for other reasons: it symbolically contains the threat to the plantation order implicit in Pauline and Bonbon's love. Jim notes that whenever Pa Bully "cut[s] his eyes toward the other side of that fence where they had no business going," Aunt Ca'line warns him to avert his gaze, as she has done ever since Bonbon began his visits. Thus, by destroying the fence and calling attention to the physical and social boundaries that divide the plantation, the twins threaten to expose their parents' relationship to the rest of the plantation, an exposure that would have deeply unsettling results.

Lest we too quickly assume that Gaines simply means to celebrate the disruptive power of the racial mixing embodied in the "two mischievous mulattoes" as containing the potential to break down the boundaries of plantation society, we should note that the twins' chaotic presence often has negative effects on the poor working people of Hebert's plantation. For example, when Bonbon gives them a BB gun for their fifth birthday, "nobody and nothing was safe on the place. If they weren't shooting at another child, they were shooting at a dog or a chicken. They put a hole in the back of Jobbo's little girl's neck, and Jobbo had to take the girl to the doctor and pay the doctor bill himself. They shot the mule that Charlie Jordan was riding and the mule threw Charlie in the ditch." They even shoot Aunt Ca'line's irreplaceable "number one rooster"—who could do the work of five—in the eyes (68). Thus the disregard for borders and boundaries suggested by the twins' indiscriminate gunplay does not automatically carry positive connotations; their chaotic behavior sometimes further deprives the already downtrodden workers of the resources they need to survive. Gaines suggests, then, that simply disrupting the oppressive but stable plantation system is not enough; what is needed is a better, more equitable system to replace it.

Another instance in which Gaines resists imbuing racial ambiguity with implicitly positive connotations is in his description of Marcus and Louise's relationship. When Marcus first appears, Jim notes, "It was too dark to tell if he was white or colored" (3). Elsewhere, Jim observes, "Marcus had a lot of Indian blood in him, and he probably had a lot of white blood in him, too" (57). Moreover, Marcus and Louise's plan to escape involves exploiting the slippery nature of racial identity. Louise covers her face and her daughter's with soot so that they can pass as black, and she so skillfully manages the difficult task that, according to Aunt Margaret, "Tite looked more like a little nigger than Jobbo's little girl Edna ever did" (241). Moreover, "you couldn't tell Louise wasn't colored. She had blacked up her face just the right amount. She had put on a hat with a veil. You couldn't see her yellow hair at all, and you had to raise the veil to see her eyes or her mouth" (243). However, Gaines suggests that this alteration is strictly superficial, without any corresponding shift of perspective for Louise. Aunt Margaret notes that, as Louise powders Tite's face with soot, "Louise didn't look like a woman, she looked like a child playing with a doll," a description that suggests that the same immaturity that characterizes her relationship with Marcus is still at work in this attempt to escape. Most significantly, Louise does not develop any new attitudes about race. When Aunt Margaret attempts to dissuade her from going through with the plan, Louise flies into a rage and threatens to hit her (242). Gaines links this outburst, one which indicates that Louise still sees Margaret as her inferior, to the inevitable failure of their attempt to escape by exploiting racial ambiguity: when Tite sees the violent confrontation between Louise and Margaret, "The water started running down Tite's face, leaving a white trail from her eyes to her mouth" (242). Tite continues to cry and further expose her white skin as Margaret faces down her mother. Thus, Gaines suggests that performances of racial ambiguity do not inherently generate any kind of positive social change unless individuals are willing to accept the larger political implications of the slipperiness and instability of the color line.

If Louise utterly fails to realize this essential truth, other characters in *Of Love and Dust* come closer, at least, though they, too, may fail in the end. Gaines continues to explore the potential for resistance to the plantation order through violating racial boundaries when Bonbon and Pauline seek out a space where they can be together outside the strict segregation of the plantation. They find it, however briefly, when Jim drives them to Baton Rouge. Not incidentally, Bonbon uses Jim's mechanical expertise as an excuse to have him along to pose as Pauline's husband and allay suspicions: he tells Jim he wants him to help him "pick up a piece for that hay machine" (131). The errand is only a diversion. According to Jim, "We found a bar where a lot of mulattoes hung out" (143). Jim observes, "I suppose they took Bonbon for a mulatto, too. He was darker than many of them" (143–44). Significantly, Bonbon divests himself of the outward symbols of his whiteness in this mixed-race space: he takes off his white cowboy hat—though he leaves it on the table, a gesture that suggests he is incapable of fully relinquishing his whiteness (143). Here Pauline and Bonbon find momentary comfort. Alas, their bliss does not last long, because Bonbon proves incapable of extending the political implications of their relationship, their togetherness in this "mulatto bar," into the larger social sphere. Bonbon relies on Jim in this situation; he needs Jim to ask the black proprietor of the establishment for a room for him and Pauline because he sees such an economic and social transaction with an African American as beneath him. According to Suzanne Jones, "Playing pimp for Bonbon forces Jim to take a long hard look at how he is implicated in maintaining the status quo for black people when he facilitates the southern racial customs that discriminate against them" (154). Further, it is interesting that as long as they are laboring together on the plantation, in a setting where Bonbon is most clearly in a position of power (even if he has relinquished the whip), Bonbon treats Jim with respect, as almost an equal, someone in whom he can confide in matters personal and professional. But in a "mulatto bar," ostensibly a place of free and easy racial mixing, Bonbon is so uneasy that he pressures Jim to assume a labor role—a pimp—that is stereotypically associated with black men. Away from the plantation, where he wields definite if conditional power, Bonbon quickly begins erecting the sorts of racial and class barriers he transgresses so casually at home. Jim does not feel bound to respect those boundaries, however, to Bonbon's chagrin: "He didn't like it when I said I wasn't going to be his pimp. . . . He was helpless in a case like this. He wanted to be with her. . . ; but he had to go to a black man, in a respectful way, and ask that black man for a room. He didn't know how to do that. He didn't know how to talk to a black man unless he was giving orders" (145).

Bonbon does, finally, ask the bar owner for a room, a gesture that suggests he begins to see the necessity of transgressing the rules governing racial interaction if he and Pauline are ever to be together. Gaines qualifies Bonbon's progress, however, by pointing out that the overseer finds it impossible to give up all signs of his power. When they enter the bar, Jim notes that Bonbon has brought his gun in with him: "He needed it everywhere he went. He needed it around his own Cajuns, he needed it around the Negroes in the field, and even needed it around these mulattoes who didn't know him at all" (144). Upon Jim's return to the bar, when he finds that Pauline and Bonbon have in fact rented a room, the proprietor notes Bonbon's weapon as well: "I see he bring his gun. . . . Bad, a man need a gun all the time—no?" (149). Bonbon's reluctance give up his weapon foreshadows the tragic consequences of his inability to imagine a new way of living in the segregated South. Here, Gaines suggests that those most insecure about their status in the traditional southern hierarchy of race and class may be the least willing to relinquish those signs by which they maintain their tenuous hold on that status, and that that reluctance threatens to doom any possibilities for meaningful community. If Bonbon is willing to open up to Jim or to others outside his own race and class only in a setting in which he knows he holds more power, then the possibilities for creating any sort of transgressive alliance are bleak indeed.

Although Bonbon fails to break away from the traditional codes governing race and class, he does learn to see his plight as connected to Jim's, to see the oppression that he suffers as part of the larger oppression of all the laborers on the plantation. He tells Jim, "Me and you—what we is? We little people, Geam. They make us do what they want us to do, and they don't tell us nothing. We don't have nothing to say 'bout it, do we, Geam?" (258). Bonbon's statement ties him and Jim together as "little people" who live under the control of the powerful planter and who, perhaps, therefore have common interests. Bonbon's murder of Marcus initially keeps Jim from reciprocating the feeling of solidarity. He says, "I couldn't feel any pity for him. Far as I was concerned, all the human understanding we had had between us was over with now. He saw this in my face and I could see how it hurt him" (277–78). However, as Jim's anger fades, he begins to see Bonbon's impossible position: "If he hadn't killed Marcus, he would have been killed himself. The Cajuns on the river would have done that" (277). Most importantly, Jim's growing comprehension of Bonbon's difficult situation leads him finally to reject the paternalism that the other African American plantation workers cling to, for he ultimately understands how paternalism divides workers who, aside from their racial differences, have a great deal in common. Aunt Margaret and the other old folks on the plantation quickly return to the old ways, forgetting the recent conflict except to worry that "them Cajuns might start some mess" (280). Jim, however, realizes that the Cajuns are not the real enemy: "[Hebert] killed Marcus; Bonbon didn't" (279). Jim's realization motivates him to opt out of the oppressive system. When Hebert warns him to leave the plantation, he claims to be concerned about marauding poor whites attacking Jim in retaliation: "These Cajuns know you and that boy lived in the same house, and they might get it in their heads to do you something" (278). Jim, however, understands that his knowledge of the way in which Bonbon and Marcus disrupted the caste and class system—and of Hebert's complicity in that disruption—has made Hebert uneasy. According to Jim, "He wanted me to leave because I knew the truth about what had happened" (278). In his most crucial act, Jim refuses Hebert's paternalistic charity: Hebert offers him "a recommendation. . . . Telling people that you're a good worker" (278). However, Jim declines the recommendation, prompting Hebert to a red-faced rage, and he leaves the plantation behind.

Of Love and Dust exposes racial paternalism not as the evidence of selfless goodwill but as a tool whereby powerful whites maintain the loyalty of their African American workers and keep them from perceiving their common interests with poor white workers. Gaines challenges the rigid distinctions between race and class that make that separation possible by examining the disruptive potential of those individuals who cross race and class lines and the ramifications for traditional social customs if people truly understand the slipperiness and mutability of the color line. Moreover, in the figure of Jim Kelly, Gaines offers hope that individuals who can perceive the truth about paternalism and can understand the ways in which workers of all races are oppressed by the plantation system may begin to forge alliances—even if complicated, tenuous, and transient at first—across lines of race and class.

And yet—Jim walks away alone. His solitude stands in sharp contrast to the vision of joyous interracial working-class community in Reverend Goodyhay's congregation in *The Mansion,* and it certainly complicates a reading of the novel that focuses on the importance of forming interracial and cross-class coalitions. Gaines continues to probe this dilemma in "Bloodline," the long story from which his 1968 collection of short fiction takes its name. Though three of the stories collected in *Bloodline*—"Just Like a Tree," "A Long Day in November," and anthology staple "The Sky Is Gray"—had been completed and published before *Of Love and Dust* appeared, "Bloodline" marks Gaines's return to the issues of race, community, and paternalism with the tale of Christian "Copper" Laurent, the illegitimate, mixed-race nephew of a dying planter, who has returned to the plantation to claim his birthright.

Like Marcus, Copper defies the rigid stratification of race on the plantation as embodied by thresholds and doorways. When Copper's uncle, plantation patriarch Frank Laurent, insists that he enter the big house through the back door, he refuses. Frank's insistence on this piece of traditional racial protocol serves as an attempt to erase Copper's difference, an attempt to see him as essentially the same as any other African American in his employ: "That nigger is on my place. . . . Any nigger on my place comes to my house when I say come" (175). Significantly, Frank feels himself to be as much a prisoner of racial codes as Sidney Bonbon does. He tells Felix, an elderly worker on the plantation and the story's narrator, "I didn't write the rules. . . . And I won't try to change them. He must come through that back door" (187). And like Bonbon, Frank must fear the wrath of the Cajuns, who have no respect for him and who depend just as strongly on a clearly demarcated color line. He asks Felix, "How long do you think they'll let him live if I let him force his way through that front door?" (199). Clearly, then, Frank's power is a sham; he teeters precariously atop a volatile social structure, and any false move might send him tumbling; his position of power is also a prison.

When Copper handily bests even the strongest men that his uncle sics on him, Frank finally submits to a meeting—but in the quarters, not in the big house. Copper lays out his plan: he intends to claim the plantation, lead his armies to revolt, restore the land to the full potential it has been denied by generations of oppression, and share its bounty with others like him. Copper feels that the land has not been allowed to thrive in the way that it could because of the cruel system of labor used to farm it: "The land has been wasted and is still being wasted, but it's not beyond saving. . . . As for the houses, they'll have to be torn down and built from the ground up" (210–11). Significantly, he argues that Frank has not truly understood the suffering that motivates his desire to revolt because his paternalism has kept him from really paying attention to any of his subordinates. Copper tells him, "You've always been in a position to give them a dime. Dimes clear all conscience" (214). Most interestingly, Copper imagines his army of the dispossessed as interracial; he intends to form a community of those who are oppressed for any reason, not just skin color. He tells Frank, "There's millions just like me. Maybe not my color, but without homes, without birthrights, just like me" (213). Thus, as opposed to Marcus, who was only concerned with his own salvation, Copper recognizes that his suffering unites him with others in similarly dire straits. Rather than simply burning down the plantation for the selfish joy of watching the flames, he has a plan, a model of affiliation and cooperation that builds upon the positive traditions of the past without repeating its injustices.

Of course, the implication that Copper may be delusional undercuts the hopefulness of his revolutionary vision. His sojourn in prison, where he was forced to clean the blood from cell floors and even from the electric chair, has inspired his new plan of action, but it may have also unbalanced him. He temporarily breaks down in front of Frank, revealing that he sees visions and hears the voices of those who have been destroyed by oppression, voices which may be guiding him: Felix often reports Copper touching his head and staring off into the distance, as if listening to barely audible whispers, before speaking. Although insanity would obviously undercut Copper's credibility, the particular nature of his alleged dementia is intriguing: unlike Marcus, the epitome of individualism, Copper is a kind of medium through whom the voices of the oppressed can speak. Still, as in the case of Willy and Billy Guerin, Copper's revolutionary potential is ambiguous. At the end of "Bloodline," Copper simply leaves, promising to return and "bathe this whole plantation in blood" if they continue to deny him his birthright, but deferring any actual struggle until some unnamed future date (217).

By overemphasizing Copper's abrupt departure and the question of his sanity, we may miss Gaines's more subtle treatment of the evolution of Felix's character and beliefs. When we first meet him, Felix seems fairly complacent in his role on the plantation. Although hardly as cringing and deferential as Bishop, he has apparently made his peace with the plantation system. Felix occupies himself by continuing to perform the job that he had as a young man, a job that has become obsolete as the plantation has begun to decay. Says Felix, "Every time I found something kind of rusty and needed working over, I brought it to the shop and cleaned it up. Once, there, this was my special job. From Monday morning till Saturday night, my job was to keep everything in good shape to work in the field. Ah, but that was long, long ago. Now all the old ones are dying, and the young ones are leaving—and the Cajuns are taking over a little more every year. So I came up to the yard now just to keep the old hands busy. Because once the hands had stopped, the man wasn't no more" (163). Felix makes clear that, at this point in the story, his work in the shop is purely a matter of habit. He has so long defined himself by his job that he must keep it up even when the plantation is crumbling around him; he believes that without his work, futile as it may be, he would cease to exist. He cannot conceive of himself as existing outside of the plantation system.

However, Felix's attitude about his labor begins to shift subtly when he meets Copper. Gaines indicates a connection between the young would-be usurper and the elderly metalworker. Both times that Felix meets

Copper, he describes his shoes as polished and shining like "new tin" (167, 206)—a description that calls to mind, even as it contrasts with, the rusty, worn-out metal in Felix's shop. Significantly, after he first encounters Copper, Felix has an exchange with Frank that indicates that he has begun to find new meaning in his work beyond simple self-preservation. Frank, in a fit of pique, tells Felix he can leave the house and go back to the shop, and wonders aloud why Felix spends so much time there. Felix replies,

> "Maybe some day somebody'll use it again . . ."
> "And who may that somebody be?" he said. "Copper?"
> "I don't know, Mr. Frank," I said. "Maybe it will be Copper." (177)

Felix's response here clearly runs counter to his earlier ruminations on finding meaning in his labor; whereas before he merely performed his old job as a way of maintaining his identity in a world where the structure that gave him that identity is crumbling, here he seems to hold out hope, however fragile, that his work will not be simply individual and futile, but that it may be part of a larger project of reclaiming and re-creating the plantation. The shining "new tin" of Copper's shoes represents the beginning of a new age, one in which Felix's work benefits a new coalition of the formerly outcast.

In addition to Copper's shoes, Gaines draws another connection between Copper and Felix. When Frank sends a group of men to bring Copper to his home by force, Copper fends them off with nothing but a new scythe blade handle. As one of his vanquished foes reports, it was "a brand new one—like it hadn't left the store, yet. Could still see the label" (196). Significantly, when Felix lists the farm implements he has been maintaining in his shop, a scythe blade figures prominently among them (162). Thus, he and Copper have two parts of the same tool—the new handle and the old but well cared-for blade, symbolizing the complicated mixture of the traditional and the revolutionary that characterizes Copper's vision of a new plantation for the dispossessed. When joined together, they will create a scythe that symbolizes the final death of the old plantation system.

Ultimately, then, if "Bloodline" represents the next step in Gaines's thinking after *Of Love and Dust*, we can see that Jim Kelly's biggest mistake was leaving on his own, giving up on the older, more complacent African Americans on the plantation as beyond hope or help. In "Bloodline," Gaines argues that real change can come only through joining the old generation and the new, through combining the best of traditional ideals with an egalitarian, perhaps even revolutionary, political ideology. But, he argues, in order to make that combination possible, a leader like Copper must make those African Americans who have so long toiled on the plantation aware of the potential they have to change the system. As Jones, who also notes Copper's influence on the plantation's older workers, observes, Copper recalls the "figure of the mulatto as race leader, a man with more cosmopolitan experiences than most black people who chooses to identify with the black masses in order to lead them" (216). Gaines thus suggests that interracial and cross-class alliances must be grounded in the particular traditions and culture of the geographical area in which they take place if they are to succeed.

5

"SUPER-NEGROES" AND HYBRID ARISTOCRATS

Race and Class in Walker Percy's *The Last Gentleman* and *Love in the Ruins*

In an essay written shortly after the publication of his first novel, *The Moviegoer,* Walker Percy asserted the inescapable commitment of the writer—especially the southern writer—to the issue of race: "Every Southern writer must come to some kind of terms with the Negro. He can no more avoid it than a Negro writer can avoid writing about the white man" (*Virtues and Voices* 182). As one might expect, Percy focuses his attention on racial issues in many of his novels, from the subtly nuanced interchanges between Binx Bolling and his Aunt Emily's butler Mercer in *The Moviegoer* to the satirically exaggerated chaos of the Bantu revolution in *Love in the Ruins* (1971).[1] Like Hurston, Faulkner, Welty, and Gaines, Percy inevitably writes about race when he writes about class, and his work is crucial to understanding the relationship between racial paternalism and the construction of aristocratic class identity as the South moves from a society and an economy rooted in the agricultural life of the plantation to a society and an economy firmly planted in the business world of the cities and suburbs.

Percy evinced an interest in the breakdown of racial paternalism as early as his 1956 essay "Stoicism in the South." In this piece he notes that "the old alliance of Negro and white gentry has broken up," and he muses, "What is the reason for this dissolution of the old alliance? . . . Does it not, in fact, reflect a profound cultural change which, as it has turned out, cannot be accommodated within the ethos of the upper-class white?" (84). He further argues, "The fact is that neither the ethos nor the traditional worldview of the upper-class white Southerner is any longer adequate to the situation" (84). In *The Last Gentleman* and *Love in the Ruins,* Percy explores the implications of this truth, searching for an ethos that *would* be adequate for a South in which paternalism no longer serves to organize relationships among races and classes. In the earlier novel,

Percy explores the concept of racial hybridity; though he sees some hope in the potential of hybrid figures to disrupt the traditional, strictly binarized hierarchies of race and class that organize southern life, his depiction of privileged whites as the only successful hybrids suggests that, far from being a subversive or revolutionary concept, hybridity may simply serve to reaffirm those hierarchies. In *Love in the Ruins,* Percy satirizes white paranoia about the collapse of essentialist racial categories and offers a vision of coalition and community that contrasts sharply with *The Last Gentleman*'s problematic privileging of aristocratic whiteness.

Percy's treatment of the relationship between racial hybridity and paternalism is much influenced by the theories of his adoptive father, Delta planter William Alexander Percy (to whom Walker and his cousins referred as "Uncle Will"). The elder Percy played a major role in the political and social development of the early-twentieth-century South, and Walker's perceptions of the relationship between race and class could not have escaped his enormous influence. However, though he pays warm tribute to Will Percy in his introduction to *Lanterns on the Levee,* his adoptive father's memoir, he significantly chooses his attitudes about race as a representative example of the significant differences in their philosophies: "The views on race relations . . . diverge from my own and have not been helpful, having, in my experience, played into the hands of those whose own interest in these matters is deeply suspect. But even when I did not follow him, it was usually in *relation* to him, whether with him or against him, that I defined myself and my own direction" ("Uncle Will" 56).[2] These "views" are most succinctly and comprehensively expressed in a passage from the *Lanterns on the Levee* chapter "A Note on Racial Relations": "To live habitually as a superior among inferiors, be the superiority intellectual or economic, is a temptation to dishonesty and hubris, inevitably deteriorating. To live among a people whom, because of their needs, one must in common decency protect and defend is a sore burden in a world where one's own troubles are about all any life can shoulder. . . . And, last, to live among a people deceptively but deeply alien and unknowable guarantees heart-aches, unjust expectations, undeserved condemnations. Yet such living is the fate of the white man in the South" (298). Will Percy's paternalistic noblesse oblige shines through clearly here: he takes up the white man's burden with a resigned acceptance that he must dutifully care for and protect these ignorant subordinates, even from himself. Further, he obviously believes that all his paternal efforts will ultimately come to no good end and that African Americans will forever live as immoral inferiors.

However, no matter how ostensibly benevolent his intentions, Will Percy certainly participated in the subjugation, exploitation, and marginalization of Mississippi's black populace. According to James C. Cobb, although Delta blacks hoped that the end of slavery and the demand for labor might open the way to economic and political independence, their hopes were thwarted by the "region's planters, who . . . fought to regain their political, racial, and economic dominance and, insofar as possible, recapture the dream of a Delta where the planter's power was absolute and his wealth unrestricted" (*Most Southern Place* 47). The primary economic system eventually created as a means of accomplishing this goal was sharecropping, which, as Cobb states, "shift[ed] some of the risks of cotton growing onto the laborers and provid[ed] greater incentives for the workers to give their best efforts . . . and remain on the plantation until the harvest was complete" (55). Sharecropping became in many ways as abusive as slavery: the dream of economic advancement was frequently deferred each year at settlement time, when workers were often cheated out of their rightful earnings (59). And although historian Neil McMillen singles out Will Percy's plantation as a "model estate" where violence was rarely employed, the threat still hung over the black tenants (125).

Significantly for both Percys, in *Lanterns on the Levee* William Alexander Percy attempts to justify his domination of African Americans as merely the natural result of the essential differences between his aristocratic white identity and their childlike immaturity. Will Percy sees this contrast as the heart of the relationship between the races, a relationship central to the formation of any proper, aristocratic white individual's personality from the earliest stages of youth. He claims that "any little boy who was not raised with little Negro children might just as well not have been raised at all" (46), for in his own youth, his black playmates tempered his essentially intellectual nature with the knowledge not only of "gaiety and casualness and inventiveness, but the possibility that mere living may be delightful and that natural things which we ignore unless we call them scenery are pleasant to move among and gracious to recall"

(54). Indeed, for Will Percy the white person's need for this access to the natural world that the black person provides extends into adulthood. He asserts, "In the South every white man worth calling white or a man is owned by some Negro, whom he thinks he owns, his weakness and solace and incubus" (287). Will Percy's so-called incubus in this case, a black man named Ford, serves in much the same capacity as his younger incarnations: in exchange for Percy's paternal care, he keeps him in touch with the magical, primitive side of nature that white people have sacrificed for their enlightenment. Ford spins his master tall tales and creates a mythology of folktales mingled with his own invented absurdities. As Percy puts it, "Ford is my fate, my Old Man of the Sea, who tells me of Martin and admonishing cooters and angels that do the loop-the-loop, my only tie with Pan and the Satyrs and all earth creatures who smile sunshine and ask no questions and understand" (296). Again, by defining the African American race as childlike and inferior, Will Percy not only justifies his paternal authority over their affairs but also constructs his own identity as a civilized, rational aristocrat. His ability to know himself rests largely on his ability to know the Other according to strictly defined terms. Therefore, the elder Percy thought it of supreme importance that no individual violate these terms or take on characteristics of the Other, lest this system of identity lose its defining power.

While Will Percy reminds whites that "the black man is our brother, a younger brother, not adult, not disciplined, but tragic, pitiful, and lovable" (309)—a theory of race that ostensibly implies a fundamental similarity between white and black southerners—he also expresses a clear uneasiness with the practical outcome of such a theory. If intermarriage between races became common, Percy argues, "the end of the century would behold a Delta population neither white nor black, but hybrid" (21). Further, he asserts that the white southerner believes that "the hybrid is not a desirable product . . . [;] amalgamation is not the answer" (21–22); thus, he suggests that he in fact thinks African Americans should never leave their essentially different, subservient position. Crucially for Will Percy, his paternalistic attitude toward African Americans maintains not only racial distinctions but also class distinctions within the white race; paternalism separates elites like himself from another class of whites who have populated the Delta, "the poor whites, who owned no slaves, whose manual labor lost its dignity from being in competition with slave labor, who worked their small unproductive holdings ignored by the gentry, despised by the slaves" (19). Percy places them lower than the African Americans, whose childlike nature so delights him. He writes, "Intellectually and spiritually they are inferior to the Negro, whom they hate. Suspecting secretly they are inferior to him, they must do something to him to prove to themselves their superiority. At their door must be laid the disgraceful riots and lynchings gloated over and exaggerated by Negrophiles the world over" (20). Thus, just as tolerant affection characterizes the descendants of the aristocratic gentry, violent hatred characterizes poor whites.

However, the traditional system of race and class from which Will Percy derived his identity, dividing black from white and aristocrat from trash, had already begun to fail when the planter-poet published his memoir in 1941. While Will Percy saw this collapse as an occasion for regret and lamentation, Walker Percy came to see it as an opportunity. We know both from his novels and from his biography that he eventually grew beyond the biases he inherited from Uncle Will.[3] True, he does at times defend the fundamental honor of Will's intentions. For instance, in his introduction to *Lanterns,* he writes, "Take the words 'paternalism,' 'noblesse oblige,' dirty words these days. But is it a bad thing for a man to believe that his position in society entails a certain responsibility towards others? Or is it a bad thing for a man to care like a father for his servants, spend himself on the poor, the sick, the miserable, the mad who come his way? It is surely better than watching a neighbor get murdered and closing the blinds to keep from 'getting involved.' It might even beat welfare" ("Uncle Will" 58). However, though he may praise the abstract ideals of paternalism, he also realizes the potential for exploitation inherent in a social system that treats an entire race as ignorant children.

In *The Last Gentleman,* Percy explores the opportunities for change made possible in the collapse of racial paternalism as a means of organizing race and class in the South, and, most interestingly, he focuses much of his attention on the phenomenon that so terrified his adoptive father: hybridity. The novel follows Williston Bibb "Will" Barrett on his quest for identity and reconciliation with his family's tradition over the course of his return to his much-altered ancestral homeland, the Delta country of the American South. Will lacks the allegedly stable identity required of the proper paternalist aristocrat. Although he comes from an aristocratic family whose identity at least in part depends upon a subjugation and objectification of African Americans that masquerades as protection, he cannot perform his aristocratic whiteness; he cannot interact with African Americans in the manner prescribed by his family's paternalist tradition. As the narrator ironically remarks, "The engineer [Will] was the only white man in the entire South who did not know all there was to know about Negroes" (151). Unlike the typical southerner, who "looks at a Negro twice: once when he is a child and sees his nurse for the first time; second, when he is dying and there is a Negro with him to change his bedclothes" (152), Will "actually look[s]" at black people in an attempt to understand them in some way of his own. Will truly holds no single worldview: the narrator describes him as "a Southerner who had crossed up his wires and was something betwixt and between" (251).

Such an in-between position makes Will a confusing anomaly in the world of elite southerners. The aristocratic southern white gentleman constructed his identity in large part through his interaction with African Americans, whom he necessarily considered his helpless inferiors. Though men like Will Percy made much of their paternalistic attitudes toward black people and claimed they wanted to help their "junior brothers" advance to a white standard of civilization, these paternal identities paradoxically depended on the fixity of the black Other in a downtrodden situation. After all, if African Americans attained enlightened whiteness, they would no doubt lose that connection to the perfect innocence that Will Percy so craved (and would likely gain a considerable disgust with their constant exploitation). By maintaining a strictly defined Other against whom they could define themselves in utter opposition, aristocratic whites constructed a system of identity predicated on binary polarities. Individuals who have invested their identities in such a system would fear any notion of a racial hybridity, either sexual or cultural, any incoherence in the structure of their selves. After all, if members of either race shift from what theorist Homi Bhabha, the most prominent theorist of hybridity, calls their "primordial polarities" and begin to operate in an interstitial space, then they threaten to "elude the politics of polarity," to create new forms of identity which render any claim to an identity based in segregated binarism unworkable (39). In a "third space" that "entertains difference without an assumed or imposed hierarchy" (4), allegedly essential racial and cultural characteristics merge, blur, and take on new forms—an instability that threatens not just racial binaries but also class hierarchies, since aristocratic whites depend upon the childlike otherness of African Americans so that they may demonstrate the paternalism that separates them from low-class whites; if the otherness that separates blacks and whites begins to break down, then so also will the supposedly essential class distinctions separating different groups of white southerners, thus challenging the aristocrats' claims that they are inherently most fit to lead.

Thus we may read Percy's chronicle of Will's attempt to reconcile his own uniquely hybrid nature with the binaristic, paternalistic tradition of identity handed down by his father as an affirmation of the power of hybridity to complicate and undermine traditional hierarchies of power. In this reading, Percy's novel functions, in Bhabha's words, to "authorize cultural hybridities that emerge in moments of historical transformation" (2).[4] However, Percy's text also resists a merely celebratory interpretation; rather, it calls attention to the ways in which the hybridity that ostensibly serves to disrupt conventional power relations often becomes instead the unique province of the privileged.[5] Indeed, hybridity may simply become assimilated into the system of race and class relations that Percy deplores.

Will Barrett's father, suicidal lawyer-planter Ed Barrett, finds hybridity threatening. Like "Uncle Will," Ed Barrett articulates his fear of cultural hybridity through his diatribes against the mingling of black and white sexual behaviors. However, the type of hybridity that he fears has little to do with genuine cultural differences but with characteristics he perceives as essential to each race. Not surprisingly, his ideas owe much to those espoused by Will Percy in *Lanterns on the Levee*. Will Barrett recalls that as he watched his father pace the street before their house in Ithaca, Mississippi (the primary setting of Will's flashbacks and a clear analog to Greenville, Will Percy's hometown), they could see that "west, atop the levee, couples sat in parked cars," and they could hear that "east, up De Ridder . . . came now and then the sound of Negro laughter" (78). However, Ed Barrett considers this physical segregation inconsequential in comparison to a far more grave cultural exchange: sexual license. Mr. Barrett nods east toward the African Americans and claims that "they fornicate and the one who fornicates best is the preacher." He perceives their supposedly loose sexuality simply as another aspect of their essential amorality. However, while he believes this behavior is intrinsic to black nature, he rails against it when practiced by whites because for him their adherence to a moral, ethical system sets them apart from the "savages" and guarantees their position of power. In order to maintain their authority as "elder brothers" who help black people attain their level of civilization, decent white southerners must also adhere to the rules that they claim define civilized behavior. Says Mr. Barrett of the levee-goers, "They fornicate too and in public and expect *them* back yonder somehow not to notice. Then they expect their women to be respected" (78). Ed Barrett's concern here goes far beyond a simple fear of miscegenation. He believes that by bringing their sexuality into public view, white people undermine their morally superior position—built upon the pedestal of exalted Southern Womanhood—and give blacks a vantage point from which to question white authority. Significantly, Will's father seems less concerned with the actual fornication than with its nature as spectacle; perhaps he recognizes on some level the arbitrary constructedness, the performative nature, of these identity-granting boundaries.

Whatever the case, Mr. Barrett sees nothing but destruction and degeneracy in this trend: "One will pick up the worst of the other and lose the best of himself. Watch. One will learn to fornicate in public and the other will end by pissing in the street" (78). Thus, Mr. Barrett can conceive of this cultural hybridity only negatively; for him, true identity depends on the perpetuation of dramatically different characteristics for each race. When he eventually realizes that the white people of Ithaca have begun to flaunt characteristics that he considers "black," he also realizes that his old-fashioned aristocratic system must inevitably fail. Consequently, Mr. Barrett suffers a dramatic crisis of identity that culminates in suicide (though Will represses this last detail until nearly the end of his trip home). Ed Barrett recognizes in his fellow whites the same capacity for ethical immunity that his class posits as the exclusive domain of blackness. He can no longer construct a culture of difference if his compeers refuse to act differently.

Ironically, however, for a culture that ostensibly abhors hybridity, aristocratic southern culture as practiced by men like Will Percy and Ed

Barrett promoted a close (if controlled) interaction between African Americans and whites, especially at a young age. This interaction, in the case of Will Barrett, provides the grounds for an authentic experience of cultural difference at least partially divorced from his father's impositions. The narrator claims that, as Will Percy might have prescribed, Will Barrett "like many others . . . had had a little black boy for a friend" (151). Although the narrator ironically remarks that Will had not "enjoyed perfect love and understanding" with his black playmate and that "unlike the others . . . , he had been from the beginning somewhat fuddled and uneasy," Will obviously preferred his company to other white children in at least one instance. Once, he fled his summer camp in North Carolina and returned home, where he "with the help of a Negro friend built a tree house in a tall sycamore. They spent the summer aloft, reading comics while the tree house tossed like a raft in a sea of dappled leaves" (9).

Further, aristocratic households would naturally employ African American servants to assist the lady of the house with menial duties as well as with child rearing. Significantly, Percy makes only the briefest mention of Will's mother, and Will's stepmother hardly seems an adequate substitute. Rather, Will's black nurse, D'lo, fills the maternal role. Indeed, his only indoor childhood memory involves watching D'lo cook. Moreover, when he returns to his father's house, he does not seek the help of the quartet of stern aunts rocking on the porch. Instead, he goes to the kitchen, D'lo's domain. Although a certain formality still informs their interactions (Will pays/bribes her for her help), their relationship closely resembles that of a mother and her wayward child. For instance, Will believes that D'lo intuitively "had somehow known that he was here," and when he describes his recent adventures, he "could not have sworn she did not know all about it" (263). Further, D'lo supplies him with a hearty meal and helps him look presentable (263).

Perhaps, then, we may usefully read Will Barrett as the hybrid product of two racial cultures. As Bhabha helpfully observes, "The effect of cultural power is seen to be the production of hybridization rather than the noisy command of colonial authority or the silent repression of native traditions" (112). Will's cultural hybridity manifests in one of his most intriguing characteristics: his "radar," his "knack of divining persons and situations" (37). He can tune in to a person's narrative wavelength, intuitively understand what sort of listener that person's narrative requires, and shape himself accordingly. Val Vaught notes Will's amorphous nature when she tells him, "Everyone thinks very highly of you—though for strangely diverse, even contradictory reasons" (164). Although most of Percy's readers have made some comment about Will's radar, they have failed to notice that Percy often figures this radar in terms distinctively associated with African Americans. Percy describes it as the chief characteristic that has enabled them to survive in such an oppressive society for so long:

> The Vaught servants were buffaloed by the engineer and steered clear of him. Imagine their feeling. They of course lived by their radars too. It was their special talent and it was how they got along: tuning in on the assorted signals about them and responding with a skill two hundred years in the learning. And not merely responding. Not merely answering the signals but providing home and sustenance to the transmitter, giving him, the transmitter, to believe that he dwelled in loving and familiar territory. He must be made to make sense, must the transmitter, must be answered with sense and good easy laughter: sho now, we understand each other. (151–52)

Although it may seem as though Percy indulges in a bit of racial essentialism here, he takes cares to describe the radar as "two hundred years in the learning," a phrase that stresses that this talent does not lie intrinsically in every person of African descent but that African Americans since the time of slavery have necessarily developed this trait to survive. Through this process, the servants satisfy what Bhabha calls the "colonialist demand . . . that the Other should authorize the self, recognize its priority, replete, indeed repeat, its references" (98). They alter themselves to serve their masters' need for constant reauthorization of their identity. Thus, not surprisingly, Will's anomalous presence confounds the Vaught servants. They do not know how to deal with Will because, unlike other white people, he does not "transmit" but, rather, only "receives"; he, "like them, was all ears and eyes and antennae."[6] Significantly, they conceive of his condition in terms of hybridity: "He was like a white child who does not grow up *or rather who grows up in the kitchen*" (152, my emphasis). This phrase is significant, given that Percy takes care to depict how in both the

Vaught and Barrett households maternal African American figures hold sway over this site of domestic power. Thus Will's appropriation of "Negro radar" stands as the clearest evidence of his hybrid nature. Perhaps this helps explain his discomfort around Lamar Thigpen, Mr. Vaught's racist-joke-telling step-son-in-law. Will dislikes jokes because he must "attend to the perilous needs of the joke-teller" (181), and Lamar's jokes in particular force him to answer a narrative demand that conflicts with the very part of himself that makes him such a good listener.

However, Percy challenges notions of hybridity's subversive potential by demonstrating that this gift does not necessarily work to the overall benefit of any of its possessors, Will included. That is, this perpetual contingency, however necessary for survival, may ultimately destroy any coherent identity. For instance, Lugurtha, the Vaughts' African American cook, more than anything else wants "to find fervent areas of agreement" and so voices her opinions only on such trite and simple subjects as juvenile delinquency (she's against it) (155). Will, too, suffers this loss of selfhood. His almost involuntary transformations into whatever those around him desire prevent him from inspecting and coming to terms with his own identity. Even though he spends five years ostensibly looking inward via psychoanalysis, Will learns nothing because he simply divines what his analyst wants to hear and gives it to him.[7]

Inevitably, Will's "betwixt and between" hybrid identity comes into conflict with itself. His father's aristocratic, paternalistic identity rests on "knowing" the Other according to very specific, limited terms that may bear little or no relation to the Other's actual characteristics. On the other hand, his "mother's" radar helps provide Will with a more authentic knowledge of others that would make such a willful ignorance impossible, yet it also denies him any truly individual identity of his own. This tension between an identity founded upon false knowledge and a truer knowledge that precludes identity lies at the heart of Will's return to the South. We may read his quest as an attempt to come to terms with his family's paternalist, aristocratic white identity and to find a system of racial interaction that will accept his hybridity without destroying his identity. As he journeys through the South, Will repeatedly faces social systems that promise him a coherent identity yet which he eventually perceives as fundamentally racist.

As the novel opens, we find Will seeking temporary refuge from his dilemma in New York City, where he works as a humidification engineer for Macy's. From this outer region, far removed from the day-to-day realities of southern life, Will can fantasize about returning to an aristocratically idealized South. He imagines that once he retires from Macy's, "he could retire and go home ... [;] he might restore Hampton plantation to its former splendor" (13). Tellingly, Will does not figure his dreams of agrarian glory in terms of updating or modernizing; rather, as the phrase *former splendor* implies, he imagines a return to the glorious aristocratic past. He expresses this desire in even more explicitly paternalistic terms after he has begun his trek South, when he thinks, "I am returning to ... recover Hampton plantation from the canebrakes and live out my days as a just man and *little father to the faithful Negroes working in the field*" (118, my italics). Even in New York, though, Will still exhibits evidence of his hybridity. For instance, he falls in with two radically (and racially) disparate crowds: an "interracial group" from Greenwich Village and "the Siberian Gentlemen, a nostalgic supper club of expatriate Southerners, mostly lawyers and brokers, who ... spoke of going back to Charleston or Mobile" (14). Despite the obvious cultural and philosophical differences of these two groups, his joint association does "not strike him as in the least anomalous" (14), perhaps because Will, as a product of two cultures who belongs to neither, necessarily requires community with both.

Will's hybrid nature comes most strikingly into conflict with his desire to take on his family's paternal role almost immediately as he begins his trip South. On several occasions, Will attempts to reduce race into simple binaries, only to find himself thwarted time and again by the variety and complexity of racial experience; for Percy, such reductive readings of race blind individuals to the true nature of the world around them. For instance, when the Vaughts semi-accidentally abandon Will in New York, Will must hitchhike his way home. He gets his first break from "pseudo-Negro" Forney Aiken, and through their misadventures Percy first begins to problematize Will's efforts to reinsert himself into his father's paternalistic mold. Forney, a white photojournalist from the North, has decided to infiltrate the "cotton curtain" as a burial insurance salesman to do a "series on behind-the-scene life of the Negro" (101). With the help of a dermatologist, Forney has made his entire body appear black, save one small patch on his forearm.[8] However, despite his physical disguise, Will sees—or rather hears—through his deception. Forney does not speak as Will believes an "educated Negro" would: "with a certain relish and a hearkening to his own periods" (98). Of course, the fact that Will presumes to know exactly what a black person of a certain type should sound like (he even gives Forney tips on the proper African American way to pronounce *insurance*) suggests that he has begun his attempt to reenter his father's Other-knowing paternalist tradition. Ironically, by not speaking as Will expects a black man to speak and then revealing himself as in fact not a black man at all, Forney actually if incidentally reaffirms Will's false position as a "knower" of the African American Other.

However, Will's first attempt to put paternal ideals into practice meets with disaster, largely because of his forcible suppression of his radar's warnings. Will and Forney sojourn into the all-white neighborhood of Levittown, a suburb of Philadelphia, to pick up author Mort Prince. As they approach Prince's house, Forney greets a throng of surly homeowners. The other suburbanites see only a black man followed by Will, who they believe works as a "blockbuster," a realtor who sells homes in all-white neighborhoods to black families. Will sees this case of mistaken identity as an opportunity for him to defend the helpless black race as paternally as his aristocratic grandfather might have, although the posse of householders certainly presents a less formidable threat than the KKK. But Will has trouble keeping his anger "pure and honorable" (113). His desire to fight the worthiest foe among the householders, a burly fellow whom Will dubs the "alpiner," for the rights of the African American conflicts with his desire to accommodate himself to the situation via his "radar," and "despite himself" he begins "to tune him in to see how it stood with him." Will desperately wants two-fisted paternalism to win out over his radar: when he sees the alpiner "advance upon the writer, hand outstretched, perhaps for the 'papers,' perhaps to shake hands," he chooses to ignore the possible alternatives and to interpret the advance as an attack. Unfortunately for Will, in the midst of all this chaos, he gets slugged, not by the villainous alpiner but by a decidedly less impressive foe (at least in his grandfather's terms): an irate housewife. The contrast between the farcical nature of the skirmish and the imagined gravity of Will's grandfather's noble showdown emphasizes Percy's ironic critique of traditional southern race relations. Thus Will's first attempt to ignore his radar and live only according to the rules of his father's "pole" meets with humiliating defeat.

The confusion and dislocation Will feels on his jaunt with Forney serve as a preview for what follows in Alabama. There, as Michael Kobre notes, Will realizes that "the old paternalistic relationships of white gentleman and black servants are no longer stable or clear-cut" (93). When Will does finally reunite with the Vaughts and arrives at their house in Birmingham, he confronts another means of mediating cultural interaction, a modern interpretation of the Old South colonial ideals. Though the Vaughts live in a suburban "castle fronting on the golf links" rather than on a plantation, they still maintain their identity in the world through strictly defined racial roles. Indeed, the Vaughts see their African American servants much as Binx Bolling's Aunt Emily saw Mercer, as living connections to the Old South way of life. When a large contingent of Vaughts and assorted hangers-on leave for a football game, the three servants stand "waving farewell on the back steps, Lugurtha fluttering her apron" (214–15). This display prompts Lamar to remark, "There's nothing like the old-timey ways!" (215). The servants "remind Lamar of an earlier, more gracious time, even though the purple castle didn't look much like an antebellum mansion and the golf links even less like a cotton plantation." The Vaughts participate in a trend that Grace Hale identifies in her study *Making Whiteness*. According to Hale, although "profound differences existed between the relatively self-sufficient agrarianism of the Old South and the more urban and consumer-oriented domesticity of the new," white southerners "of the rising middle class" nevertheless "insisted on conflating the plantation household and the post-Reconstruction white home in order to ground their own cultural authority within the power . . . of the plantation-based planter class" (87).

At the Vaught household, Will at first has no trouble fitting in: he plays golf with Mr. Vaught and his cronies and prepares for college. However, as time passes, he increasingly realizes his incompatibility with the Vaughts' system of racial interaction. When a group of young people from his native Delta country come to visit, he proves unable to enjoy their company, particularly when they discuss the integration of their formerly whites-only university. In contrast to his fellow Deltans who "[knew] what they wanted and who they hated," Will remains "so mystified by white and black alike that he [can]not allow himself the luxury of hatred" (210). Significantly, he even thinks of them as "lordly" in their hatred, a term that recalls the aristocratic nature of plantation race relations. His refusal, indeed his inability, to separate race into simple binaries deprives him of the identity that comes so easily for them.

Will does find a temporary refuge for his hybridity in a rather peculiar room in the Vaught castle: the pantry. He most often and most comfortably situates himself here in this interstitial space, a space "not properly a room at all but rather the space left over in the center of the house when the necessary rooms had been built. . . . It fell out somehow or other that both Negro and white could sit in the pantry, perhaps because it was an intermediate room between dining room and kitchen, or perhaps because it was not, properly speaking, a room at all" (152). The fact that this room exists because "Mr. Vaught, who also did not know what he did not know, had been his own architect" suggests that any construction of white culture that assumes omniscience in making allowances for the presence of African Americans has at its heart the potential for hybridity and therefore resistance. Bhabha's reading of Renee Green's architectural art project *Sites of Genealogy* might apply equally well to the Vaught pantry: Green uses the attic and basement of the museum to signify binary opposites, and the stairwell, like the Vaught pantry, "prevents identities at either end of it from settling into primordial polarities. This interstitial passage between fixed identities opens up the possibility of a cultural hybridity that entertains difference without an assumed or imposed hierarchy" (Bhabha 4). In the pantry Will finds his hybridity satisfied (if only briefly), for its curious nature frees him from the requirement to choose an identity based on any particular racial binary.

However, Percy also problematizes the notion of the pantry as a site of ideal hybridity. Although this curious room does function as a space for intercultural interaction, those interactions still occur in an area ultimately ruled by paternalistic white authority. Even though "many doors and vestibules" lead out of the room, they all lead simply to another area on the Vaught estate. Thus any cross-cultural exchanges do not occur unmediated in a vacuum but rather in the heart of an authority that controls the kinds of hybridity generated. Percy addresses this issue through the character of the Vaughts' butler David Ross, who, in Will's words, "ain't black nor white nor nothing" (248). David, the pantry's other chief occupant, also has difficulty fitting into any racial role. Will, who still clings to his father's binaries, thinks of him as "different from the other Negroes" because "he had not caught onto either the Negro way or the white way" (152). However, while this intermediate position eventually provides Will with a position from which to critique these binaries and forge an identity separate from either, it simply leaves David open to exploitation: he cannot "be cunning with a white man's cunning or cunning with a black man's cunning" (153). Further, even his radar does not function properly: when Will unexpectedly calls him on the phone, David proves incapable of answering his narrative demand: "David, feeling summoned, cast about for the right response—was it surprise? joy?—and hit instead on a keening bogus cheeriness" (247). When Will tells David he is sick, David, "aiming for the famous Negro sympathy, hit[s] instead on a hooting incredulity" (248).

David, son of Lugurtha the cook, has no biological father in the novel, but he has in a sense adopted Mr. Vaught as a father figure, and he even behaves as a privileged son would. Will thinks of him as "David sure enough, of royal lineage and spoiled rotten" (177). David uncritically accepts the bootstraps-capitalist ideal that Mr. Vaught embodies. He has grown up surrounded by unbridled success, and he therefore believes that he, too, can easily attain this American capitalist ideal of success and personal achievement with no difficulty. He frequently answers "advertisements in magazines, such as *Learn Electronics! Alert Young Men Needed! Earn Fifty Dollars a Day! Send for Selling Kit!*" even though his "long black-and-pink fingers could never quite work the connections and the soldering iron" (153). Importantly, Percy does not describe David's incompetence as resulting from his blackness but, rather, because he acts "like a rich man's son," pampered and sheltered. Even with his electronics mishap, David still continues to pursue his goal, this time with the intention of going door-to-door in the Vaughts' neighborhood to sell ice dispensers.

By innocently and faithfully pursuing these endeavors, David behaves like "baby brother at home" (154) in two ways. First, he conducts himself as a spoiled younger son who expects success to come naturally. Second, he acts like "baby brother" in Will Percy's paternalist sense: he unquestioningly believes that white people genuinely want to help him attain their lifestyle, to become just like them. David acts "as if everybody was going to treat him well," but Will Barrett, more familiar with the depths of white paranoia, recognizes this blind faith in the system as David's "awful vulnerability." He knows that David will fail because "they're not going to treat [David] well. They're going to violate [him]" (154). David remains committed to an identity that promises progress but guarantees fixity in his subordinate situation. When the authoritarian culture completely controls the interactions with the subordinate culture, as in the pantry, hybridity cannot be truly subversive. In this sense, David more accurately embodies another concept closely associated with Bhabha: colonial mimicry. According to Bhabha, the aim of colonial discourse is to force the colonized other to mimic the values of the civilized colonizer. However, too accurate a mimicry might challenge colonizers' claims of essential difference—"mimicry is at once resemblance and menace," writes Bhabha; thus, as he puts it, "colonial mimicry is the desire for a reformed, recognizable Other, *as a subject of a difference that is almost the same, but not quite* . . . in order to be effective, mimicry must continually produce its slippage, its excess, its difference" (86). Or, as he more succinctly expresses it, mimicry creates a subject who is "not quite/not white" (92). That is, the colonized must reflect the colonizers' ideals, aspirations, language, and social structures, ostensibly therefore justifying the "civilizing" mission of colonialism; yet the colonized must also always manifest a difference that marks them as Other.

Bhabha sees the inevitable failure of mimicry as ultimately productive of a subversive hybridity; he argues that "in 'normalizing' the colonial state or subject, the dream of post-Enlightenment civility alienates its own language of liberty and produces another knowledge of its norms" (86). Potentially, this new knowledge could lead to disruption and rebellion. However, Percy holds out no hope that David will ever begin to question the norms he has adopted. Percy here treats mimicry and hybridity as divided by class and race. David's failed mimicry never leads to any kind of resistance or disruption of paternalistic power, never paves the way for a hybridity—like Will's—that allows him a keen insight, "another knowledge," in Bhabha's terms, into the complicated relationship between black and white southerners. Thus, while for Bhabha mimicry and hybridity exist on a spectrum, Percy raises the possibility that they may in fact be divided by race and class—by privilege.

This reading may at first seem to suggest that Percy believes that only those individuals who belong to the ranks of paternalistic authority, rich white southerners such as Will, can truly attain any politically viable sort of hybridity, for only they have the autonomy to resist the types of identity offered by their culture. Indeed, some of Will's reflections on David seem to suggest a sort of condescending anger at his failure to see the world through his hybrid eyes, a sentiment that complicates a view of Will as progressive hybrid hero. Thus, while Will can flee to the North and live off his inheritance, David must accept the meager opportunities available to him in his subservient position. This tension recalls Aijaz Ahmad's critique of hybridity as a phenomenon exclusive to wealthy migrants, those who abandon the Third World for the Western metropolis, where they gain an ostensibly more perceptive view of the land they have left behind. According to Ahmad, the embrace of hybridity as a revolutionary and subversive attack on traditional hierarchies "overlook[s] the position of class and caste privileges" from which theories of hybridity emerge (15). He points out that even "among the migrants themselves, only the privileged can live a life of constant mobility and surplus pleasure" (16). In some ways, then, Percy's vision of hybridity seems a reasonable subject for Ahmad's critique; both David and Will possess unstable, contingent identities, but only Will, who can afford to migrate to New York, has developed a "radar" better than any white or black southerner, one that offers him a deeper knowledge of southern race relations.

However, Percy also complicates any attempt to simply read hybridity as a mark of privilege. Will encounters an African American character whose hybridity has succeeded far better than even his. Later in the novel, when Will chances upon Forney Aiken again, Forney has with him a contingent of thespians and playwrights. When Will meets one playwright, "a slender pop-eyed Negro" (251), he feels a remarkable sensation: he experiences for the first time "as powerful and white-hot a radar beam leveled at him as he leveled at others." Will realizes this playwright has "done the impossible!—kept his ancient Negro radar intact and added to it a white edginess and restiveness" (251). Indeed, the playwright represents one of the very few Percy characters not trapped inside a restrictive and confining role. The narrator contrasts the playwright with an actor in his company: "Where the actor [is] all self playing itself and triumphantly succeeding, coinciding with itself, the playwright [is] . . . not in the least mindful of himself" (251). Significantly, although the playwright, like Will, has a powerful radar, he does not share Will's compulsive desire to remake himself in everyone else's image of him. Perhaps his creative vocation allows him to externalize his working through of other "selves" in a way that Will cannot. Though Percy problematically offers no hint as to how he achieved this "impossibility," the playwright's presence in the novel offers at least the possibility that a black person can escape a paternalist-imposed identity, can escape the "moral scheme," as Jack Kirby puts it, of paternalism. Still, however, the fact remains that the main figure through whom Percy develops his examination of hybridity is in fact a wealthy white male, a fact that suggests that hybridity can sometimes simply be another permutation of privileged whiteness.

At any rate, Will realizes that he cannot stay in the pantry forever because of its position within the power of traditional paternalist authority. But even when he leaves the Vaughts, he discovers that paternalist ideology is not confined to the updated plantation of the golf links suburbs. When the Vaught sons, Jamie and his brother Sutter, steal away in the night, the other Vaughts want Will to pursue them. He follows Sutter's map down through Mississippi to Tyree County, where Valentine Vaught, a Catholic nun, directs a mission for poverty-stricken African American children. Percy's readers have usually treated Val fairly generously, as a flawed but fundamentally holy woman committed to the spiritual advancement of her charges. Gary M. Ciuba argues that "she teaches her Tyree children out of a desire to give them back the world rather than from the potential haughtiness of noblesse oblige" (113). Indeed, perhaps Will at first perceives her as the critics do. After all, Val ostensibly represents a system of racial interaction different from either the Vaughts' or Mr. Barrett's. Mr. Vaught considers her the "worst of all" his children because she took his hundred-thousand-dollar gift and "gave it to the niggers" (65). Further, Val purports that she does not participate in the southern racial theories proposed by men like Will's father. She claims that while she once heard Mr. Barrett "make a speech to the D.A.R. on the subject of *noblesse oblige* and our duty to the Negro" (162), she does not necessarily share his views: she tells Will, "I can't say that I agree with your father on his reasons for treating Negroes well rather than beating them up" (164). Even the location of her school seems at first hopeful: Will recalls that in years past the school "was one of the old-style country academies" where privileged children could study under "Dr. so-and-so who taught Greek and Colonel so-and-so who taught military science" (232). But now he finds "instead a raw settlement of surplus army buildings, Quonset huts, and one geodesic dome, stretching out into the piney woods, each building fed by a silver butane sphere. It looked like a lunar installation" (232–33). Thus, it would seem that Val has productively taken a site once used for the perpetuation of aristocratic ideology and converted it into a place where a new way of thinking about race might begin.

Nevertheless, Will quickly realizes that Val offers no more useful a means of mediating cultural interaction than did the Vaughts or his father. Rather than revising the past, she merely repeats it; her new structures symbolize not a fresh, different racial ideology but a reconstruction of the old. Will can find no means for understanding his hybridity here. When Will tunes her in with his radar, he sees that Val's ideology, benevolent though it may appear, would replace African American culture with a version of her own. Val claims she stays in Tyree because of her fascination with a "linguistic phenomenon" (237). The black children grow up almost completely mute: she tells Will, "Nobody at home speaks. They don't know thirty words. They don't know words like pencil or hawk or wallet." Val stays so that she may give them language: "What's that? they ask me. That's a hawk, I tell them, and they believe me." She describes this as an empowering process. As she informs Will, "When they do suddenly break into the world of language, it is something to see. They are like Adam on the First Day." Critics have generally taken this claim at face value: Ciuba argues that "by giving her silent students the word . . . she gives them back the entire world that she affirms as well as their very selves as Adamic namers" (111). However, Val's statement articulates a powerful contradiction. The children have little in common with Adam, for Adam gave the things of the world names of his own creation and constructed a knowledge of the world on his own terms and without the burden of history. The Tyree children, by contrast, receive the names of things from Val and thus learn to understand the world only in terms prescribed by an authority who bears a closer relationship to aristocratic ideology than she admits. Val does not teach the children to speak so that they may use the power of language to understand the world and their culture in some way of their own but, rather, so that they will understand the world through her belief system. Thus she perpetuates the "moral scheme" of paternalism that Kirby identifies: "Most insidiously, paternalism bound blacks to whites, apprenticed them not only as laborers but also as moral creatures" (16). Thus, for Percy, even religious attempts to aid or educate the oppressed and impoverished may be tainted by racial paternalism.

Percy does, however, provide a sliver of hope for the Tyree children. When Jamie reaches his lowest point, he asks Will to call Val, but when Will eventually gets through, he reaches not Val but one of her students, Axel. Will inquires about Val using her full religious name, Sister Johnette Mary Vianney, buy Axel refers to her by a name of his own creation: "Sister Viney" (308). Thus, perhaps Val's attempt to control completely the terms of their knowledge must finally fail. Even as she gives their world her names, Axel and his classmates give her a name of their own creation. Less hopefully, Axel's misspoken name for his teacher may simply be a linguistic manifestation of the "reformed, recognizable Other," the "not quite/not white" mimic created by colonial discourse.

I do not mean to suggest that Val's work has no value or is unnecessary; certainly, these children will be better off with an education. However, Percy nevertheless suggests that something sinister underlies Val's apparent benevolence; rather than creating something new on the grounds of the old-fashioned southern academy, she merely repeats its ideology. As Will listens to Val's spiel, he realizes that she "has her hooks out" for him. Will then begins to perceive the danger if he remains: "Another hour in this gloomy cancerous wood and I'd be laid out stiff as a corpse, feet sticking straight up" (238). He no longer sees Val's school in terms of a hopeful new beginning but rather in terms of a decaying and decrepit ending: "Seven-Up machines, plastic crucifixes, and worn, gnawed-at woodwork such as is found in old gymnasiums" (238). Val's religion offers nothing new, so Will continues to follow Sutter's map even deeper into his father's Delta country, where he must most directly confront his father's aristocratic tradition.

To this point, every alternative to his father's paternalistic binarism that Will has encountered has proven equally corrupt and incapable of providing any useful framework in which Will's hybridity might find some resolution. So, it should come as no surprise that when he reaches his hometown Will once again attempts to quash his hybridity and reassert the role of paternal defender, although in a somewhat different manner than he did with Forney Aiken in Philadelphia. Yet in depicting Will's conflicted acceptance of his father's mantle, Percy again demonstrates that the unique perceptions granted Will by his hybridity, his radar, prevent him from accepting traditional stratifications of race and class that paternalism relies upon. Will once again encounters Forney and his entourage (inconveniently *sans* two-fisted writer Mort Prince) taking refuge from the racist local constabulary in the Dew Drop Inn, a bar run by an effeminate African American improbably named Sweet Evening Breeze. Breeze identifies Will with his father and, specifically, with his father's paternalism: he tells Forney's compatriots, "This here's Will Barrett, Lawyer Barrett's boy. Lawyer Barrett help many a one" (253). Placed in a situation in which someone actually needs his protection (as opposed to the incident in Philadelphia, when he simply created a need), Will has no trouble slipping into his great-grandfather's role; indeed, in this case it almost seems as though he uses his "Negro radar" to shape himself into the champion that Breeze apparently needs. When the town deputies, Beans Ross and Ellis Gover, exemplars of the violent poor white that Will Percy so despised, arrive on the scene, Beans takes a blackjack "as soft and worn as skin" and routinely knocks Breeze unconscious with it (255). This act inspires Will to slug Beans; as Ciuba observes, Will "acts like his father's noble son" (131).

However, Percy questions the possibility and even the desirability of being that "noble son," for Will still cannot stay completely within his great-grandfather's role. His ancestor fought only the unreservedly evil Grand Wizard and therefore did not have to worry about how his foe might look in front of the other Klan members. But Will has a friend of sorts among his opponents: Ellis Gover, who played halfback to Will's quarterback in high school. While Will does defend Breeze and Forney's troupe from these policemen, he cannot help tuning into Ellis's needs as well. He recognizes that Ellis will likely face considerable trouble for letting him assault Beans, so he provides Ellis with a cover story. Will tells him to report that Forney's group "got in behind" him and then bring charges against Will to clear himself (256). Will thus sees even more clearly the impossibility of maintaining his family's system of identity, as his hybrid radar prevents him from easily sorting people into heroes and villains. For Percy, hybridity compels an acknowledgment of the complexity that challenges traditional hierarchies of power in the South.

This realization of the folly of trying to separate the irreducible complexity of black and white in the South into easily understood binaries prompts Will to a better understanding of the pitfalls of his father's worldview. Seeking temporary refuge in his ancestral home, Will remembers once again his father's diatribes against the apparent intermingling of black and white cultures, but this time he remembers the tragedy that his father's commitment to that binary scheme of identity caused. He does not simply tell Will that he does not "have to choose that" and then withdraw from society; instead, he goes inside (despite Will's desperate request that he not leave him) and takes his own life. Will finally understands the type of identity that he has so long idealized, the standard to which he has held himself, as ultimately flawed. Ed Barrett, himself a product of his family's paternalist tradition, died because he could not make a new identity when the old one had obviously lost its validity, when the boundaries separating black from white and aristocrat from trash had begun to dissolve. Will thinks, "I think he was wrong and that he was looking in the wrong place. No, not he but the times. The times were wrong and one looked in the wrong place. It wasn't even his fault because that was the way he was and the way the times were, and there was no other place a man could look" (261). Because of his adherence to the tradition handed down by men like Will's great-grandfather, Mr. Barrett believes that "there was no other place" to look for an identity, for a way of living in the world.

This realization immediately alters Will's perception of his relationship with African Americans, and he begins to embrace his own unique identity. No longer does he feel obligated to behave as a protector of childlike African Americans. However, Percy questions the notion that hybridity necessarily leads to profound cultural change; although Bhabha and others see hybridity as offering a way to challenge the "politics of polarity" (39), Percy suggests that it may instead offer the privileged the illusion of an escape from politics, period. As Will stands under a streetlight outside his father's house—the very place where Ed Barrett would hold lofty and uplifting discourse with black passers-by on the necessity of good character—a young black man Will's own age comes "whistling toward him under the street light" (262). When these two men confront each other, they have "nothing to say," even though "their fathers would have had much to say." While their fathers' discourse would have involved a complex and racially determined reinforcement of cultural roles, Will's new understanding of the falsity of those roles allows him to begin to cast off the burden of paternalist identity and to say nothing, to demand no narrative. It is troubling, however, that only Will seems aware of their new status and does not believe himself capable of helping his black companion. He thinks, "You may be in a fix and I know that but what you don't know and won't believe and must find out for yourself is that I'm in a fix too and you got to get where I am before you even know what I'm talking about and I know that and that's why there is nothing to say now" (262). Thus the white individual has ostensibly transcended his old role and left the black individual behind. The worrisome sense of condescending superiority that inflects this scene, much as it did Will's earlier reflections on David's failed hybridity, again complicates a view of Will as a progressive figure. A charitable reading of this scene might hold that Will's reluctance to tell the black man about his "fix" results from a fear of replicating his father's noblesse oblige, of patronizingly offering the black man a model of identity to which he should aspire. A less charitable reading might point out that Will only assumes that his African American peer has not somehow acquired wisdom and insight equal to his own. By refusing to engage him in dialogue, Will ensures that his own superiority will go unchallenged. Whatever the case, the black individual loses out. Indeed, when the young African American finally leaves, he does so "as if it were required of him" (262); Percy's use of this phrase suggests that the black man still perceives himself in a culturally subordinate role. Again, the allegedly disruptive powers of hybridity have simply proved to benefit only the privileged, the wealthy. The aristocratic young white man may have gained a new perspective on his life, but he is incapable of sharing it with others who might benefit from it, incapable of putting it into meaningful practice.

However, Will quickly thereafter encounters two men who have largely escaped their old race-class roles and formed new ones. Will receives final confirmation of the inevitable deconstruction of paternalist binaries when he crosses the river to visit his Uncle Fannin and his black servant Merriam. On the old family plantation, he sees that even those who do not choose suicide cannot maintain the old ways entirely. Critics have generally read Fannin and Merriam's relationship as a rather pathetic remnant of the Old South master-slave relation. William Rodney Allen claims that Fannin and Merriam "are living in a world completely 'shut off' from the racial changes going on . . . throughout the South" (71). However, these readings neglect the subtle ways in which Fannin and Merriam's relationship has changed. True, when Will first arrives in Shut Off, Fannin and Merriam do seem on the surface to maintain a relationship much like that of an aristocratic master and his deferential servant. That is, they at first act very conscious of their traditional roles: as they ride in the truck, Merriam occupies as little seat as is humanly possible, and Will believes "that Merriam could have sat in the air if it had been required of him" (267). Further, when they hunt, Merriam plays Ford to Fannin's Will Percy: Fannin treats Merriam as his link to all things natural and "tak[es] due notice of the magic and incantatory faculty that Negroes are supposed to have—they know what animals are going to do, for example" (268).

However, Will also notices a slippage in their rigidly defined roles, a slippage that indicates that their roles are deliberate performances. For instance, Fannin carries a particularly decrepit gun, a "Browning automatic worn to silver, with bluing left only in the grooves of the etching" and with a trigger guard "worn as thin as an old man's wedding ring" (266). Merriam, on the other hand, carries "a brand-new single-shot nickel-plated sixteen-gauge from Sears Roebuck which look[s] like a silver flute" (267). Further, Will observes that when Fannin asks Merriam for his preternatural insight, he does so "ironically" (268). Also, when Will arrives unexpectedly on the scene, "blackness . . . seemed to rush forward in [Merriam's] face" (266); perhaps this curious phenomenon implies that when outsiders arrive, Merriam must emphasize his blackness to satisfy their expectations. After all, Fannin and Merriam make their money by providing businessmen from New Orleans and Memphis with a place to hunt quail, so maybe this elaborate façade simply gives them the look of inauthentic authenticity that white men from the city would expect to find on an old-style plantation.

Inside their house, the almost complete disintegration of their binary roles becomes most evident. In the living room, the modern has replaced the old: a "round-eyed Zenith and two leatherette recliners, the kind that are advertised in the back page of the comic section," now occupy the "clearing that had been made long ago by pushing Aunt Felice's good New Orleans furniture back into the dark corners of the room" (269). Again, Will's outsider presence causes Fannin and Merriam to revert superficially back to their act. Will and Fannin sit in the two recliners, but Will "perceive[s] immediately that the recliner" that Fannin gives him belongs to Merriam, but Fannin "pretend[s] the recliner had been brought out for the engineer . . . and Merriam pretend[s] he always roost[s] high in the darkness." However, Fannin forgets this supposedly ordinary arrangement, and "sometimes . . . forgetting, would speak to the other recliner" as though Merriam occupied it. Indeed, the manner in which they watch television implies an almost equal footing for the two men: they argue and debate about the gunslingers in their western with no sense of social or racial rank or station, and they both cackle "like maniacs" at children's television shows (272). Their old master-servant relationship has completely disintegrated in the flickering light of a vacuum tube. Though they may, as Allen says, live "shut off" from the rest of the South, these "sad gags from Madison Avenue" have the power to "transport" (272) them out of their roles. Nevertheless, Will cannot stay here either, for Fannin and Merriam, although they live mostly free of the trappings of the Old South's paternalistic ideology, also live apart from society. Their only interactions with the outside world come from the television or from the businessmen who pay for their anachronistic entertainments. Hybridity can find no home in this funhouse of a plantation. Indeed, Percy's depiction of Fannin and Merriam's easy—and highly profitable—transition into and out of racial roles suggests the limits of the subversive power of Bhabha's "interstitial space": though their contingent, flexible identities are profoundly antiessentialist, this flexibility is too easily recouped into an exploitative capitalist system. Thus their antiessentialism does not imply a subversive politics; indeed, their privilege affords them an escape from the political. Rather than disrupting traditional hierarchies of power, Fannin and Merriam use their role-shifting skills to make a buck by conforming to a romanticized image of those hierarchies.[9]

Through his recollection of his father's suicide and his experience in Shut Off, Will finally realizes that the old system of southern paternalism no longer works as it once did. However, none of the other ideological systems that he has encountered upon his way has proven any more helpful; indeed they, too, provide opportunity for both the violation of individual black people and for the annihilation of their culture rather than a productive cultural interplay from which hybridity might emerge. Percy offers no pat, easy answers. For him, all ideologies—particularly those controlled by white authority—have the potential for corruption. However, hope remains. When Will finally arrives in New Mexico to attend to Jamie in his last days, he rejects suicide and asserts his intentions for the rest of his life to Sutter: Will plans to marry Kitty and to settle down in Alabama. But he takes care to emphasize that he does not intend to adopt their racist viewpoints, nor does he intend to re-create the plantation system. Will wants to "promote tolerance and understanding between the races, surely the most pressing need before the country" (303). While Will's statement of purpose here somewhat recalls the sort of banal platitudes that Binx Bolling so despises in *The Moviegoer*, perhaps Will's complex, life-changing experiences have reinvested the used-up words with new force. His understanding of the potential good he can do may allow him to overcome his fear of repeating his father's paternalistic attitudes. Will realizes that because of his unique, hybridized position he can work as a force for change within the system. Perhaps he even means that he will work for a new racial ideology literally from "*between* the races," from an interstitial space.

Of course, even this reading is optimistic. The hybridity that Percy depicts as so potentially salvific apparently only appears under fairly specific circumstances, and it does not always succeed. Though he describes African Americans with hybrid identities, he either represents them as failures (David) or he insufficiently elaborates upon them (the playwright). Indeed, if the successful hybrid who works for racial equality and for new ways of formulating racial identity can only be the product of an aristocratic white family, then we are in some ways left with the noblesse oblige that Percy criticizes. Percy exposes a system of class identity based on racial paternalism as fundamentally flawed, dependent upon an essentialist binary distinction between black and white that inevitably breaks down. Nevertheless, in *The Last Gentleman* he at best only partially succeeds in creating a meaningful alternative to that flawed system, leaving us once again with the figure of an aristocratic white man who allegedly possesses a truer understanding of the relationship between white and black cultures as our savior—a figure who perhaps bears more resemblance to Will Percy's planter-father-figure than we, or Walker Percy, can be comfortable with.

If in *The Last Gentleman* Percy explores the necessity of deconstructing the false ideology of paternalism, in his next novel, *Love in the Ruins*, he examines what happens to a society that remains committed to that ideology. Further, instead of placing hope for the future in the figure of an unusual aristocratic white man, Percy offers an alternative, more communal model of resistance, an odd, patchwork assemblage—reminiscent of Reverend Goodyhay's congregation in Faulkner's *The Mansion*—that stands in stark contrast to the alienating conformity of the futuristic southern suburbs in which most of the novel is set. In the earlier novel we see a continuity between the plantation and the suburb; the gleaming purple golf-links mansion where Barrett's New South friends (whose money comes from selling cars, not cotton) live seems to have little in common on the surface with the aging plantation manor of southern lore, but a version of traditional plantation race relations thrives there despite the supposed encroachment of bland conformity. Thus, although Alex Harris, in his collection of photographs and short stories about the suburban south, *A New Life*, quite rightly cites Percy as a leader in the move to a southern fiction that is about more than "the legendary past of antebellum homes, poor black servants, struggling white farmers," and so on (xv), I would suggest that we should not too quickly treat the southern suburb—of the 1960s and 1970s at least—as antithetical to southern traditions of race and class; instead, we should look for the ways in which those traditions that we associate with the plantation survive, albeit perhaps in mutated, altered, and complicated forms, in this new environment and see what the manner of those transformations can tell us about the relationship between race and class in the 1960s and 1970s. If, as Percy has remarked, his fiction deals with the problem of a Quentin Compson who did not commit suicide, we might say that *Love in the Ruins* deals with a Will Barrett who did not leave the suburbs—and the diverse group of saviors who can rescue him from the prison of paternalist logic.

Written in 1971 but set in the near future of the early 1980s, *Love in the Ruins* chronicles the exploits of Dr. Tom More, a brilliant but delusional scientist who believes he has invented a device—an ontological lapsometer—that will enable him to heal the Cartesian rift separating mind from body and thus to save humankind. A self-confessed, self-committed mental patient as well as a psychiatrist, Tom fears an "unprecedented fallout of noxious particles" whose effects "are psychic rather than physical. They do not burn the skin and rot the marrow; rather do they inflame and worsen the secret ills of the spirit and rive the very self from itself" (5). However, Tom believes that he can both render people immune from the particles' effects and eliminate those "secret ills" entirely: he has created a device known as More's Quantitative-Qualitative Ontological Lapsometer, or MOQUOL. With this invention, he believes he can take readings of the brain's electrical activity, readings which then can "be correlated with the manifold woes of the Western world, its terrors and rages and murderous impulses" (28–29). The woes of the Western world, or at least the part of it Tom lives in, are manifold indeed. The novel's action takes place in a fictional Louisiana parish where political and racial tensions have reached a boiling point: the American Catholic Church has split from the Roman Catholic, left-wingers and right-wingers are irreconcilable, and Honey Island Swamp has become a haven for all kinds of derelicts, drop-outs, and ne'er-do-wells, including the Bantus, militant African Americans who have tired of waiting for a peaceful solution to the civil rights crisis and who now stage raids on outlying subdivisions and shopping centers. Tom More resides in one of these subdivisions, Paradise Estates, which he calls an "oasis of concord in a troubled land." According to Tom, in Paradise, "everyone gets along well, heathen and Christian, Jew and Gentile, Northerner and Southerner, liberal and conservative" (16). Such harmony conforms to Robert Fishman's concept of the suburb as a "bourgeois utopia": according to Fishman, "suburbia is more than a collection of residential buildings; it . . . [is] a refuge . . . from threatening elements in the city . . . [and] also from discordant elements in bourgeois society itself. . . . [T]he suburban world of leisure, family life, and union with nature was based on the principle of exclusion" (4).

The plantation clearly influences the particular form that this exclusive utopia takes in Percy's fiction, the specific way in which this politically diverse group of wealthy white southerners forms consensus. Significantly, Tom's definition of "everyone" completely excludes African Americans and other minorities. As Kobre argues, "conservatives and liberals can live side by side happily in the segregated utopia of Paradise Estates as long as everyone tacitly agrees to forget or abridge the real history of America's racial trouble" (129). Although strongly held political positions sharply divide the denizens of Paradise, they find common ground in an attitude of paternalism toward African Americans. The residents of Paradise have taken the trend that Grace Hale observes—grounding the middle-class home in the images of the aristocratic antebellum South—to a comical extreme. Indeed, the showplace of Paradise is Tara, a reconstruction of Scarlett O'Hara's mansion drawn from what its first owner called the "original plans"—that is, the drawings of David O. Selznick's set designer. Further, Tom tells us that even the northerners who have moved south "have taken to Southern ways like ducks to water. They drink toddies and mint juleps and hold fish fries with hush puppies. Little black jockeys fish from mirrors in their front yards. Life-size mammy dolls preside over their patios" (16–17). According to Tom, although the African Americans in the area are generally held to be a bad lot, "Our servants in Paradise are the exceptions . . . [;] faithful black mammies who take care of our children as if they were their own, dignified gardeners who work and doff their caps in the old style" (17). He further observes, "Nearly everyone treats his servants well, picking them up in Happy Hollow and taking them home, allowing 'totin' privileges' and giving them 'Christmas gifs'" (17). At Christmas, the African American waiters at the Paradise country club dress up as Santa Claus: Tom tells us, "They grin sideways from their skewed Santa hoods and shout 'Christmas gif'! I give them money, a dollar, ten dollars, whatever" (91). Tom even recognizes among the obsequious Santas a man he knows, Willard Amadie, whose put-on "goofy Gullah accent" and subservient attitude contrast sharply with his past as a tough-as-nails career soldier. This reliance on African American labor that conforms to a plantation-based stereotype characterizes Paradise dwellers of all political persuasions. Tom notes, "When conservative Christian housewives drive to town to pick up their maids in the Hollow, the latter ride on the back seat in the old style. Liberal housewives make their maids ride on the front seat" (15).

Tom's description of this community, in which African Americans occupy roles based on an idealized version of antebellum race relations and in which wealthy whites bestow economic boons on needy servants, suggests that a form of racial paternalism is the glue that binds the citizens of Paradise together despite their political differences, solidifying a class identity that is based on a romanticized version of an Old South ideal. We might even perceive Paradise as an exaggerated form of the "aristocratic delusion" that James C. Cobb argued characterized middle-class residents of the Mississippi Delta, where, according to Cobb, the absence of a middle-class tradition forced "on middle-class whites the burden of shouldering an aristocratic heritage that was not really their own" (*Most Southern* 176).

However, Tom also reveals that the ostensible happiness of even these faithful servants may actually be a sham. In fact, they refuse to assimilate completely into the faux-antebellum system of Paradise Estates. Tom notes that, in addition to nouveau-plantation manors like Tara, Paradise also contains "the 'Quarters,' a long rowhouse, a ruin of soft warm brick which housed sugar-plantation slaves and which, set just above water level of the bayou, was thought of by the Paradise developers as a kind of Natchez-under-the-hill and so restored and reroofed for domestic servants, even a chapel added so that strains of good old spirituals would come floating up to our patios in the evening" (99). But the domestic servants refuse to live in the former slave quarters, choosing instead to reside in Happy Hollow, which Tom describes as a "hot airless hole" where "the sun slants down like a laser" (141). Significantly, only the very old and the very young live in Happy Hollow; most of the young men have become militant Bantus, who, as the story opens, have attempted to kidnap the female students from Valley Forge Academy—"founded on religious and patriotic principles and to keep the Negroes out"—and hold them hostage (12). The lack of social and economic opportunity plays an important role in African American feelings of disenfranchisement. Even the menial labor of tending the golf course and caddying for wealthy whites has been made redundant by technological advances such as the golf cart and, more fancifully, Tifton 451, a new kind of grass that never needs cutting. These dire straits have even driven some African Americans who once conformed to the Paradise-approved social roles to take up arms and withdraw from society to join the Bantu revolutionaries who reside in Honey Island Swamp. Tom recognizes one Bantu gunman as a man named Ely, who, Tom says, "was a bagboy at the A&P for forty years. What a transformation! . . . Forty years as a favorite at the A&P, toting bags to cars for housewives, saluting the tips, now he looks as if he'd just as soon [shoot] me as not" (312).

Tom attempts to portray himself as above this fray, dodging Bantu snipers and other dangers only so that he can prevent his invention from falling into the wrong hands and so avert a massive catastrophe. To his credit, he does at times evince a more open attitude about race than some of his neighbors. For instance, he belongs not to the thriving, overtly racist American Catholic Church but to the barely surviving Roman Catholic Church, a ragtag multiracial flock that counts among its membership "two freejacks, light-skinned sloe-eyed men of color" (188). Nor does Tom discriminate in his medical practice: he serves white policemen and Bantu revolutionaries alike, often without hope of compensation (11). Further, he professes to be tired of the "ancient spurious friendship" between black and white that characterizes the paternalistic interaction between one of his neighbors and a young African American boy, and he has no patience with his mother's attitude toward her domestic servants (289).

Nevertheless, Percy suggests that a reductive racial paternalism can thrive even in the most ostensibly liberal of reformers. Percy also makes clear that Tom is more committed to the paternalist ideals that unite the citizens of Paradise than he reveals, that his profession of disinterest simply disguises a deeply rooted sense of paternalism. In fact, Tom believes that many of the problems befalling his future American society stem from the failure of whites to behave in the paternalist manner that William Alexander Percy would have found familiar—a failure to "protect and defend" their "younger brother." Tom speculates, "Was it the nigger business from the beginning? What a bad joke: God saying, here it is, the new Eden, and it is yours because you're the apple of my eye . . .

and all you had to do was pass one little test . . . [;] here's a helpless man in Africa, all you have to do is not violate him. That's all. One little test: you flunk!" (57). Though he will of course not admit it, Tom sees himself as the greatest paternalist of all, the enlightened white scientist who best understands the South's racial situation and will gladly put it right for little more than the thanks of an adoring throng. Tom hopes to, through his lapsometer, correct this terrible mistake, to bridge "the dread chasm that has rent the soul of Western man." Indeed, Tom believes that this healing is necessary to bring an end to racial strife: in a moment of grand delusion, he sees himself as the new Christ who will bring the races together (153). Significantly, Tom's vision of himself as the new Christ follows quickly after a scene in which Victor Charles urges Tom to forsake his solitude and rejoin him, the racist Leroy Ledbetter, and the rest of the community at the "shrimp jubilee," a now-defunct annual festival. Tom expresses shock at Victor's request: "Here's a black Southerner making common cause—against me!—with a white Southerner who wouldn't give him the time of day" (149). The class implications of the word "common" here are suggestive: Tom's messianic hallucination represents a fearful response to the possibility that an African American man might choose to make "common cause" with a less aristocratic white man, thus threatening the paternalistic relationship that gives his life meaning. Paternalism, Percy suggests, exerts a powerful influence over even those who claim to have grown beyond such traditional boundaries.

Tom continues to reveal inadvertently that his vision for the salvation of Western man is as exclusive as his posh suburb. In an interesting choice of words, he claims that his device will allow humans to "reenter paradise, so to speak" (36). Percy's pun makes us aware that all may not be as it seems with Tom's lapsometer. Though he claims that it will ostensibly protect "humankind" from the coming catastrophe, he also claims that it will not work on African Americans. As he tells the mysterious Art Immelman, "My sensors won't penetrate melanin pigment in the skin" (200). Thus, only white people could attain the metaphysical wholeness and freedom from rage and depression that Tom's device promises, and only white people could survive the imminent catastrophe unscarred. Significantly, Tom's friend Dusty Rhoades shrewdly notes that the device seems intended to affirm and reinforce only a specifically classed form of whiteness, as well. He asks Tom, "Is that thing nonpartisan? . . . Does it also measure alcoholism, treachery, laziness, and white trash morals?" (87).

Thus, paternalism proves to be particularly insidious. Tom desires the nationwide spread of what he imagines to be "mature" Western values, the extension of the wonders of whiteness even to his "junior brothers." While we might wish to consider the MOQUOL's bigotry as an incidental design flaw, Tom's own contradictory narration actually suggests that he has imposed this limitation himself, whether consciously or not. Though he insists on the lapsometer's inability to "read" black people, he also, with no acknowledgment of the apparent paradox, claims that he has used it to diagnose the mind and soul of his colleague, the African American scientist Colley Wilkes: "He had good readings at layer I, little or nothing at layer II. Diagnosis: a self successfully playing at being a self that is not itself" (112). I would suggest that this contradiction results neither from novelistic ineptitude on Percy's part nor from an insignificantly anomalous quirk on the lapsometer's part. In fact, this curious irregularity supports the notion of Tom as a crusader committed to preserving not all of humanity but only that portion of it that conforms to certain norms. Tom always carefully sets Colley apart from the novel's other African Americans. He labels him a "super-Negro," an epithet that implies that he believes Colley has somehow transcended the supposed limitations of his race. However, Tom suggests that Colley has not gained his equality simply as an intelligent and talented black man but, rather, by overcoming his blackness: Colley is "one of those super-Negroes who speak five languages, quote the sutras, and are wizards in electronics as well" (29). Later, he reemphasizes the point, calling Colley "a super-Negro, a regular black Leonardo. He is the chief encephalographer, electronics wizard, ornithologist, holds the Black Belt in karate, does the crossword in the Sunday *Times*" (107–8). Thus Tom's lapsometer will diagnose Colley because Colley has assumed the type of identity that Tom recognizes and accepts as valid and worthy of salvation and preservation. Tom inadvertently reveals this prejudice in a conversation with Uru, the Bantu leader. Uru asks Tom point blank, "You really don't think we're any good, do you? . . . I'm talking about greatness, Doctor. Or what you call greatness. I'm talking about the Fifth Symphony, the *Principia Mathematica*, the Uranus guidance system" (299). When Tom does begin to suggest an area of greatness, Uru cuts him off: "And don't tell me about music and rhythm and all" (300). Tom falls silent, for he cannot apprehend "greatness" according to any terms but those of the dominant culture, and he therefore considers African American culture unworthy of preservation. Clearly, then, Percy suggests that Tom's device fails to work on African Americans because of a cultural bias, not a dermatological one.

Thus, though Tom wishes to portray himself as above the political, racial, and class differences that fracture the South, he reveals himself as committed to maintaining the values of an oppressive status quo. At bottom, his aims are still those of the racial paternalist—to impose an allegedly superior set of values on an ostensibly ignorant Other. Indeed, in the novel's final chapter, Percy reveals just how committed to this order Tom really is. Though no great catastrophe befalls the citizens of Feliciana Parish, great social upheaval occurs when the Bantus discover oil in Honey Island Swamp. They use their new wealth to purchase all the houses in Paradise Estates and establish a new social order only superficially different from the old—that is, they represent their success in the terms of the paternalist, faux-antebellum system that so long oppressed them. Aside from their colorful Bantu robes and the fact that they worship Longhu6, the god of the winter solstice, and not Jesus, little has changed; the Bantu mayor of the town lives in Tara, and the Bantus charitably care for poor whites in the area: Tom tells us that Colley Wilkes and his wife fixed over a hundred Christmas baskets for impoverished "peckerwood" children. Nor has this new system ushered in an age of integration and equality—Tom can't use the hospital because the Bantu medical society won't let him in, and his African American friends caution him, "You can sometimes accomplish more by not rocking the boat" (389). Colley tells him, "Rome wasn't built in a day. . . . These things take time, Tom. . . . Rest assured . . . that some of us are working on it" (389).

Significantly, however, Tom has few complaints about the new arrangement because, I would argue, he is in fact so committed to the system of rigid class and race distinctions that validate life in Paradise that, if he cannot play the role of the wealthy paternalist in that system, he will gladly accept the role of simple, rural, humble Other. Tom notes, "I don't have to listen to 'Christmas gif,' Doc!' and I don't have to worry about tipping. Instead, I get tipped" (395). Moreover, Tom still uses his lapsometer for the maintenance of the status quo: now that nearly all the Bantus have attained the sort of Western "greatness" that he recognizes, Tom has no trouble making "magic passes" with his machine and diagnosing their metaphysical selfhood. Indeed, Tom even refers to one of his Bantu patients as an "Orientalized heathen Englishman" (393). Most significantly, he and his new wife make their home in the slave quarters the domestic servants once disdained: he says, "Ellen and I are poor. We live with our children in the old Quarters. Constructed of slave brick worn porous and rounded at the corners like sponges, the apartments are surprisingly warm in winter, cool in summer" (381). Tom claims for himself those qualities which he—and William Alexander Percy—once claimed the African American servants possessed. For instance, as he hoes collard greens, he tells us, "Poor as I am, I feel like God's spoiled child" (383). Colley need not worry about Tom "rocking the boat." Indeed, he claims to enjoy his new life, and most of Percy's readers have taken him at his word here as well; they believe that Tom's new position greatly improves upon his last. For instance, Lewis Lawson claims that "although he is poor, he is happy" (203). Howland believes that Tom "ekes out a happy life" (80), and Ciuba argues that Tom "gains a renewed sense of the world" because the "sensuous bounty found in poverty's bare simplicity differs from his former surfeit of objects and experiences in the old world of Paradise Estates" (166). J. Gerald Kennedy, who refers to Tom's "theory of poverty" as "mawkish" (134), is one of the few critics who sees any irony in Tom's situation. Still, I would suggest that, positively as we might take Tom's claim to be "God's spoiled child" in a more religious-centered reading of this novel, no one so well-versed as Percy is in the clichés and language used to characterize and justify the oppression of African Americans could write such a sentence without being aware of, for instance, his own adoptive father's characterization of African Americans as the fortunate spoiled children of nature, people "who smile sunshine and ask no questions and understand" (*Lanterns* 296).

Ultimately, then, Percy satirizes this type of blind commitment to a class structure founded in racial paternalism as leading to an inability to imagine alternate forms of race and class interaction, alternate, nonoppressive models of identity and of political participation—a failure of imagination that Will Barrett ultimately transcends. However, although

Tom's myopia makes him a bad savior, Percy locates some hope in the character of Victor Charles, an African American who, though he once conformed to the paternalist conception of what African Americans should be and do, has managed to cast off that yoke without repeating the mistakes of the Bantus; he approaches Tom to tell him he is running for Congress and to invite him to join his new political coalition. He tells Tom, "I got the Bantu vote . . . [; they] are willing to go with me. Chuck Parker's helping me with the swamp people. Max is working on the liberals. Leroy Ledbetter's got the peckerwoods. You could swing the Catholics" (401). While Tom slavishly adheres to the nouveau-plantation ideology that offers him an identity, Victor demonstrates his ability to work outside that system, to put together what Tom calls a "funny fouled-up coalition" in the spirit of "Kennedy, Evers, Goldberg, Stevenson, L. Q. C. Lamar" (401), one that will work for social justice and possibly break the deadlock between the opposing political factions. Victor, it seems, can see contemporary southern society in all its complexity. Perhaps Tom can learn to see it the same way; his acceptance of Victor's offer might well be the necessary first step.

As *The Last Gentleman* and *Love in the Ruins* indicate, the legacy of racial paternalism in the post–World War II, civil-rights-era South was of crucial concern for Walker Percy. In both novels, he suggests that traditional attitudes toward race and class, especially the emphasis on paternalism as a way of defining the aristocrat, have failed, and that those who seek to perpetuate them will ultimately find themselves trapped and isolated as southern society continues to change. Tom More's humble position at the end of *Love in the Ruins* is but a comically exaggerated example of the marginalization facing southerners who cling to an ideology of race and class drawn from a romanticized ideal of antebellum race relations. Instead, Percy argues, white southerners should put aside any claim to aristocracy or class that depends on ignoring the complexity of individuals of other races or classes and embrace a "funny fouled-up coalition" that better exemplifies the complicated nature of southern life. Such a vision of coalitional politics is not necessarily radical, even for 1971; however, Percy dramatizes just how difficult realizing the necessity of even such a practical solution can be when southerners are blinded by outmoded ideologies of race and class.

CONCLUSION

FROM "PET NEGRO" TO "MAGIC NEGRO"
Hyperreal Paternalism

I want to linger for a moment over Walker Percy's wry prophecy about the golf course of the future. Extending a curve whose literary origin point is *The Sound and the Fury,* Percy in *The Last Gentleman* describes a South in which aristocrats live in golf communities, not plantation manors. In *Love in the Ruins,* Percy extends this arc to a comical extreme and imagines that the invention of Tifton 451, a self-maintaining grass, has ushered in an ostensibly utopian age in which duffers amble across links that never need cutting. Thus, though the labor of landscaping and groundskeeping may have temporarily served as a modern version of the plantation's agricultural work for the South's African American workers, the development of Tifton 451 has rendered even that labor unnecessary. The already thin tether of labor relations binding together white and black Louisianans in the novel is thus frayed almost to its final strand. Percy identifies a moment in which the only need that whites have for African Americans is strictly symbolic, in which black people continue to help them satisfy a certain ideal of themselves, but the traditional network of social and economic relations from which that ideal developed has become almost unrecognizable. The "plantation airs" put on by his white characters are gradually losing their reference even to a distorted view of their current relationship to black characters or to a skewed interpretation of history. Instead, they are beginning to refer solely to other simulations, as in the case of Tom's paramour Lola's suburban "Tara," modeled on the set designs for *Gone with the Wind*—"a real without origin or reality: a hyperreal," as Jean Baudrillard would have it (166).[1]

If I can keep us on the links just a little longer, I'd like to draw a connection between *Love in the Ruins* and the 2000 film *The Legend of Bagger Vance* in order to help us understand one important way in which racial paternalism has survived into the contemporary moment as a kind of hyperreal. Set in Depression-era Savannah, Georgia, the film tells the story of Rannulph Junuh, a Savannah golf hero who, emotionally devastated after the horror of World War I and withdrawn deep into a bottle (and even deeper into his family's decaying, gothic mansion, all cobwebbed chandeliers and musty-sheeted furniture), is lured back onto the course to play a high-stakes game against legends Bobby Jones and Walter Hagen. Although he is hailed as a "gentle-born chevalier" by an adoring hometown crowd, he only regains his former confidence and athletic prowess with the aid of Bagger Vance, a mysterious African American caddy who emerges during a particularly dark and stormy night of Junuh's soul with a mouthful of folksy-cum-new-age wisdom about harmony, rhythm, and the "authentic swing" inside all of us.

It is not hard to see Bagger as an updated (if only barely) version of Will Percy's Ford or Fannin's servant Merriam in *The Last Gentleman*, black men alleged to have "magic and incantatory facult[ies]" (*Last Gentleman* 268) that give them special insights into the workings of nature, men who embody a connection to the rhythms of the world that ostensibly more civilized white paternalists have lost. But what interests me here is that while Will Percy had a long-term, complicated personal and economic relationship with Ford (as did Fannin and Merriam, or Jim Meserve and Joe Kelsey, or the Fairchilds and their workers), Junuh's relationship with Bagger Vance is of a singularly fleeting and even spectral nature. Bagger has no history with Junuh or his family: Junuh didn't frolic under the watchful eye of Bagger's mother, nor did their fathers once fish together as children in an ostensible Edenic golden age. The economic relationship between the two men is complex as well. Bagger only accepts compensation for his services as a caddy according to a curious agreement: he will take exactly five dollars for his services. Although it may seem as though naming his price for his expertise would mean that he is placing himself outside a mystified paternalistic relationship to mansion-dwelling Junuh, the film makes a point of stressing that as his caddy Vance is actually entitled to 10 percent of Junuh's winnings; with a top prize of $10,000, Vance stands to take home a thousand of his own, and during the Great Depression no less. Thus the five-dollar fee he charges is so meager as to be purely symbolic. In this transaction, as on another occasion when he asks Junuh for his castoff golf shoes, Vance deliberately places himself in a position similar to that of the "pet Negro," receiving favors, not wages, from his aristocratic employer. But, unlike other "pets" such as Joe Kelsey or Merriam, Vance does not otherwise have anything to do with Junuh's life, does not stick around to caddy for him again or to take up residence on the grounds of Junuh's surely soon-to-be-restored manor. Instead, he vanishes before Junuh sinks his last putt to win the match, resisting what I can only assume must be an overwhelming temptation to say, "my work here is done."

The relationship between Junuh and Vance in *The Legend of Bagger Vance* is an allegory for one way in which racial paternalism is deployed in the contemporary South. This paternalism is very much of the sort predicted by Percy, a paternalism that is simply a series of strictly symbolic gestures on the part of the white paternalist—and, I should say, *profitable* symbolic gestures, as Junuh's appearance in the tournament guarantees that his long-suffering sweetheart Adele can keep the debt-ridden golf resort that she inherited. These gestures are only for the benefit of the gesturer: they have no meaningful influence on the lives of the African Americans who are ostensibly their objects, nor do they forge even the most fraught and blinkered bond between paternalist and "pet." The crucial aspect of Bagger's character is that, as far as the political, social, and economic life of Savannah is concerned, *he does not exist:* he is a specter, a cipher, a wraith who wanders through town simply so that Junuh can make a few public demonstrations of lordly goodwill and thereby both earn some money and regain his sense of himself as a "noble-born chevalier." As Rita Kempley has noted, Vance is the very embodiment of what director Spike Lee has called the "magical Negro," a mystical supporting player who only exists in order to help the white protagonist become a better person.[2] It is telling that the final shots of Bagger Vance are of him alone and in silhouette: his individual features are lost to shadow, and he is represented as an absence, a hole, a receptacle into which Junuh can very publicly deposit his "waste" (as Veblen might put it) without fear that the receptacle will demand anything in return.

Thus, *The Legend of Bagger Vance* allegorizes contemporary southern racial paternalism as consumption in its purest form, narcissistic in the extreme. Amy Elias suggests that this narcissism is widespread and insidious in her essay "Postmodern Southern Vacation," in which she offers an insightful analysis of the ways in which travel advertisements in *Southern*

Living magazine appeal to middle- and upper-class southerners' desires to identify with the images and ideals of an imagined version of Old South aristocracy, including racial paternalism. Elias describes the South of *Southern Living* as "a stylized magazine country with an almost adolescent narcissism—consumed with itself, checking itself out in the mirror, practicing its walk, yet also filled with a defensive confidence about who it is" (257). In a South where "lives become 'lifestyles,'" she continues, "southern regional identity is fast being redefined as postmodern simulation, which Jean Baudrillard defined some time ago as an image, created by the media and the market, without a referent" (258). Not surprisingly, the golf course figures prominently in one ad for the Hyatt Regency at Hilton Head Island. Elias argues that this advertisement, which features an image of a young African American man on a golf course dressed in a manner that evokes images of the "lawn jockey," "encode[s] subliminal references to Old South plantation-slave economies in order to sell the values of that former time" (267).

As Elias goes on to assert, the advertisements that appear in *Southern Living* emerge from a complicated nexus of regional, national, and international business interests—as does *The Legend of Bagger Vance*, of course. Elias urges that rather than simply pointing out that the South has become hyperreal, we instead "pay more attention to how this fantasy South, the postmodern South of simulation and desire, is being constructed" and examine the "ways communities are taking charge of this representation" in an era of globalization (275). This attempt to "take charge" of representation is at the heart of Tom Wolfe's *A Man in Full* (1998), a novel which chronicles the fall of Charlie Croker, a poor Georgian who rises to become a powerful real estate developer in Atlanta. Croker's ruination is brought about partly because he is caught in the transition that Elias describes between "lives" and "lifestyles." Though a clever manipulator of paternalism, Charlie also clings to the belief that applying the old rules of reality to the new world of hyperreality will produce similar results. In one sense, it is possible to read Croker's downfall as a result of his failure to fully grasp the underlying truth spoken by *Bagger Vance*—that contemporary paternalism is only profitable insofar as it treats the objects of its attention as ephemeral.

In his youth, Charlie was but a hard-luck "Cracker" whose father worked in the pulp mill, "a horrible freak show of men with fingers and eyes missing" (77). Now, however, that young boy has reinvented himself as "Cap'm Charlie Croker," the lord of Turpmtime Plantation, a striking blend of antebellum and modern attributes: "Twenty-nine thousand acres of prime southwest Georgia forest, fields, and swamp! And all of it, every square inch of it, every beast that moved on it, all fifty-nine horses, all twenty-two mules, all forty dogs, all thirty-six buildings that stood upon it, plus a mile-long asphalt landing strip, complete with jet fuel pumps and a hanger—all of it was his" (4). Charlie uses the plantation to identify himself with an aristocratic antebellum ideal. His African American employees call him "Captain Charlie, or just Cap'm" (40–41) in the manner of the master/slave relationships of yore. Indeed, the workers Charlie employs are the descendants of the plantation's first laborers, and Charlie sees himself—and his corporation—as filling the same paternalist role that their masters did then: "He told of how Croker Global was today one of the biggest employers of unskilled black labor in that part of Georgia. He told of black workers tending the plats, black workers tending the horses, black workers tilling the soil, black workers preserving the ecology of Turpmtime's eight thousand acres of swamp" (55). He continues, "These are Turpmtime folks who count on Croker Global as the one steady rock in their lives" (55).

Most importantly, however, Charlie's pretensions to paternalism do not merely signify his upper-crust status. In fact, Charlie uses his antebellum, aristocratic associations as a tool to gain more wealth. Certainly, Jim Meserve does the same in *Seraph;* however, while paternalism simply helps Jim organize African American labor, it helps Charlie attract powerful investors. As Martyn Bone, a perceptive and insightful reader of this novel, notes, "Charlie uses the plantation's simulated Old Southernness to woo potential corporate tenants" (214), and his servants "perform a crucial role in the seduction of Charlie's real-estate clients: they provide an authentic sheen of slavelike labor to the plantation's simulated Old South" (214–15). Charlie deploys the images and symbols of the Old South to affirm his own authority and desirability as a business partner. When financier Herb Richman comes to visit, Charlie reflects that the magic of Turpmtime lies in creating a "luxurious bygone world in which there were masters and servants and everybody knew his place" (277). He tells an affectionate story about one of his employees, Uncle Bud, and the narrator notes, "He didn't have to explain who Uncle Bud was. He merely had to say his name in a certain way, and one and all would realize that he was some sort of faithful old retainer, probably black" (277). Further, Charlie forces another employee, Mason, to detail the wonderful deeds Charlie has done for his family so that his guests will be awed by his paternalistic benevolence (282). Charlie's paternalism is a self-conscious act, a performance he deliberately deploys because he perceives that creating himself in the image of a plantation lord makes him seem like a sound investment.

Of course, unlike the more spectral "magic Negro" figure of Bagger Vance, Cap'm Charlie's employees do get something out of this deal, and at times Charlie's affection for them seems quite genuine. However, later in the novel we discover that his commitment to the ideals of paternalism does not place him above staging other types of racial performances when it suits the needs of his pocketbook. Charlie's creditors, fed up with his constant evasions, threaten to expose the shenanigans by which he lowered the price of some much desired real estate in Cherokee County enough for him to acquire it. Charlie enlisted the aid of Andre Fleet, a crusading African American politician, and Darwell Scruggs, a former high school classmate and current Ku Klux Klan member, to stage a racially charged confrontation that made Cherokee County seem like an undesirable place to develop indeed. As Charlie watches the old news footage his creditors sent him to remind him of his shady dealings, he sees "Andre Fleet leading his placard-carrying black protestors from Atlanta through Canton, the county seat. There was Darwell Scruggs, albeit not in white raiment and pointy hood, screaming vile racial imprecations along with a pack of raggedy youths" (596). This display allows Charlie "to assemble his land in this viciously slandered county for about $200,000, one-twentieth of what it would have cost before Andre Fleet and Darwell Scruggs did their duet" (596). However, to characterize Charlie as simply a shrewd, capable, and cynical manipulator of race and class would not be entirely accurate; after all, when he is faced with the necessity of laying off a large part of his work force, he chooses to retain the servants at Turpmtime and drastically reduce the number of employees at a California warehouse. As Bone notes, "Charlie's desire to maintain his paternalistic, simulated, Old South sense of place at Turpmtime has an all-too-real impact on the lives of workers elsewhere in the Croker Global corporation" (215). Thus, in this novel the drive of acquisitive, competitive capitalism does not entirely supersede the moral obligations of paternalism. Nevertheless, this desire to maintain his ideal of himself as an Old South aristocrat is undercut because his strategy—making room on his payroll for his plantation workers by eliminating warehouse laborers—is ill suited for a contemporary South in which, as *The Legend of Bagger Vance* demonstrates, racial paternalism is most effective as a purely symbolic construct with no reference to real labor relations.

My purpose in briefly discussing *A Man in Full* and *The Legend of Bagger Vance* is not to offer an exhaustive analysis of their engagement with race, class, and economics but, rather, merely to suggest some of the complicated ways in which the ideas discussed in this book continue to have relevance in the contemporary South. A detailed study of the ways in which race and class overlap and inform one another in the South since the early 1970s must take into account the influence of a wide array of events including the Vietnam War, the return of large numbers of African Americans to the South from which their ancestors fled, and the increasing suburbanization of the South. Certainly, the growth of African American political power in the South has further complicated the use of paternalism to establish an aristocratic class position. As David Goldfield points out, "between 1975 and 1985 more than 850,000 blacks moved south, compared with slightly more than 500,000 blacks who left" (244). These immigrants were attracted, he says, "without ancillary pulls such as kin or place but with the promise of upward mobility" (245). He cites in particular an ironic reversal in the electoral landscape of rural Alabama. Writing in 1990, Goldfield notes, "So thorough is black power in rural Alabama that outnumbered whites are calling for federal examiners, while black leaders urge the federal government to stay out of local politics—a familiar refrain from an unfamiliar source" (230). Such power both reflects and furthers the growth of the black middle class, though, to be sure, African American poverty continues to be a major problem in the rural south, and a rise in income and status does not necessarily protect more well-to-do African Americans from the effects of racism (247). However, the South's larger economic progress sometimes obscures this suffering.

As I hope I've demonstrated, the idea of "class" in the South is much more complicated and confounding than readers of southern literature have fully understood. Fred Hobson has written that "any honest discussion of contemporary southern life must increasingly lie" at the "treacherous intersection of race and class" (147). I would extend Hobson's claim here simply by making it plural: there are many such intersections, not only one, each with its own set of internal dynamics that requires close attention. In many ways, the relationship between racial paternalism and class is the most slippery of these intersections, precisely because of the ways that paternalism seeks to mystify and conceal the very idea of class itself, to render the construction and maintenance of class invisible as an object of critical inquiry. It is my hope that by rendering class and the multiplicity of its "treacherous" intersections with race visible in southern studies we might come to a better understanding of the various ways in which southern literature has been affected by these intersections as well as the ways in which it has attempted to intervene—to direct (or divert) traffic through the intersection.

NOTES

INTRODUCTION

1. Such critical studies include Sylvia Jenkins Cook's important *From Tobacco Road to Route 66: The Southern Poor White in Fiction* (1976), Duane Carr's *A Question of Class: The Redneck Stereotype in Southern Fiction* (1996), and Matthew Guinn's illuminating *After Southern Modernism: Fiction of the Contemporary South* (2000). Patricia Yaeger's *Dirt and Desire: Reconstructing Southern Women's Writing, 1930–1990* (2000) takes aim at a number of the field's familiar shibboleths, but I am most interested in her treatment of the ways in which "literature by southern women explores a radically dislocated surface landscape filled with jagged white signifiers and pallid detritus that bespeaks a constant uneasiness about the meaning of whiteness" (20). Her insightful readings of works such as Eudora Welty's *Delta Wedding* and Ellen Douglas's *Can't Quit You, Baby* note in particular how the wealthy white women of those texts build their posh lifestyles on the backs of African American servants, a system that threatens to break down when they are forced, sometimes in shocking and violent ways, to view their servants as individuals. Of course, the analyses discussed above represent only a sampling of the work on race and class in southern fiction. Some critics have dealt with more complicated issues of class in articles or books on particular authors, and I will deal with those studies in later chapters.

2. I should stress that "paternalism" in this study always means "interracial paternalism" unless otherwise specified. Intraracial *white* paternalism also existed in the South, of course. As Joel Williamson points out, contemporary observers of the rapidly growing textile industry in the turn-of-the-century South saw the relationship between the nearly all-white mill town and the mill owners as "a direct translation into the realities of the New South of the Old South values of *noblesse oblige*, paternalism, loyalty, and service," but with poor whites instead of blacks as the recipients of elite benevolence (431). At the time, the popular conception held that the mill represented "the southern community in harmony with itself and with the real and modern world. Master, trained to care for slaves on the plantations of the Old South, now brought capital and a kindly management to the white workers in the factories of the New" (434). Indeed, many textile managers believed they were effecting "the salvation of the lower class of whites by a patrician leadership" (432), and they "were convinced of their own paternalism. There was a feeling among them that they not only protected their white neighbors and cousins from the threat of black labor, but they also provided them with a life well above the level of bare subsistence" (434). I would not wish to ignore the significance of this white paternalism for the South, and I am particularly interested in the manner in which this system, as Williamson describes it, seems to equate lower-class whites with African Americans and thus complicates the

"whiteness" of a poor white. However, I would argue that, as my readings of individual texts will demonstrate, white paternalism did not do the same social work in creating social class in the South that racial paternalism did.

3. I should note that the collaboration between planters and industrialists that Cobb identifies was not only a phenomenon of the late nineteenth and the twentieth century. George Fitzhugh, for instance, argued in pre–Civil War works such as *Sociology for the South* (1854) and *Cannibals All! or Slaves without Masters* (1857) that the South should welcome industrialization but should preserve the institution of slavery and avoid the capitalist system of free wage labor at all costs. In *Cannibals All!* he claims that "the unrestricted exploitation of so-called free society, is more oppressive to the laborer than domestic slavery" (5), and that "capital, irresponsible capital begets, and ever will beget, the *immedicabile vulnus* of so-called Free Society" (202).

CHAPTER 1. Zora Neale Hurston's *Seraph on the Suwanee*

1. Though I am treating Hurston's rendering of Larraine and Carl's dialect as a straightforward attempt to represent a poor white southern style of speech that did, as Hurston claimed, have much in common with poor *black* southern styles of speech, Claudia Tate has offered a compelling and intriguing alternative hypothesis. According to Tate, Hurston intentionally put black dialect in the mouths of white characters, a strategy that "carnivalizes the presumption that discernible racial differences are the natural basis of segregation and discrimination" (390).

2. Of course, this essay is not the first to address issues of class in *Seraph on the Suwanee*. In "From the Suwanee to Egypt, There's No Place Like Home," Cynthia Ward discusses the implications of literacy for class formation. Ward does touch on issues of race, as when she claims that Arvay's "secure place in the ethnic hierarchy—embraced by her in numerous demonstrations of racism—is threatened by Jim's class position, which has less need for overtly racist classification" (81). I would agree that Jim's class position is not authorized by "overt racism," at least not in the ways that Arvay demonstrates, but, as I will discuss, it is absolutely bound up with if not rac*ist,* then rac*ialized* systems of classification. I would disagree with Ward, then, when she argues that Arvay "initiates an identity based on not a fixed racial or ethnic other but a classed other," her sister Larraine (82); clearly, Arvay's separation from Larraine is crucial, but she fully manages this separation only through a performance of a class role that requires a "fixed racial other." Similarly, I would agree with Laura Dubek's claim in "The Social Geography of Race in Hurston's *Seraph on the Suwanee*" that Hurston exposes "race as a social construct and racism as a system of oppression inextricably linked to the production and perpetuation of an upwardly mobile, morally impoverished white middle class" (344). Moreover, she notes that Jim, "because of his class background . . . knows the social behaviors and manipulations that make for gender, race, and class power" (350). Yet Dubek often includes very different kinds of racialized practices under the "white power" umbrella and does not explore the class implications of these variations that are the focus of my study. John Lowe, in turn, highlights the importance of class in *Seraph* when he argues that "Hurston wrote her 'white book' partly because removing race from her central field of interest made possible a more

intense focus on gender but particularly class" (261). I would argue, however, that while class is indeed central, Hurston's depiction and critique of class in the South is inextricably bound up with her ideas about race. Most recently, Christopher Rieger has persuasively argued in "The Working-Class Pastoral of Zora Neale Hurston's *Seraph on the Suwanee*" that the novel offers an "ambivalent portrait of the conversion of the Florida wilderness for human subsistence and profit" (107). However, Rieger argues, Hurston ultimately resolves this ambivalence by "present[ing] Jim's relationship with nature in positive terms and [. . . thus creating] what I call a 'working-class pastoral' that affirms the value of knowing nature through labor. . . . Hurston presents the natural world as a relatively egalitarian arena in which an individual like Jim can improve his family's economic and class standing" (107). I find Rieger's argument compelling, though I argue that Hurston treats Jim's rise to power and prominence must less positively; I will engage with some of the specific areas at which Rieger and I differ in the essay.

3. Despite Hurston's growing conservatism, her letters from the 1940s indicate that, while she might not have agreed with all the ideals of liberal white reformers, she remained an ardent opponent of Jim Crow and a keen observer of racial politics. When journalist Douglas Gilbert quoted Hurston as endorsing segregation, Hurston wrote him a letter in which she insisted that though she described middle-class southern African Americans as "hold[ing] a sort of prestige in their communities, which they would lose in the North" (477), she did not intend this to mean that "Negroes are better off in the South than in the North" (476). Near the end of the letter she puts her feelings bluntly: "My stand is that the South is wrong, but the North is not guiltless. It is only a matter of opportunity and degree" (477). In a letter to Claude Barnett regarding the interview, Hurston wrote, "I deny categorically that I ever said that Negroes were better off in the South. . . . Neither did I approve of segregation in the South or anywhere else. I said that it was frankly established" (474–75).

4. Delia Konzett claims that Hurston "saw herself as depicting and imagining a New South in which the sociocultural bonds between blacks and whites are staged and thereby acknowledged, leading to a better understanding of the complex relationships between these two races" (134). Moreover, continues Konzett, "Hurston suggests . . . that this publicly staged and official racialized behavior is only the veneer of a much stronger and deeper bond that [Jim and Joe] acknowledge and confirm in private actions" (140). Similarly, John Lowe argues that Jim has a strong "appreciation for black people and their culture" and that Joe Kelsey and his family "bring laughter, rich folk culture, and a sense of community to Jim and Arvay. Jim, and eventually Arvay as well, find social fulfillment and companionship through their relationship with the Kelseys, especially through verbal joking and dueling and humor-infused gossip and tale-telling" (285–86). I would agree with Lowe and Konzett that a measure of genuine friendship and camaraderie exists between the Kelseys and the Meserves; however, because their verbal and physical interactions in the text fit so easily into an insidious paternalist framework that permits, even encourages, affection and exploitation to exist simultaneously, I would argue that the possibility that that friendship will develop into a true, deep understanding is always constrained, and perhaps completely foreclosed, by the complicated nexus of race and class relations the characters inhabit and by the roles they are expected to perform.

5. Moreover, we have good reason to doubt Hurston's faith in paternalism in the citrus industry specifically. In a piece entitled "The Ocoee Riot" written for the WPA, Hurston describes racial violence and the failure of paternalism to protect even an innocent African American man, July Perry, in Florida's citrus country. When a mob of angry whites, searching for a black man who had the temerity to attempt to vote, hear that the man has been seen with Perry, they decide to burn his house down and kill him. As Hurston writes, Perry "loaded his high-powered rifle and waited, at the same time unwilling to believe that the white people with whom he had worked and associated so long would permit the irresponsibles from the Winter Garden to harm him or his things" (149).

6. As Susan Meisenhelder has noted, "being Jim's 'pet Negro' does not fundamentally alter Joe's servitude" (96). She further argues that "even though Jim sees his role as one of benevolent protector of his pet (a role Joe never disputes), the money Joe receives from Jim cuts him off from his roots and finally culturally impoverishes him" (114). Though he does not deal explicitly with class, in *The Fugitive Race: Minority Writers Resisting Whiteness* Stephen P. Knadler offers an intriguing reading of this scene and other intimate moments shared by Jim and Joe and Jim and Jeff as highly eroticized, homosocial if not homosexual, and part of Hurston's project to "destabilize sexual and racial borders from within the New South's nationalism by confronting the reader with a similar anxiety about the legibility of the homosexual. As often as the novel scripts the story of Jim and Jeff in terms of southern plantation myths, it as frequently displaces this commonplace view with oppositional forms of white and black homo-masculinity" (174–75).

7. Though *Seraph*'s narrative, focused as it is on Jim and Arvay, depicts the black workers' favorable disposition toward Jim as more or less sincere and uncomplicated, a telling passage from a Hurston piece specifically about the citrus industry suggests that that friendliness may, of course, be a pose intended to secure their material well-being. Hurston interviews John C. "Seaboard" Hamilton, "reputed to be the fastest orange picker in Florida," who tells her about the "field foreman" (Jim's first job in the citrus business): "Sometimes we get mad at him, but we are careful not to *call* him anything" (135).

8. Here, Dubek argues that Arvay's objections reveal "a selfish but also racist attitude: Drawing on the pervasive stereotype of blacks as thieves, Arvay cannot recognize them as unpaid or underpaid workers who desperately need any scrap they can use. Arvay's social position within the racist order not only prevents her from recognizing the labor of people of color, it guarantees that she will profit from such labor" (346). But, in fact this commonplace type of racism that Dubek ascribes to Arvay's position in the "racist order" prevents her from fully attaining the highest class position and from getting the most profit out of black labor.

9. Although the model of "conspicuous consumption" that I utilize in this study is drawn from the works of Weber and Veblen, Thomas Haddox has noted in "The Logic of Expenditure in *Their Eyes Were Watching God*" that the work of sociologist Georges Bataille is also an important and influential referent for examining Hurston's treatment of consumption, expenditure, and class mobility.

10. Arvay demonstrates her low-class roots in other ways, of course. For instance, Jim flies into a rage when he finds her eating clay to satisfy a pregnancy-induced craving. As John Lowe rightly notes, "Her behavior introduces a class barrier between her and the horrified Jim" (292). Although here I focus primarily on the narrative of class mobility and

aristocratic becoming that at first divides and then unites Jim and Arvay, there are also important ways in which Jim's "scuffling" to place Arvay "higher up" on a pedestal are part of a patriarchal attitude toward women that divides them even after their reconciliation, an attitude perhaps equally characteristic of a romanticized version of Old South society. As Ann duCille observes, "Jim is so caught up in his own manhood—in playing the role of patriarch—that he can neither see nor hear the woman he has married. And Arvay is so thoroughly blinded by her own insecurities that she invariably misreads the obvious and misunderstands the simple to the point that the reader, much sooner perhaps than her husband, loses patience with and sympathy for her myopia" (133). Susan Meisenhelder argues that *Seraph* represents Hurston's "most subversive attack on the values of what she called 'Anglo-Saxon' civilization. . . . [S]he exposes the foundation of that culture as one resting on oppression of white women, exploitation of people of color, and domination of Nature" (95–96). More specifically, "Hurston gives us quite a critical view of life on a pedestal, revealing the specific ways in which love is 'de prong' even well-to-do white women get hung on" (96).

11. As Chuck Jackson notes in "Waste and Whiteness: Zora Neale Hurston and the Politics of Eugenics," "Earl's resemblance to 'queer' Uncle Chester connects him to a maternal line of bad blood"; thus, he "lets loose a slew of insecurities about [Arvay's] white trash self" (647). Jackson offers a compelling reading of the ways in which Arvay's anxieties about class in general and about Earl in particular spring in part from debates about eugenics prevalent in the 1940s. He argues that observers concerned about maintaining the purity (and supremacy) of the white race were much vexed by the problem of "white trash," whose benighted condition threatened their ideas about what, essentially, a white person *is*. Writes Jackson, "The moment of anthropological eugenics works to signify 'white trash' culture as the defiling element *of white America*, polluting not only genetically, but structurally as well. That is, under the eugenic gaze, the cacogenic family blocks biological and intellectual 'progress' while simultaneously threatening to taint the purity of racial and economic categories. A normalized white body functions as an icon for the white race, which must keep itself clean, avoid abjection, and, to be blunt, get rid of its shit" (645). Thus, for Jackson, Earl's death symbolically "purifies" Arvay and enables her to achieve a normative whiteness. I would agree with Jackson, and only note that Earl is *taken* from Arvay, not freely given, and it is the active enactment of paternalistic racial ideals that I find crucial to Arvay's ascent to the aristocratic throne.

12. Ward argues that Arvay's "adoption" of Belinda is undercut by the way in which she describes Belinda as "my little girl." According to Ward, "In Arvay's formulation . . . the possessive adjective is proprietary rather than familial" (82). Yet I would argue that this elision of property and family lies at the very heart of the paternalist ethic. After all, as Eugene Genovese notes, the relation of master to slave represented "an extension of the relationship of father to perpetual child" (121), and he elsewhere observes that "not accidentally, and by no means as a petty propaganda device, acts of the Confederate Congress referred to the obligations of citizens to their black and white families. Not infrequently, planters recorded births and deaths of slaves in their family Bibles" (196).

13. Though I have described Arvay as subordinated to Jim in her (still relatively privileged) position as a nouveau-plantation matriarch, certain elements of Hurston's final

description of the Meserves may initially seem to challenge this reading. In the novel's closing scene, Arvay reflects upon her marriage as Jim sleeps in her arms: "Inside he was nothing but a little boy to take care of, and he hungered for her hovering. Look at him now! Snuggled down and clutching onto her like Kenny when he wore diapers. Arvay felt such a swelling to protect and comfort Jim that tears came up in her eyes. So helpless sleeping there in her arms and trusting himself to her" (919). Arvay sees Jim as "trusting" and childlike, needing her "hovering" mothering. Yet by accepting her role as mother to her entire family, Arvay has also accepted a traditional model of plantation gender relations that may seem to offer her a limited degree of authority but which ultimately constrains her. Elizabeth Fox-Genovese argues that elite antebellum southerners often praised "women's special capacities for gentleness and nurture" and "were wont to view women as especially attuned to moral concerns and as especially suited for the early education of children. Above all, they emphasized women's obligation to manifest piety, purity, chastity, and obedience and to cultivate their special calling for motherhood" (202). Yet the lauded talents of women were often used as proof of essential gender differences that justified the squelching of women's voices when it came to topics outside their limited domestic purview. I would concur with Carol P. Marsh-Lockett's evaluation of this scene in her study of images of motherhood in *Seraph on the Suwanee.* Lockett argues that Arvay "consciously conspires in her own oppression when she concludes peacefully that she must love Jim like a 'mother'—which, in this context means self-effacing, unconditional capitulation to sexist dogma and failure to expect any growth on the part of her partner" (102).

CHAPTER 2. Eudora Welty's *Delta Wedding* and *The Ponder Heart*

1. Indeed, while I read *Delta Wedding* as an exposure and critique of paternalist values, many reviewers of the time, including Diana Trilling and John Crowe Ransom, read it—favorably or not—as a nostalgic celebration of the aristocratic Delta lifestyle. However, Welty resisted readings of *Delta Wedding* as a reverie for the southern past. In an interview, Linda Kuehl cited Ransom's claim that the novel might stand as "one of the last novels in the tradition of the Old South." Welty replied, "I revere Mr. Ransom, but his meaning here is not quite clear to me. I wasn't trying to write a novel of the Old South. I don't think of myself as writing out of any special tradition, and I'd hesitate to accept that sanction for *Delta Wedding.* I'd hesitate still more today, because the term itself, 'Old South,' has a connotation of something unreal and not quite straightforward" (*Conversations* 91–92).

2. A number of Welty scholars have noted the influence of contemporary events in the Delta on *Delta Wedding.* For instance, in *Eudora Welty's Chronicle: A Story of Mississippi Life,* Devlin observes that "the plantation system could still assume the fertility of the Delta, but in the 1930s the growing of cotton was made precarious by a depressed world market, while in the 1940s the planter was asked to meet unusually high wartime standards of production. The mule . . . [,] the Negro. . . [,] the landowner. . . [,] all were forced to readjust their traditional relations when the mechanization of agriculture turned time into a form of money" (92). However, I would argue that this contemporary state of flux for the Delta has a more destabilizing effect on plantation race relations than Devlin claims. My own reading has more in common with Susan V. Donaldson's "Gender and

History in *Delta Wedding.*" Donaldson has also pointed out that "it was during the decade that Welty wrote *Delta Wedding* that white planters in the Delta like the Fairchilds began to lose their rigid control of the black laboring population" (7), and she rightly claims that "the narrative itself resists and questions the Fairchilds' unexamined sense of entitlement to property and social standing in the Delta" (8).

3. Welty's readers have observed how central this fragility was to her project in *Delta Wedding.* As Albert Devlin notes, "Welty has selected a time and a place that foresee only difficulties for Shellmound and in retrospect reveal the historical vulnerability of the plantation to cultural change" (97). Jan Nordby Gretlund has pointed out that, in fact, 1923 was not quite the calm, quiet year Welty imagined it to be: "In 1922 there had been an overflow of the river, and it had been difficult to retain enough labor for 1923. Blacks by the thousands left the Delta and went north to work in industrial plants. They were anxious to leave, as their circumstances were often those of 'latter-day bondage' with coercion, severe economic deprivation, dietary problems, and a high rate of pellagra, rickets, and death. The uneasy planter-businessmen who saw their black laborers head north tried to restrain them from leaving in many ways, at times by force" (156).

4. For a good discussion of domestic ritual in *Delta Wedding,* see Ann Romines's study *The Home Plot: Women, Writing, and Domestic Ritual,* as well as Peggy Whitman Prenshaw's essay "Woman's World, Man's Place: The Fiction of Eudora Welty."

5. Welty's father, Christian, was a native Ohioan who met his future wife, Chestina, while they were both schoolteachers in West Virginia. They moved to Jackson, Mississippi, where Christian Welty eventually became director of the Lamar Life Insurance Company, and where Welty was born in 1909 and where she would spend the vast majority of her life. Welty's knowledge of the Delta was based partially on her trips across the state as a publicist for the Works Progress Administration and on her visits with her friend John Robinson's family. These visits provided important material for the novel; as Welty put it in an interview with Linda Kuehl, "Some family tales and sayings are right in the book, though by now I can't remember which are true and which are made up" (*Conversations* 91). Further, as biographer Ann Waldron notes, John Robinson's great-great-grandmother, plantation mistress Nancy McDougall Robinson, kept a diary from 1832 to 1870, which Welty drew upon to provide context, detail, and historical background for *Delta Wedding* (154–55).

6. In his early review of the novel, Ransom perceived the Fairchilds' performative nature: "The Fairchilds have so much self-consciousness along with their naturalness that it is as if they were actors, and their common life the drama they enacted daily. They are brought up to have this sense of themselves, and it affects them with a certain sophistication, and a public responsibility" (73). M. E. Bradford also highlights the performative aspect of Fairchild identity in "Fairchild as Composite Protagonist in *Delta Wedding,*" though he does not connect that performativity explicitly to issues of race and class (205).

7. As Gretlund notes of the Fairchilds in *Eudora Welty's Aesthetics of Place,* "Their everyday ways of experiencing and behaving keep alive the family past and with it much of what we consider Old South ways." He goes on to point out that the Fairchilds treat their black employees "like children who at times will get in trouble and need their employers' 'parental' guidance and protection. Even the old and supposedly wise blacks are treated like children" (169). In "*Delta Wedding* as Region and Symbol," Hardy rightly observes that "it is

at the expense of [African Americans] that the Fairchilds can be the 'gentle swains'. . . that they are" (87). Kreyling states that "as the novel opens . . . the blacks make their entrance in a way familiar to a thousand plantation novels and the films later to be based on them: they are arrayed as a roster of willing adjuncts to the lifestyle of the plantation" (*Understanding Eudora Welty* 104).

8. As Kreyling puts it, "Battle Fairchild, who has ceded all practical control of the plantation to Troy, lifts himself to the podium of soft-hearted gentleman on the strong and merciless arm of his overseer" (97). Romines concurs, noting that "as overseer, Troy has the duty of maintaining relationships [of power], so that white landowners will be relieved of the burden of doing so" ("Reading the Cakes" 614).

9. In a recent article exploring "the black characters' positions in the white characters' perceptions of their own identities in *Delta Wedding*," Betina Entzminger also offers an analysis of this scene as the moment Dabney acquires "the painful knowledge that her Uncle George has an identity separate from the family group" because "he cares for outsiders whom she considers unworthy" (62). Entzminger argues that Dabney's anxious meeting with Man-Son and the resulting reverie "carries the hint of sexual threat, a threat that is paradoxically linked to the memory of naked men and the hint of awakening desire" (62). She raises an intriguing idea that calls for further elaboration, especially considering the homoerotic undercurrents in the passage, though such elaboration is beyond the scope of this essay. Entzminger's piece offers a number of interesting ideas about the intersections of blackness and white identity generally in *Delta Wedding*; my analysis of both this scene specifically and the racial relations at Shellmound in general differs from hers by focusing particularly on Welty's handling of the complicated intersection of race, class, labor, and economics.

10. Troy and Robbie Reid Fairchild are both low-class interlopers who threaten the Fairchild status quo; though I focus mainly on Troy, the Fairchilds may be even more concerned with Robbie. As Tempe tells Shelley, "when people marry beneath them, it's the woman that determines what comes. It's the woman that coarsens the man. The man really doesn't do much to the woman, I've observed" (270); as Shelley understands her, "Troy's not as bad for us as Robbie" (271). I would suggest, however, that Tempe and Shelley have little to worry about from Robbie. Though she does often betray her unspeakably parvenu nature, she also at times earnestly desires to relate to George as a Fairchild would rather than forcing him down to her "coarse" level. For instance, in her version of the Yellow Dog story, Robbie reflects that the Fairchild women take pride in the fact that their men will do anything they ask of them. Robbie thinks to herself that even though she "was not that kind of woman" and "she did not want to," nevertheless "she had to ask him for something—life waited for it" (192). She settles upon the right thing to ask for when George stands in the path of the Yellow Dog to wrest Maureen's leg free. Then, "in terror . . . she had held the Fairchilds' own mask in front of her. She had cried out for him to come back from his danger as a favor to her" (192). Her exclamation when George declines—one which draws hoots of derision from the Fairchilds upon each retelling of the story—is a protest that he has not played by the rules of the game, has not accepted her Fairchild performance: "George Fairchild, you didn't do this for me!" Although, as I have discussed, George's Fairchild identity is ambiguous, it would seem that Robbie does not inspire that ambiguity, does not "coarsen" him. Perhaps she is an exception to Tempe's rule. By contrast,

as I will discuss, the fact that Troy—so essentially othered by the Fairchilds—can so easily become a Fairchild is fundamentally threatening to the Fairchild status quo.

11. Danielle Fuller argues compellingly that "by shooting at Root's shaking hand, Troy commits an act that maintains and marks his position as a white, working-class male within the hierarchy of the plantation" (299). I would argue that Fuller's assertion is correct as far as it goes but that in this scene Troy behaves not just like an overseer but also like a paternalist; his behavior is influenced not just by his position as Fairchild employee but also as aspiring Fairchild.

12. Romines and Donaldson each offer convincing readings of this passage, though with different emphases than mine. In her essay "Gender and History in Eudora Welty's *Delta Wedding*," in which she asserts that the project of *Delta Wedding* is "not just an ironic portrayal of a society on the verge of drastic historical change but something very like a feminist interrogation of history and historical perspective" (3), Donaldson argues that this scene reveals that "to see white male authority as only a performance, a role assumed in imitation of men who, in turn, imitate others, raises profound questions about the assumed differences between masculinity and femininity, and ultimately about the boundaries between historical agent and historical background and between the public and the private sphere" (11). My own interpretation of this scene has much in common with Donaldson's and differs mainly in that I wish to emphasize the scene's implications for Welty's treatment of class rather than gender or history. In her compelling "Reading the Cakes: *Delta Wedding* and the Texts of Southern Women's Culture," Ann Romines has also argued that because of this scene, "Shelley can no longer believe in the fundamental fixity or the benignity of the plantation order" (614). Although she also sees Troy transgressing certain boundaries of identity, she initially renders that transgression in terms not of class but of gender: Troy's ministrations for Big Baby make him appear "as a grotesque imitation of a child's caretaker and cook, roles that—in this book—belong entirely to women" (614). I would note, however, that George also appears in the caretaker role in this novel; moreover, though Romines focuses on the culinary significance of the ice pick to connect Troy to the female cooks of the novel, I would argue that Welty's pointed comparison of the ice pick to a knife at the beginning of the passage forges a stronger link between Troy and George than between Troy and Roxie, Partheny, and other cooks. Betina Entzminger offers a specifically race-conscious reading of this scene. She rightly asks, "Is Troy, the lowly overseer whose job it is to associate closely with the black field hands so the land owners will not have to do so, a real white man? Or is he somehow tainted, whether physically or metaphysically, with black blood?" (61). However, though her questions implicitly raise the subject of class and labor, my reading differs from hers in that I see the black blood not merely as representing racial otherness but also as representing the violence and physicality implicit in plantation labor relations, a crucial aspect of life at Shellmound of which the Fairchilds strive to remain willfully ignorant in order to preserve their class position. Entzminger reads Shelley's anxiety over the performative nature of "real" Deltans primarily in terms of race, not class: she takes "Shelley's use of the word 'real' to mean, at least in part, 'white,'" and, continuing, points out that "for Shelley and most other people of her time and region, a black man from the Delta could never be a Deltan, but only a colored man. His black blood was believed to make him genetically unfit for the leadership and

gentlemanly behavior required of a Deltan" (61). Entzminger is certainly correct that an African American man could never be a "real Deltan," but she does not explore the ways in which a "real Deltan" is not only a racial but also a class identity. I would argue that Shelley is most affronted by Troy's crossing of class lines she believes are natural and essential, though of course the crossing of these class boundaries both here and in George's bayou scene is often rendered in terms of racial otherness.

13. As Ted Ownby puts it in *American Dreams in Mississippi*, Bonnie Dee "asserts herself by becoming a spender" (149). He further claims, "For Welty . . . no ultimate judgment awaits characters who buy new goods to define and enjoy themselves. Even if they offer no ultimate solutions or redemptions, goods allow significant forms of freedom" (148). Julia Eichelberger argues that "Edna Earle regards Bonnie Dee as a kind of consumer glutton with poor taste. Yet Welty's narrative suggests that electricity, a washing machine, and a telephone are only unimportant to someone who already has a cadre of servants to wash their clothes, carry fuel, and run to town to deliver messages and summon doctors" (17). My interpretation follows Ownby's and Eichelberger's in reading Bonnie Dee as a consumerist; however, no one has yet extended the scope of Bonnie Dee's consumerism to her attitude toward marriage or discussed the ways consumerism disrupts the class hierarchy of Clay. I should stress that although Bonnie Dee's attitude toward money seems consistent with Veblen's ideal of conspicuous consumption—she keeps her purchases on the front porch for all to see, after all—Veblen also argues that conspicuous consumption *alone* is not enough to propel an individual into the upper classes. Rather, that consumption must conform to a society's accepted norms. As Veblen cautions, "it must not be understood that the motive on which the consumer acts in any given case is this principle in its bald, unsophisticated form. Ordinarily his motive is . . . to live up to the accepted norms of decency in the kind, amount, and grade of goods consumed" (115). Clay's consumption patterns are based on a paternalist model, in which one must engage in a form of conspicuous waste that proves one's adherence to certain romanticized versions of antebellum attitudes toward African Americans.

14. Though Edna Earle comments that she does not "believe for a minute" that Bonnie Dee saw the ad—she thinks "somebody with bright eyes, who did, went and told her" (59)—it seems unlikely that an avid ad-watcher like Bonnie Dee could have missed it, especially as it runs over the course of three days. Edna Earle even seems to contradict this statement later when she informs us that Bonnie Dee has begun to subscribe to the *Commercial Appeal*: "With her name in it that one time, she tried a whole year of it, and here it came, packed with those big, black ads" (67).

15. Weiner's essay briefly discusses the ways in which a move to a cash economy threatens families like the Ponders; she addresses the legal ramifications of the cash economy and the way that it threatens to "corrupt" Grandpa Ponder's easy life by letting in an outside world full of strangers; however, I am more interested in the way that the cash economy serves to undermine essentialist claims to aristocratic class positions.

16. In "Welty's Philosophy of Friendship: Meanings Treasured in *The Ponder Heart*," Sharon Deykin Baris also reads Narciss's dissatisfaction at the novel's end as a form of resistance (68). I agree with Baris; my reading differs from hers primarily in that I see Narciss's resistance as having a specific origin in her relationship with Bonnie Dee.

17. Peggy Whitman Prenshaw has written eloquently about the role of "private relationships" in Welty's political ideology, in "Welty's Transformations of the Public, Private, and the Political" in the volume *Eudora Welty and Politics*. As Prenshaw puts it, "Welty shows unmistakably that what she regards as the politics of substance and courage, politics that is truly public, civil, and communal, is the human connection between freely operating individuals who confront issues that directly affect their lives. The domain where such connection occurs for Welty the writer, and also, I think, for Welty the human being, is typically personal, private, and interior" (46). Other essays in the same volume by Noel Polk, Suzanne Marrs, and Daniele Pitavy-Souques take up the same issue.

CHAPTER 3. William Faulkner's *The Mansion* and *The Reivers*

1. As Theresa Towner notes, "many contemporary critics" find in the manner and content of Faulkner's speech evidence that, "even upon the death of a woman so important to him and his family," Faulkner could not react with genuine emotion but, rather, clung to "his plantation-owner pose," pressing the complicated and individual Barr into the decidedly uncomplicated mold of the "black mammy" (124). Towner cites, in particular, essays by Judith Sensibar and Minrose Gwin. Towner reads the Barr eulogy in the context of Faulkner's other public statements on race in order to critique easy dismissals of Faulkner as a racist whose "go-slowist" ideology merely masked his true desire to maintain the southern status quo. She rightly finds the issue more complicated than that: she argues that "the question 'Was Faulkner a racist?' is not only unanswerable but also a kind of hermeneutic red herring" (121).

2. Here I would like to note briefly how I engage with and differ from two of the most significant discussions on class in Faulkner scholarship. Myra Jehlen offers one of the earliest attempts to think of Faulkner's work in terms of class in her *Class and Character in Faulkner's South* (1976). Jehlen argues that "it is his strong awareness of class that animates Yoknapatawpha County" (10), and that his novels often deal "with maintaining, resenting, or refurbishing a social situation which is first of all class defined and only then regional or racial" (10). I would argue, however, that we cannot so easily separate class and race, and that Faulkner's fiction is invested in the project of showing the ways in which they mutually determine one another. The most valuable recent examination of Faulkner's treatment of class is Kevin Railey's *Natural Aristocracy: History, Ideology, and the Production of William Faulkner* (1999). Railey sees Faulkner's work as grappling with a central tension between the paternalism of the Old South and the liberalism of the New. He defines paternalism broadly: paternalists believe in "a social order that is stable, hierarchical, consciously elitist, and therefore fundamentally antithetical to liberalism. A paternalist assumes an inherent inequality of men; some are born to rule, others to obey" (7). Further, he argues that when Faulkner was born "paternalism had already become mostly a residual ideology, liberalism was well on its way to rising to dominance, and populism was in the process of being co-opted by the forces of liberalism and progressivism" (28). Out of this complicated ideological soup, Faulkner emerged with an ideology combining tenets of liberalism and paternalism, says Railey: Faulkner accepted "certain tenets of liberal ideology, namely reward based on merit and the content of one's achievement," while at the same time he

held "fast to a belief in the possibility of a naturally ordered society whose most powerful figures are men who are, in theory, naturally better and more superior than others" (43). Ultimately, according to Railey, "Faulkner can never, it seems, break from a deep allegiance to paternalism and the social stratification it requires" (45).

Railey offers a compelling vision of Faulkner's relationship to art, history, and ideology, and I find his readings of novels such as *The Sound and the Fury* and *Absalom, Absalom!* compelling. However, I would argue that Faulkner's ideas about paternalism and the intersection between race and class evolve quite dramatically by the late 1950s—so much so, in fact, that I resist reading the Snopes trilogy as a unified whole. Such treatment of the Snopes trilogy is common in Faulkner scholarship and not unique to Railey's study; and indeed, there are good reasons for reading the three novels in this fashion. However, the nineteen years between *The Hamlet* and *The Mansion* are crucial in southern history, and include such major historical events as the United States' entrance into World War II, the *Brown* decision, and the Emmett Till murder. So, while I agree that we may read *The Mansion* as part of a project criticizing "an aristocracy of wealth that engenders a repressive and exploitative system concerned with business and profit," I would resist Railey's assertion that it upholds Faulkner's "belief that if power in a society is not preempted by a benevolent paternal class of rulers, dispensing largesse according to the moral deserts of the individual, then society will always fall victim to Snopesism" (148). Thus, although I will demonstrate that Faulkner does indeed place his hope in a group of benevolent individuals, I will also argue that by the late 1950s he has come to see the ideal constitution for such a group as in fact radically opposed to the ideal of "natural aristocracy" that Railey sees Faulkner as endorsing in the Snopes novels and in *The Reivers*.

3. In *Fictions of Labor*, Godden reads Faulkner's work of the 1930s, primarily *The Sound and the Fury* and *Absalom, Absalom!* as texts which grapple with "founding and ramifying anxieties about the legacy of violently maintained labor relations" (2) as southern planters experience a "dramatic transformation . . . from lords of bound labor to payers of a wage" (1). Godden further argues that Faulkner's work of this period is about "how a revolution at the center of the southern economy releases from the forms of life that have made that economy typifying contradictions whose resolution takes shape as narrative options and stylistic habits that are, quite literally, forced out of a historically determined and pervasive structure of feeling" (3). Though my study is less concerned with narrative practice than is Godden's, the transition of southern aristocrats from slave owners to employers is of course central to the collapse of paternalism that is central to my project; I would argue that this transition, combined with the New Deal, World War II, and the civil rights movement, produced anxieties about class and labor not just for the planters but also for an entire social structure rooted in idealized versions of the southern past which lasted well beyond the 1930s.

4. Corrine Dale has also noted the way in which Flem blurs the boundaries between Old South and New; she compares Flem and Thomas Sutpen, arguing that both men "self-consciously imitate the paternalistic Southern gentleman, accruing the necessary domestic symbols—mansion, wife, and family" (323). Further, "Both serve to acknowledge the financial basis of Southern paternalism and to suggest the kinship of Old South planter and New South businessman" (323). Though Dale goes on to talk about how "Sutpen and

Snopes fail because they apply financial ethics to family relationships" (325), my reading is more concerned with the racial and class aspects of paternalism.

5. Further, as Polk points out, Gavin's righteous fulminations about the immorality of Flem's greed are fundamentally hypocritical. Gavin marries Melisandre Backus, an old sweetheart and the widow of a New Orleans mobster. Polk notes, "It is an irony worth noting, then, that the highminded idealistic Stevens, the self-proclaimed foremost opponent of 'Snopesism,' lives out his days as the direct beneficiary of Harriss' ill-gotten gains" ("Idealism in *The Mansion*" 116).

6. Mauri Skinfill contends that *The Hamlet* argues against "the desperate fetishization of money produced by the demands of underclass subsistence living, demands already determined by the operations of a market economy" (168). Richard Moreland sees Ratliff as the primary vehicle for that critique; according to Moreland, the salesman's tales (again in *The Hamlet*) caution Yoknapatawpha's citizens that they "must not accept uncritically and humorlessly New South capitalism's fetishized 'cash money' as the arbiter of social exchange" (142).

7. I should also note here that some critics have seen Linda Snopes Kohl, Communist Party member and Flem's legal, though not biological, daughter, as a resistant figure. Certainly, Linda's flight from Jefferson to New York City, marriage to Jewish sculptor Barton Kohl, and participation in the Spanish Civil War (participation which renders her deaf when an exploding shell bursts her eardrums) would prepare us for such a reading. Keith Louise Fulton has argued that Linda represents an "alternative vision of America" because she "walks out of the mansion and closes the door on the American dream of a patriarchal dynasty after achieving what no other female or male character in Faulkner's fiction achieves, an act of justice that settles her conflicts with the past and empowers her move into the future" (425). Further, Hee Kang asserts that "her participation in the war and her being a Communist and later a teacher of black children demonstrates her political radicalness; and her job as a riveter in an airplane factory proves her economic independence. Such experiences allow her to shape her feminine consciousness that will collapse men's belief system" (26). Certainly, Faulkner does present Linda's communism sympathetically, and I would agree that, initially, we may read her as a hopeful character. However, such hopeful readings of Linda quickly become complicated. For instance, though her attempt to educate Yoknapatawpha's African American children is obviously laudable, her plan for doing so is somewhat problematic. She intends to "establish a kind of competitive weekly test, the winners, who would be the top students for that week in each class, to spend the following week in a kind of academy she would establish, with white teachers, details to be settled later but for temporary they would use her sitting-room in her father's house for a sort of general precept" (531–32). Thus, Linda plans to reward merit with separation from other members of the African American community in favor of education in the very heart of the symbol of patriarchy and paternalism, a plan that indicates she perhaps has not fully shaken the influence of a corrupt form of southern society. Even if we are inclined to give her the benefit of the doubt, we cannot avoid considering that, in addition to conspiring to kill Flem—an only questionably (if that) justifiable action—she ends the novel not with a gesture of solidarity with the poor and marginalized but with the wealthiest consumers: she drives away in a brand-new British Jaguar.

8. Polk argues compellingly that "Flem is not the completely dishonest, evil person he has been depicted by most critics" ("Faulkner and Respectability" 120); as he notes elsewhere, Flem's experience of "that nomadic life of sharecropper poverty and insecurity" goes a long way to explain "why middle-class emotional and financial security should be so attractive to him" ("Idealism in *The Mansion*" 115). With that in mind, "If violence, if murder, is the only way we can deal effectively with Snopesism, if the world has to depend on the likes of Mink Snopes to save it, then we are in sorry shape indeed" ("Idealism in *The Mansion*" 125). As Joseph Urgo claims in *Faulkner's Apocrypha*, "Snopesism" is not demonic; rather, "to be a 'Snopes' is to refuse class typification and identification as 'fate,' to refuse subordinate status based on class position, and to say no (or nope) to class stigma and class-based economic determinism in general" (153). Frances Louisa Nichol rightly argues that "Flem is not a 'force' or 'power' but merely one man adapting vestiges of the Old South's ability to manipulate the truth" (493), though I disagree with her ultimate conclusion that Mink "achieves heroic dimensions . . . [because he] displays a moral responsibility toward himself" (505). Most recently Matthew Lessig has argued that while the "New Critics nee Agrarians found in Faulkner's Snopes clan an embodiment of the social forces they felt were menacing the traditional Southern order," neither they nor their like-minded successors "questioned the historical or ideological implications of burdening poor-white tenant farmers with the responsibility for the modernization of the South" (80).

9. Goodyhay's church may not be Faulkner's first attempt to describe such a community. Barbara and Wesley Morris note that in *Intruder in the Dust* (1948), Chick, Aleck Sander, and Miss Habersham represent "an alternative community consisting of blacks, women, and children; it is a community of minorities, marginalized on the threshold of the dominant community of adult, white men" (224). I would suggest that *The Mansion* advances the depiction of community in the earlier novel by focusing in particular on the community's alternative economic practices.

10. In his reading of this passage, Kevin Railey chooses to emphasize the hierarchical nature of the afterlife Faulkner describes here. Railey argues that Faulkner rewards Mink in death because of "his recognition of other values besides those of money as well as his recognition of the natural ties and responsibilities between people." Most importantly for Railey, Mink "reveal[s] his acceptance of the proper social structure. This acceptance involves Mink's realization of his place within the overall scheme of society" (163). Thus, as Railey sees it, Faulkner celebrates Mink to the degree that he recognizes his own essential downtroddenness—an interpretation of Faulkner's late career ideology that I argue strongly against in this piece.

CHAPTER 4. Ernest Gaines's *Of Love and Dust* and "Bloodline"

1. For a further discussion of Faulkner's influence on Gaines in general and *Of Love and Dust* in particular, see "Bloodlines and Patriarchs: *Of Love and Dust* and Its Revisions of Faulkner" by David Lionel Smith.

2. As Carmean notes, "To sustain the illusion of order, perpetuate tradition, and support his belief in white superiority, Bishop must believe Hebert deserving of his position. And to support his faith, he must absolve him of all responsibility" (52).

3. Valerie Babb argues, "Implicit in Marcus's assessment of Bonbon as a 'catfish-eating Cajun' is a disapprobation based on caste and power. To him Bonbon is not a 'real' white man but merely a pretender to the throne of white power, because he has not descended from the old lines of social power that a Marshall Hebert has. While Marcus has been accustomed to the rule of established southern families, he sees in Bonbon a parvenu usurper and resents the authority given to Sidney and refused him" (67). Though I would agree that this description of Bonbon applies to most of the other African Americans' attitudes toward Bonbon, I would suggest that Marcus is much less enthralled with planter power than Bibb indicates here.

4. Herman Beavers has also noted the way in which Jim's mechanical expertise gives him a unique status on the plantation, though Beavers's analysis is more concerned with narrative and memory than with class. Beavers reads *Of Love and Dust* as a fiction "in which the individual, in order to reach a new state of awareness or self-recovery, must break free from repressive paradigms of folk memory," and in which "the protagonist must break out of an older, restrictive circle of memory in order to move into a space where he or she can begin to utilize the past in new ways" (68). According to Beavers, "Jim's mechanical ability leads Bonbon to cross the boundary of racial difference into the space of sanctioned remembrance. Trucks and tractors provide the means for Bonbon to ignore Jim's inequity of social status, to add flesh, blood, and bone to his authoritarian presence as overseer" (73). Beavers claims that Jim's in-between status "works to cement, rather than challenge, the status quo" (76). Similarly, Frank Shelton rightly claims that Jim "owes the trust whites place in him and his responsible position on the plantation to his knowledge of machinery" (23). However, he further asserts that "it is suggestive that Gaines associates them [Cajuns] with the tractor, which has become for him 'the machine in the garden.' While Gaines certainly feels that social change is necessary, such mechanization of agriculture is portrayed as dehumanizing, and it does not bring with it improvement in the lot of his black characters" (21). I would argue that Gaines's treatment of the relationship between mechanization and social change is somewhat more complicated than Beavers and Shelton would have it; in fact, it is only from his unique—albeit admittedly compromised—perspective that Jim can come to understand the best ways in which to challenge the status quo.

5. My reading of Marcus and Louise's relationship is less sympathetic than Suzanne W. Jones's in her excellent *Race Mixing: Southern Fiction since the Sixties*. Jones argues that "the vengeful sexual encounters that each separately engineers metamorphose into a mutually satisfying emotional relationship, transformative for them as individuals" (156). Similarly, Joseph Griffin asserts that "their relationship rapidly develops into a mutually satisfying and transforming one" (79). I would agree with Jones and Griffin that Marcus and Louise do develop real affection for each other, but I contend that it does not truly lead to the transformation she identifies; even at the novel's end, Marcus still displays his selfish arrogance, and, most importantly, Louise still clings to her immature, childlike ways. Neither character has transformed in any meaningful sense.

CHAPTER 5. Walker Percy's *The Last Gentleman* and *Love in the Ruins*

1. For instance, Michael Pearson claims that Percy sets up racism as a thematic counterpoint to the central theme of his work: "love, human and divine." Says Pearson, "Racism

thrives on ignorance and abstraction, love on understanding and a recognition of individuality. By implication as well as intention, everything Percy has written is a criticism of the racist mentality" (495). By framing his discussion of racism in these terms, he overemphasizes the theological dimensions of Percy's work. Indeed, Percy himself claims that he would have to eliminate Christianity from any viable formula for better race relations "because the Christians left it out" ("Questions They Never Asked Me" 421); Percy displays here a concern for cultural realities that his readers sometimes ignore. John Edward Hardy does briefly discuss race in Percy's novels but he ultimately asserts that "it is most important that we not miss the novelist's design to transcend *all* social issues, the racial one most troublesomely included" (80). For Hardy, "the problem, and its solution if any, like all other problems of human enmity, is rooted most deeply in the individual, personal conscience" (115). Jac Tharpe characterizes Percy's position on race as that of a "Southern moderate," but he also frames the racial struggle in terms of existential angst: "Blacks must reach the economic level the whites have attained, and then suffer the alienation the whites endure, to discover that nobody has any home" (24). Most recently, Farrell O'Gorman has offered an intriguing examination of Percy's changing racial views, and their presentation in his fiction, by focusing on "the inherent connection of his religious conversion, his personal shift from segregationist to civil rights advocate, and the treatment of race in his writing . . . as not only generally Christian but also specifically Catholic" (68).

2. Although Will Percy did not publish *Lanterns* until 1941, considerably after Walker's adolescence in Greenville, it no doubt accurately reflects the sorts of racial attitudes implicit in the household in which Walker grew up. Further, its publication came considerably in advance of Walker's first attempts at fiction in the late 1950s and early 1960s.

3. His active participation in the civil rights movement indicates that Walker Percy found the political and social equality of African Americans a worthy goal. Patrick Samway notes that "Walker was deeply concerned about the civil rights issue, and gradually, through friends and acquaintances, he had begun to make decisions about how he could personally contribute to the movement" (243). In particular, Percy helped found the interracial Covington Community Relations Council, an organization that chartered both a credit union accessible to economically disadvantaged blacks and a Head Start program (270). Percy even spoke as an expert witness for the black students of Covington High School in their campaign to have the Confederate flag removed from their school (281). Significantly, he felt that this struggle for equal autonomy extended to selfhood as well: in a review of Ralph Ellison's *Invisible Man*, he warned of the "fatal pitfall" that lies in the path of the young African American writer: "the temptation to see the Negro and even himself through the sociologist's abstraction" (10–11). Even before his first attempts at fiction, Percy asserted the inevitable reductiveness of perceiving African Americans as members of a stereotyped class.

4. Ania Loomba criticizes Bhabha's construction of hybridity; she claims that as he develops the idea, it "swells from its previous colonial context to become paradigmatic of all oppositional theory and politics." Loomba finds this quality "illustrative of how feebly it was grounded in the colonial encounter to begin with" (309). However, I would suggest that we may still productively utilize Bhabha's formulation by continuing to supply the specific cultural context that Loomba finds lacking.

5. In "Walker Percy and Albert Murray: The Story of Two 'Part Anglo-Saxon Alabamians,'" Roberta S. Maguire also takes up the issue of hybridity in Percy's work, albeit from a different angle. Maguire argues that Percy's relationship with fellow novelist Murray "played an important role in the evolution of Percy's thinking about race, or, more precisely, his thinking about the relationship between black and white southerners" (10). According to Maguire, when Murray visited Percy in 1969, Murray "emphasized his view of the complexity of black-white interrelatedness—that the hybridity of American culture does not mean that differences become indistinguishable, but rather that differences and similarities become interwoven" (18). Maguire argues that Percy was particularly influenced by Murray's character Scooter, from *Train Whistle Guitar* (1973), a protagonist who is "a role-player *par excellence*" (22). Maguire's essay is valuable, especially for its tracing of the Percy/Murray relationship (one that goes unremarked upon in both of the major Percy biographies) and for its discussion of the Murrayan influence on Percy's African American character Elgin from *Lancelot* (1976). However, I would suggest that Maguire somewhat overstates Murray's influence on Percy's thinking about hybridity; though she cites *The Last Gentleman*'s David Ross as a kind of failed version of the role-playing figure that both Percy and Murray write about, she neglects the ways in which Will Barrett operates as an ultimately successful hybrid figure.

6. I should note that at one point, Percy's narrator claims that *all* southerners, not just African Americans, possess a "radar": "It was unsettling, too, coming among a people whose radars were as sensitive as his own," a group of people who are "as light-footed and hawk-eyed and God-fearing a crew as one could imagine" (145). However, he also quickly notes that Will's "radar was remarkable, even for the South. After standing around two or three days, as queer and nervous as a Hoosier, he quickly got the hang of it" (145–46). I would suggest that Will's radar is so exceptional because it is so akin to the radar that African Americans have had to develop to survive.

7. Will's radar keeps him from learning anything about himself even in New York. Though he sees an analyst, he simply responds to his analyst's desires: "Never had [Dr. Gamow's] own theories found a readier confirmation than in the free (they seemed to be free) associations and the copious dreams which this one spread out at his feet like so many trophies" (24). Even when Gamow realizes Will's game and confronts him, Will makes "an equally charming confession, exhibit[s] heroic sweats and contortions to overcome his bad habits, offer[s] crabbed and meager dreams, and so ma[kes] another trophy of his disgrace" (24). For the entire duration of his treatment, Will satisfies Gamow's every wish and never once uncovers anything about himself. We may wonder why Will persists in his visits to Dr. Gamow's office at all. Though it seems a small point, Will may continue his analysis because this man, whom he thinks of as "a father of sorts" (30), also participates somewhat in the essentializing and objectification of black people. For instance, he has decorated his office "in a Bahama theme, with a fiber rug and prints of hummingbirds and Negresses walking with baskets on their heads" (25). Perhaps Gamow uses what he (wrongly) perceives as an image of native tranquillity and innocence (and ignorance?) as a contrast with the ultracivilized, clinical practice that takes place in the room. Further, when Gamow entreats Will to join a therapy group, he describes one of its participants as "an extremely sensitive Negro who is *not* success-oriented—a true identity problem there"

(30). Thus, Gamow posits driving ambition as central and essential to African American identity.

8. Forney's quest obviously has its roots in John Howard Griffin's *Black Like Me*.

9. Fannin and Merriam's relationship also usefully recalls that of Will Percy and Ford, his black servant, especially in its suggestion of homosexuality. Will Percy refers to Ford as his "incubus," and he figures his dismissal of Ford as an "annul[lment]" of a "contractual relationship," a phrase that may imply a marriage of sorts. Historian John Barry makes that suggestion more explicit when he reports that "some [blacks], it was rumored, might know Will far too well" (301). Fannin and Merriam carp at each other about the hunting dogs, and Fannin strongly wants Barrett to approve of Merriam; when he chastises Merriam, he does so "shyly, watchful of the engineer, lest he, the engineer, think too badly of Merriam"; Barrett realizes that "his uncle was pleading with him!" (270). However, the similarities end there: William Percy must dismiss Ford because he violates his racial boundaries. On one occasion, he invades Percy's morning shower and criticizes his body: "You ain't nothing but a little old fat man. . . . Jest look at your stummick!" (*Lanterns on the Levee* 287). Percy cannot tolerate such impertinence, and so he sends Ford away to preserve his self-image. He resists the deconstruction of colonialist identity caused by his relationship with Ford; Merriam and Fannin, by contrast, seem to accept willingly the depolarization of their racial roles. Indeed, while, as Robert Young observes, colonialists often used same-sex sex as a way of circumventing the ever-present threat of "racial amalgamation" (26), here Walker Percy seems to suggest that an interracial homosexual relationship may in fact promote a sort of cultural hybridity. However, the insular nature of their relationship, one which survives no doubt in part because of their relative isolation from the gaze of the outside world, remains essentially useless to Will.

CONCLUSION

1. For an excellent discussion of the hyperreality of the contemporary South, see Scott Romine, "Where Is Southern Literature? The Practice of Place in a Postsouthern Age."

2. See Rita Kempley, "Movie's 'Magic Negro' Saves the Day—But at the Cost of His Soul," and "Black Angels" by Krin Grabbard.

WORKS CITED

Ahmad, Aijaz. "The Politics of Literary Postcoloniality." *Race & Class* 36.3 (1995): 1–20.

Allen, William Rodney. *Walker Percy: A Southern Wayfarer.* Jackson: UP of Mississippi, 1986.

Babb, Valerie Melissa. *Ernest Gaines.* Boston: Twayne, 1991.

Baker, Houston A., Jr. *Turning South Again: Re-Thinking Modernism / Re-Reading Booker T.* Durham: Duke UP, 2001.

Baris, Sharon Deykin. "Welty's Philosophy of Friendship: Meanings Treasured in *The Ponder Heart.*" *Southern Literary Journal* 27.2 (1991): 65–76.

Barry, John M. *Rising Tide: The Great Mississippi Flood of 1927 and How It Changed America.* New York: Simon and Schuster, 1997.

Bartley, Numan. "The Era of the New Deal as a Turning Point in Southern History." *The New Deal and the South.* Ed. James Cobb and Michael Namorato. Jackson: UP of Mississippi, 1984.

Baudrillard, Jean. "Simulacra and Simulations." *Selected Writings.* Trans. Mark Poster. Stanford: Stanford UP, 1988. 166–84.

Beavers, Herman. *Wrestling Angels into Song: The Fictions of Ernest J. Gaines and James Alan McPherson.* Philadelphia: U of Pennsylvania P, 1995.

Bernard, Shane K. *The Cajuns: Americanization of a People.* Jackson: UP of Mississippi, 2003.

Bhabha, Homi. *The Location of Culture.* New York: Routledge, 1994.

Black, Earl, and Merle Black. *Politics and Society in the South.* Cambridge: Harvard UP, 1987.

Bloom, Jack M. *Class, Race, and the Civil Rights Movement.* Bloomington: Indiana UP, 1987.

Bone, Martyn. *The Postsouthern Sense of Place in Contemporary Fiction.* Baton Rouge: Louisiana State UP, 2005.

Bourdieu, Pierre. *The Logic of Practice.* Trans. Richard Nice. Stanford: Stanford UP, 1980.

———. *Practical Reason: On the Theory of Action.* Stanford: Stanford UP, 1998.

Boyd, Valerie. *Wrapped in Rainbows: The Life of Zora Neale Hurston.* New York: Scribner, 2003.

Bradford, M. E. "Fairchild as Composite Protagonist in *Delta Wedding.*" *Eudora Welty: Critical Essays.* Ed. Peggy Whitman Prenshaw. Jackson: UP of Mississippi, 1979. 201–7.

Brasseaux, Carl A. *Acadian to Cajun: Transformation of a People, 1803–1877.* Jackson: UP of Mississippi, 1992.

Burton, Orville Vernon. "Race Relations in the Rural South since 1945." *The Rural South since World War II.* Baton Rouge: Louisiana State UP, 1998. 28–58.

Carmean, Karen J. *Ernest J. Gaines: A Critical Companion.* Westport, CT: Greenwood, 1998.

Carr, Duane. *A Question of Class: The Redneck Stereotype in Southern Fiction.* Bowling Green: Bowling Green State U Popular P, 1996.

Cash, W. J. *The Mind of the South.* 1941. New York: Vintage, 1960.

Ciuba, Gary M. *Walker Percy: Books of Revelations.* Athens: U of Georgia P, 1991.

Cobb, James C. *The Most Southern Place on Earth: The Mississippi Delta and the Roots of Regional Identity.* New York: Oxford UP, 1992.

———. *Redefining Southern Culture: Mind and Identity in the Modern South.* Baton Rouge: Louisiana State UP, 1999.

Cook, Sylvia Jenkins. *From Tobacco Road to Route 66: The Southern Poor White in Fiction.* Chapel Hill: U of North Carolina P, 1976.

Dale, Corrine. "*Absalom, Absalom!* and the Snopes Trilogy: Southern Patriarchy in Revision." *Mississippi Quarterly* 45.3 (1992): 321–37.

Daniel, Pete. "The New Deal, Southern Agriculture, and Economic Change." *The New Deal and the South.* Ed. James Cobb and Michael Namorato. Jackson: UP of Mississippi, 1984.

Devlin, Albert J. *Eudora Welty's Chronicle: A Story of Mississippi Life.* Jackson: UP of Mississippi, 1983.

Dollard, John. *Caste and Class in a Southern Town.* 1937. 2nd ed. New York: Harper, 1949.

Donaldson, Susan V. "Gender and History in Eudora Welty's *Delta Wedding.*" *South Central Review* 14.2 (1997): 3–14.

Dubek, Laura. "The Social Geography of Race in Hurston's *Seraph on the Suwanee.*" *African American Review* 30.3 (1996): 341–51.

duCille, Ann. *The Coupling Convention: Sex, Text, and Tradition in Black Women's Fiction.* New York: Oxford UP, 1993.

Eichelberger, Julia. "Historicizing the Ponder Heart." *Eudora Welty Newsletter* 25.2 (2001): 15–19.

Eisenger, Chester E. "Traditionalism and Modernism in Eudora Welty." *Eudora Welty: Critical Essays.* Ed. Peggy Whitman Prenshaw. Jackson: UP of Mississippi, 1979. 3–25.

Elias, Amy J. "Postmodern Southern Vacation: Vacation Advertising, Globalization, and Southern Regionalism." *South to a New Place: Region, Literature, Culture.* Ed. Suzanne W. Jones and Sharon Monteith. Baton Rouge: Louisiana State UP, 2002. 253–82.

Entzminger, Betina. "Playing in the Dark with Welty: The Symbolic Role of African Americans in *Delta Wedding.*" *College English* 30.3 (2003): 52–67.

Fabricant, Dan. "Onions and Hyacinths: Unwrapping the Fairchilds in *Delta Wedding.*" *Southern Literary Journal* 18.1 (1985): 50–60.

Faulkner, William. "Funeral Sermon for Mammy Caroline Barr, 1940." *Essays, Speeches, and Public Letters.* Ed. James B. Meriwether. New York: Random House, 1965. 117–18.

———. "Interview with Russell Howe." *Lion in the Garden: Interviews with William Faulkner, 1926–1962.* Ed. James B. Meriwether and Michael Millgate. New York: Random House, 1968. 257–264.

———. Letter to the Editor. *New York Times.* 13 October 1957. *Essays, Speeches, and Public Letters.* Ed. James B. Meriwether. New York: Random House, 1965. 227–28.

———. *The Mansion. Novels 1957–1962.* Ed. Joseph Blotner and Noel Polk. New York: Library of America, 1999. 327–721.

———. "On Fear: Deep South in Labor: Mississippi, 1956." *Essays, Speeches, and Public Letters.* Ed. James B. Meriwether. New York: Random House, 1965. 92–106.

———. *The Reivers. Novels 1957–1962.* Ed. Joseph Blotner and Noel Polk. New York: Library of America, 1999. 723–971.

Fishman, Robert. *Bourgeois Utopias: The Rise and Fall of Suburbia.* New York: Basic Books, 1987.

Fite, Gilbert C. *Cotton Fields No More: Southern Agriculture, 1865–1980.* Lexington: UP of Kentucky, 1984.

Foucault, Michel. "Discipline and Punish." *Literary Theory: An Anthology.* Ed. Julie Rivkin and Michael Ryan. Malden, MA: Blackwell, 1998. 464–87.

Fox-Genovese, Elizabeth. *Within the Plantation Household: Black and White Women of the Old South.* Chapel Hill: U of North Carolina P, 1988.

Fuller, Danielle. "'Making a Scene': Some Thoughts on Female Sexuality and Marriage in Eudora Welty's *Delta Wedding* and *The Optimist's Daughter.*" *Mississippi Quarterly* 48.2 (1995): 291–318.

Fulton, Keith Louise. "Linda Snopes Kohl: Faulkner's Radical Woman." *Modern Fiction Studies* 34.3 (1988): 425–36.

Gaines, Ernest J. *Bloodline.* New York: Norton, 1968.

———. "An Interview with Ernest Gaines." Interview with William Parrill. *Con-*

versations with Ernest Gaines. Ed. John Lowe. Jackson: UP of Mississippi, 1995. 172–99.

———. "Talking with Ernest Gaines." Interview with Marcia Gaudet and Carl Wooton. *Conversations with Ernest Gaines*. Ed. John Lowe. Jackson: UP of Mississippi, 1995. 221–40.

———. *Of Love and Dust*. New York: Vintage, 1967.

Genovese, Eugene. *The World the Slaveholders Made*. New York: Pantheon, 1969.

Glissant, Edouard. *Faulkner, Mississippi*. 1996. Trans. Barbara Lewis and Thomas C. Spear. New York: Farrar, Straus, and Giroux, 1999.

Godden, Richard. "Earthing *The Hamlet*: An Anti-Ratliffian Reading." *Faulkner Journal* 14.2 (1999): 75–116.

———. *Fictions of Labor: William Faulkner and the South's Long Revolution*. Cambridge UP, 1997.

Goldfield, David R. *Black, White, and Southern: Race Relations and Southern Culture, 1940 to the Present*. Baton Rouge: Louisiana State UP, 1990.

Grabbard, Krin. "Black Angels." *Chronicle of Higher Education* 6 June 2003.

Grantham, Dewey W. *The South in Modern America*. New York: Harper Collins, 1994.

Gretlund, Jan Nordby. *Eudora Welty's Aesthetics of Place*. Newark: U of Delaware P, 1994.

Griffin, Joseph. "Ernest J. Gaines' Good News: Sacrifice and Redemption in *Of Love and Dust*." *Modern Language Studies* 18.3 (1988): 75–85.

Guinn, Matthew. *After Southern Modernism: Fiction of the Contemporary South*. Jackson: UP Mississippi, 2000.

Haddox, Thomas F. "The Logic of Expenditure in *Their Eyes Were Watching God*." *Mosaic* 34.1 (2001): 19–34.

Hale, Grace Elizabeth. *Making Whiteness: The Culture of Segregation in the South, 1890–1940*. New York: Pantheon, 1998.

Hardy, John Edward. *The Fiction of Walker Percy*. Urbana: U of Illinois P, 1987.

———. "Delta Wedding as Region and Symbol." *Critical Essays on Eudora Welty*. Ed. W. Craig Turner and Lee Emling Harding. Boston: G. K. Hall, 1989. 75–89.

Harris, Alex. Introduction to *A New Life: Stories and Photographs from the Suburban South*. Ed. Alex Harris. New York: Norton, 1997. xiii–xx.

Hemenway, Robert E. *Zora Neale Hurston: A Literary Biography*. Urbana: U of Illinois P, 1977.

Hobson, Fred. *But Now I See: The White Southern Racial Conversion Narrative*. Baton Rouge: Louisiana State UP, 1999.

Howland, Mary Deems. *The Gift of the Other: Gabriel Marcel's Concept of Intersubjectivity in Walker Percy's Novels*. Pittsburgh: Duquesne UP, 1990.

Hurston, Zora Neale. "The Citrus Industry." *Go Gator and Muddy the Water: Writings by Zora Neale Hurston from the Federal Writers' Project.* Ed. Pamela Bordelon. New York: Norton, 1999. 131–38.

———. Letter to Claude Barnett. 4 February 1943. *Zora Neale Hurston: A Life in Letters.* Ed. Carla Kaplan. New York: Doubleday, 2002. 474–75.

———. Letter to Douglas Gilbert. 9 February 1943. *Zora Neale Hurston: A Life in Letters.* Ed. Carla Kaplan. New York: Doubleday, 2002. 475–78.

———. "The Ocoee Riot." *Go Gator and Muddy the Water: Writings by Zora Neale Hurston from the Federal Writers' Project.* Ed. Pamela Bordelon. New York: Norton, 1999. 146–52.

———. "The 'Pet Negro' System." *American Mercury.* May 1943: 593–600.

———. *Seraph on the Suwanee.* 1948. *Novels and Stories.* Ed. Cheryl A. Wall. New York: Library of America, 1995. 597–920.

Jackson, Chuck. "Waste and Whiteness: Zora Neale Hurston and the Politics of Eugenics." *African American Review* 34.4 (2000): 639–60.

Jehlen, Myra. *Class and Character in William Faulkner's South.* New York: Columbia UP, 1976.

Jones, Suzanne W. *Race Mixing: Southern Fiction since the Sixties.* Baltimore: Johns Hopkins UP, 2004.

Kang, Hee. "A New Configuration of Faulkner's Feminine: Linda Snopes Kohl in *The Mansion.*" *Faulkner Journal* 8.1 (1992): 21–42.

Kempley, Rita. "Movie's 'Magic Negro' Saves the Day—But at the Cost of His Soul." *Black Commentator* 3 July 2003. 12 January 2006. www.blackcommentator.com/49/49_magic.html>.

Kennedy, J. Gerald. "The Sundered Self and the Riven World: *Love in the Ruins.*" *The Art of Walker Percy: Stratagems for Being.* Ed. Panthea Reid Broughton. Baton Rouge: Louisiana State UP, 1979. 115–36.

Kirby, Jack Temple. *The Countercultural South.* Athens: U of Georgia P, 1995.

Knadler, Stephen P. *The Fugitive Race: Minority Writers Resisting Whiteness.* Jackson: UP of Mississippi, 2002.

Kobre, Michael. *Walker Percy's Voices.* Athens: U of Georgia P, 2000.

Konzett, Delia Caparoso. "'Getting in Touch with the True South': Pet Negroes, White Crackers, and Racial Staging in Zora Neale Hurston's *Seraph on the Suwanee.*" *White Women in Racialized Spaces: Imaginative Transformation and Ethical Action in Literature.* Ed. Samina Najmi and Rajini Srikanth. Albany: SUNY P, 2002. 131–46.

Kreyling, Michael. *Understanding Eudora Welty.* Columbia: U of South Carolina P, 1999.

Lawson, Lewis. *Still Following Percy.* Jackson: UP of Mississippi, 1996.

The Legend of Bagger Vance. Dir. Robert Redford. Perf. Will Smith, Matt Damon. Twentieth-Century Fox, 2000.

Lessig, Matthew. "Class, Character, and 'Croppers': Faulkner's Snopeses and the Plight of the Sharecropper." *Arizona Quarterly* 55.4 (1999): 79–113.

Loomba, Ania. "Overworlding the 'Third World.'" *Colonial Discourse and Post-Colonial Theory: A Reader*. Ed. Laura Chrisman and Patrick Williams. New York: Oxford UP, 1994. 305–23.

Lowe, John. *Jump at the Sun: Zora Neale Hurston's Cosmic Comedy*. Chicago: U of Illinois P, 1995.

Maguire, Roberta S. "Walker Percy and Albert Murray: The Story of Two 'Part Anglo-Saxon Alabamans.'" *Southern Quarterly* 41.1 (2002): 10–29.

Marrs, Suzanne. "'The Huge Fateful Stage of the Outside World': Eudora Welty's Life in Politics." *Eudora Welty and Politics: Did the Writer Crusade?* Ed. Harriet Pollack and Suzanne Marrs. Baton Rouge: Louisiana State UP, 2001. 69–88.

———. *One Writer's Imagination: The Fiction of Eudora Welty*. Baton Rouge: Louisiana State UP, 2002.

Marsh-Lockett, Carol P. "What Ever Happened to Jochebed? Motherhood as Marginality in Zora Neale Hurston's *Seraph on the Suwanee*." *Southern Mothers: Fact and Fiction in Southern Women's Writing*. Ed. Nagueyalti Warren and Sally Wolff. Baton Rouge: Louisiana State UP, 1999. 100–110.

Matthews, John T. "Faulkner and Proletarian Literature." *Faulkner in Cultural Context: Faulkner and Yoknapatawpha 1995*. Ed. Donald M. Kartiganer and Ann J. Abadie. Jackson: UP of Mississippi, 1997. 166–90.

———. *The Play of Faulkner's Language*. Ithaca: Cornell UP, 1982.

McMillen, Neil R. *Dark Journey: Black Mississippians in the Age of Jim Crow*. Urbana: U of Illinois P, 1989.

———. "Fighting for What We Didn't Have: How Mississippi's Black Veterans Remember World War II." *Re-Making Dixie: The Impact of World War II on the American South*. Jackson: UP of Mississippi, 1997. 93-110.

Meisenhelder, Susan E. *Hitting a Straight Lick with a Crooked Stick: Race and Gender in the Work of Zora Neale Hurston*. Tuscaloosa: U of Alabama P, 1999.

Messerli, Douglas. "The Problem of Time in Welty's *Delta Wedding*." *The Critical Response to Eudora Welty's Fiction*. Westport, CT: Greenwood, 1994. 108–25.

Moreland, Richard. *Faulkner and Modernism: Rereading and Rewriting*. Madison: U of Wisconsin P, 1990.

Morris, Wesley, and Barbara Alverson Morris. *Reading Faulkner*. Madison: U of Wisconsin P, 1989.

Morrison, Toni. *Playing in the Dark: Whiteness and the Literary Imagination*. New York: Vintage, 1992.

Myrdal, Gunnar. *An American Dilemma: The Negro Problem and Modern Democracy*. New York: Harper, 1941.

Nichol, Frances Louisa. "Flem Snopes's Knack for Verisimilitude in Faulkner's Snopes Trilogy." *Mississippi Quarterly* 50.3 (1997): 493–505.

O'Gorman, Farrell. "Walker Percy, the Catholic Church, and Southern Race Relations (ca. 1947–1970)." *Mississippi Quarterly* 53.1 (1999–2000): 67–88.

Ownby, Ted. *American Dreams in Mississippi: Consumers, Poverty, and Culture, 1830–1998*. Chapel Hill: U of North Carolina P, 1999.

Pearson, Michael. "The Double Bondage of Racism in Walker Percy's Fiction." *Mississippi Quarterly* 25 (1988): 479–95.

Penley, Constance. "Crackers and Whackers: The White Trashing of Porn." *White Trash: Race and Class in America*. Ed. Matthew Wray and Annalee Newitz. London: Routledge, 1997. 89–112.

Percy, Walker. "Letter to the Editor." *Harper's* May 1967: 8–9.

———. *The Moviegoer*. New York: Ballantine, 1960.

———. "Virtues and Vices of the Southern Literary Renascence." *Commonweal* 76 (1962): 181–82.

———. *The Last Gentleman*. New York: Ballantine, 1966.

———. *Love in the Ruins*. New York: Ballantine, 1971.

———. "Questions They Never Asked Me." *Signposts in a Strange Land*. 1977. Ed. Patrick Samway. New York: Farrar, Straus, and Giroux, 1991. 397–424.

———. "Stoicism in the South." *Signposts in a Strange Land*. Ed. Patrick Samway. New York: Farrar, Straus, and Giroux, 1991. 83–88.

———. "Uncle Will." *Signposts in a Strange Land*. Ed. Patrick Samway. New York: Farrar, Straus, and Giroux, 1991. 53–62.

Percy, William Alexander. *Lanterns on the Levee: Recollections of a Planter's Son*. New York: Knopf, 1941.

Pitavy-Souques, Daniele. "Private and Political Thought in *One Writer's Beginnings*." *Eudora Welty and Politics: Did the Writer Crusade?*" Baton Rouge: Louisiana State UP, 2001. 203–22.

Polk, Noel. "Idealism in *The Mansion*." *Faulkner and Idealism: Perspectives from Paris*. Ed. Michael Gresset and Patrick Samway. Jackson: UP of Mississippi, 1983. 112–25.

———. "Faulkner and Respectability." *Fifty Years of Yoknapatawpha: Faulkner and Yoknapatawpha 1979*. Jackson: UP of Mississippi, 1980.

———. "Faulkner and World War II." *Remaking Dixie: The Impact of World War II on the American South*. Ed. Neil R. McMillen. Jackson: UP of Mississippi, 1997. 131–45.

Prenshaw, Peggy Whitman. "Elegies for Gentlemen: Walker Percy's *The Last Gentleman* and Eudora Welty's 'The Demonstrators.'" *Walker Percy: Novelist and Philosopher*. Ed. Jan Norby Gretlund and Karl-Heinz Westarp. Jackson: UP Mississippi, 1991. 84–98.

———. "Welty's Transformation of the Public, the Private, and the Political." *Eudora Welty and Politics: Did the Writer Crusade?* Ed. Harriet Pollack and Suzanne Marrs. Baton Rouge: Louisiana State UP, 2001. 19–46.

———. "Woman's World, Man's Place: The Fiction of Eudora Welty." *Eudora Welty: A Form of Thanks*. Ed. Louis Dollarhide and Ann J. Abadie. Jackson: UP of Mississippi, 1979. 46–77.

Railey, Kevin. *Natural Aristocracy: History, Ideology, and the Production of William Faulkner*. Tuscaloosa: U of Alabama P, 1999.

Ransom, John Crowe. "Delta Fiction." *Critical Essays on Eudora Welty*. Ed. W. Craig Turner and Lee Emling Harding. Boston: G. K. Hall, 1989. 71–75.

Rieger, Christopher. "The Working-class Pastoral of Zora Neale Hurston's *Seraph on the Suwanee*." *Mississippi Quarterly* 56 (2002–2003): 105–24.

Romine, Scott. *The Narrative Forms of Southern Community*. Baton Rouge: Louisiana State UP, 1999.

———. "Where Is Southern Literature? The Practice of Place in a Postsouthern Age." *South to a New Place: Region, Literature, Culture*. Ed. Suzanne W. Jones and Sharon Monteith. Baton Rouge: Louisiana State UP, 2002. 23–43.

Romines, Ann. *The Home Plot: Women, Writing, and Domestic Ritual*. Amherst: U of Massachusetts P, 1992.

———. "Reading the Cakes: *Delta Wedding* and the Texts of Southern Women's Culture." *Mississippi Quarterly* 50 (1997): 601–17.

Samway, Patrick. *Walker Percy: A Life*. New York: Farrar, Straus, and Giroux, 1997.

Schulman, Bruce J. *From Cotton Belt to Sunbelt: Federal Policy, Economic Development, and the Transformation of the South, 1938–1980*. New York: Oxford UP, 1991.

Shelton, Frank W. "Of Machines and Men: Pastoralism in Gaines's Fiction." *Critical Reflections on the Fiction of Ernest J. Gaines*. Athens: U of Georgia P, 1994. 12–29.

Sitkoff, Harvard. "The Impact of the New Deal on Black Southerners." *The New Deal and the South*. Ed. James Cobb and Michael Namorato. Jackson: UP of Mississippi, 1984.

Skinfill, Mauri. "Reconstructing Class in Faulkner's Late Novels: *The Hamlet* and the Discovery of Capital." *Journal of American Fiction* 24.2 (1996): 151–69.

Smith, David Lionel. "Bloodlines and Patriarchs: *Of Love and Dust* and Its Revisions of Faulkner." *Critical Reflections on the Fiction of Ernest J. Gaines*. Athens: U of Georgia P, 1994. 46–61.

Tate, Claudia. "Hitting 'A Straight Lick with a Crooked Stick': *Seraph on the Suwanee,* Zora Neale Hurston's Whiteface Novel." *The Psychoanalysis of Race.* Ed. Christopher Lane. New York: Columbia UP, 1998. 380–94.

Tharpe, Jac. *Walker Percy.* Boston: Twayne, 1983.

Towner, Theresa. *Faulkner on the Color Line: The Later Novels.* Jackson: UP of Mississippi, 2000.

Trilling, Diana. "Fiction in Review." *The Critical Response to Eudora Welty's Fiction.* Ed. Laurie Champion. Westport, CN: Greenwood, 1994. 103–06.

Urgo, Joseph. *Faulkner's Apocrypha: "A Fable," "Snopes," and the Spirit of Human Rebellion.* Jackson: UP of Mississippi, 1989.

Veblen, Thorstein. *The Theory of the Leisure Class.* 1899. New York: Penguin, 1994.

Waldron, Ann. *Eudora Welty: A Writer's Life.* New York: Doubleday, 1998.

Ward, Cynthia. "From the Suwanee to Egypt, There's No Place Like Home." *PMLA* 115 (2000): 75–88.

Weber, Max. *Economy and Society: An Outline of Interpretive Sociology.* Ed. Guenther Roth and Claus Wittich. 1922. New York: Bedminster, 1968.

Weiner, Rachel V. "*The Ponder Heart:* The Judgment of Art." *Southern Studies* 19 (1980): 261–73.

Welty, Eudora. "The Art of Fiction XLVII: Eudora Welty." Interview with Linda Kuehl. *Conversations with Eudora Welty.* Ed. Peggy Whitman Prenshaw. New York: Pocket, 1984. 82–101.

———. *Delta Wedding.* 1946. New York: Harcourt, 1974.

———. "'The Interior World': An Interview with Eudora Welty." Interview with Charles T. Bunting. *Conversations with Eudora Welty.* Ed. Peggy Whitman Prenshaw. New York: Pocket, 1984. 43–69.

———. "A Conversation with Eudora Welty." Interview with Albert J. Devlin and Peggy Whitman Prenshaw. *More Conversations with Eudora Welty.* Ed. Peggy Whitman Prenshaw. Jackson: UP of Mississippi, 1996. 100–119.

———. *The Ponder Heart.* New York: Harcourt, 1954.

———. "Seeing Things Real: An Interview with Eudora Welty." Interview with Jan Nordby Gretlund. *More Conversations with Eudora Welty.* Ed. Peggy Whitman Prenshaw. Jackson: UP of Mississippi, 1996. 248–61.

———. "Eudora Welty: A Writer's Beginnings." Interview with Patricia Wheatley. *More Conversations with Eudora Welty.* Ed. Peggy Whitman Prenshaw. Jackson: UP of Mississippi, 1996. 120–45.

Williamson, Joel. *The Crucible of Race: Black-White Relations in the American South since Emancipation.* New York: Oxford UP, 1984.

Wolfe, Tom. *A Man in Full.* New York: Farrar, Straus, and Giroux, 1998.

Woodward, C. Vann. *Origins of the New South.* Baton Rouge: Louisiana State UP, 1951.

Wright, Erik Olin. *Class Counts: Comparative Studies in Class Analysis.* Cambridge: Cambridge UP, 1997.

Wyatt-Brown, Bertram. *The House of Percy: Honor, Melancholy, and Imagination in a Southern Family.* New York: Oxford UP, 1994.

Yaeger, Patricia. *Dirt and Desire: Reconstructing Southern Women's Writing, 1930–1990.* Chicago: U of Chicago P, 2000.

Young, Robert. *Colonial Desire: Hybridity in Theory, Culture, and Race.* London: Routledge, 1995.

Young, Stark. "Not in Memoriam, but in Defense." *I'll Take My Stand: The South and the Agrarian Tradition.* 1930. Baton Rouge: Louisiana State UP, 1983. 328-59.

INDEX